94

D0515926

Albuquerque Academy Library
6400 Wyoming Blvd. NE
Albuquerque, NM 87109

Screen Memories

Screen
MEMORIES

Hollywood Cinema on the
Psychoanalytic Couch

Harvey Roy Greenberg

Columbia University Press

New York

Columbia University Press
New York   Chichester, West Sussex
Copyright © 1993 Columbia University Press
All rights reserved

Library of Congress Cataloging-in-Publication Data

Greenberg, Harvey R.
    Screen memories : Hollywood cinema on the psychoanalytic couch /
Harvey Roy Greenberg.
        p.   cm.
    Includes bibliographical references and index.
    ISBN 0–231–07286–4 (acid-free paper)
    1. Motion pictures—United States—Psychological aspects.
I. Title
PN1995.G675   1993
791.43'015—dc20   92–41710
                                                              CIP

Casebound editions of Columbia University Press books are
printed on permanent and durable acid-free paper.

Printed in the United States of America

c   10   9   8   7   6   5   4   3   2   1

"Reel Significations: An Anatomy of Psychoanalytic Film Criticism" (with
    Krin Gabbard), *Psychoanalytic Review* 77(1):89–110, 1990;
"*Casablanca:* If It's So Schmaltzy, Why Am I Weeping?," in *The Movies on
    Your Mind: Film Classics on the Couch from Fellini to Frankenstein* (New
    York: Saturday Review Press, 1975), pp. 79–105.
"*The Maltese Falcon:* Even Paranoids Have Enemies," in *The Movies on Your
    Mind,* pp. 53–78.
"Dangerous Recuperations: *Red Dawn, Rambo,* and the New Decaturism,"
    Journal of Popular Film and Television 15(2):60–70, 1987.
"*Psycho:* The Apes at the Windows," in *The Movies on Your Mind,* pp. 106–
    137.
"Reimagining the Gargoyle: Psychoanalytic Notes on *Alien* and the
    Contemporary 'Cruel' Horror Films," *Camera Obscura* 15:87–110,
    1986.
"Improper *Bostonians,*" *Psychoanalytic Review* 73(2):213–22, 1986.
"Raiders of the Lost Text: Remaking as Contested Homage in *Always,*"
    Journal of Popular Film and Television 18(4):164–71, 1991.
"*Working Girl:* Leveraged Sell-Out," *Journal of Popular Film and Television*
    16(5):32–34, 1989.
"Awful Plausibility: *Enemies: A Love Story,*" *Psychiatric Times* 7(8):52–54,
    1990.

791.43
GRE

Contents

For Sharon

Acknowledgments

I thank the following people for sharing their insights on various films and cinematic issues addressed in *Screen Memories:* professors Robert Eberwein, Krin Gabbard, Norman Holland, Peter Lehman, William Luhr, Michael Marsden, Jack Nachbar, and Constance Penley; Irv Schneider, M.D.; Sharon Messitte, and Matthew and Paul Greenberg.

Louise Waller was instrumental in forging the idea and the format of this collection.

Introduction

No friend to cinema during his lifetime,
Freud himself takes a star turn in John
Huston's 1962 film about the origins of
psychoanalysis. Montgomery Clift as
Freud; Susannah York as a glamorous
hysteric (more or less reminiscent of
Anna O). Courtesy of Museum of
Modern Art/Film Stills Archive.

he Movies on Your Mind, my first collection of essays on cinema, was written in the early seventies. There had been little previous exploration of film by psychoanalytic clinicians, compared with a considerable body of work on the other arts. Setting aside studies like Martha Wolfenstein and Nathan Leites's *The Movies,* most analytic excursions into film were hopelessly heavy-handed. The smattering of analytically oriented film study I discovered outside my field seemed either naive (e.g., much of Parker Tyler's writings) or intuitively insightful (Robin Wood, Barbara Deming, and Pauline Kael), but nevertheless untutored about many of the intricacies of analytic theory and practice.

My research for *The Movies on Your Mind* was an improvised overview-cum-pastiche. I dipped into a few manuals about the nuts and bolts of filmmaking; the theorists I scanned predictably included Münsterberg, Kracauer, Balacz, Arnstein, and Eisenstein; Lindsey, Agee, Durgnat, and Thompson. Although I greatly admired the several famous European directors of the day, I knew little about the latest developments in continental film and literary theory beyond a tease of Barthes and Lévi-Strauss. I had heard vaguely of *Cahiers du Cinema* and not at all of *Screen* or *Communications.* Saussure and the poststructural semiologists were largely unknown quanta.

I had then no close colleagues in film academia; nor was I otherwise traveling in intellectual circles where I would have been alerted to the impact Metz's Lacanian Freud and its associated ideological freight was having abroad or to its dawning influence in the American academy. Several years previously I had completed psychoanalytic training at a "culturalist" neo-Freudian institute. There my study of Hartmann's ego psychology and the English object relations school was leavened by Sullivan and Horney, Adler and Jung. I also read the Freudian left of the day, absent Lacan.

Against this eclectic background, I undertook a sampling of analytic possibilities at the Bijou. I soon discovered scripts were expensive, as well as inaccurate. I couldn't promote a movieola, so I ran rented or borrowed 16-millimeter prints on an ancient projector at home and taped soundtracks off the TV, at dusty revival houses, or at Forty-Second Street fleapits where my mutterings into a tape recorder regularly provoked nearby cineasts to threaten to do to me what Godzilla did to Tokyo.

When completed, *The Movies on Your Mind* addressed about a hundred films produced during the previous forty years. Some were probed in great detail, others in passing or *en genre*. My selection was wildly undefinitive—Bogart to Bergman, *The Wizard of Oz* (1939) to *2001* (1968)—choices dictated by private preference often under the sway of nostalgia, as well as restricted accessibility. The book went on to be reviewed passably well, if not widely, by mainstream critics. It garnered one kind, if rather patronizing, notice in a psychoanalytic journal from a practitioner who stopped just short of saying I could probably find something more serious to do with my time.

The raw anger and contempt of a few responses astonished me then, but I have grown used to this sort of thing since. It seems that no matter how delicate, how respectful your touch, a small number of viewers—by no means are all naive—react as if an analytic critique had trod upon privileged celluloid treasure with muddy golf shoes. I am reminded of patients who object violently to the faintest inference that a favorite character in their history might occasionally have acted out of less then noble motives.

I was saddened but not surprised when *The Movies on Your Mind* eventually went out of print. Theoretical studies on film rarely sell more than a few thousand copies before hitting the remainder racks. But then the book unexpectedly began to acquire a small following in film academia; entered a few curricula; formed the basis for a festival in the Northwest. I started hearing from similarly inclined scholars in cinema and literature, some of whom have gone on to become cocontributors and friends.

While I continued to furnish the odd movie piece for various psychoanalytic journals throughout the late seventies, I concentrated chiefly on writing a self-help series about mental health for teenagers. I became definitively reengaged with film theory when Professor Norman Holland invited me to present a paper on horror cinema at a seminar held by the State University of New York at Buffalo's Center for the Psychological Study of the Arts.

That weekend marked my first exposure to the Lacanian/semiotic/feminist/Marxist approaches to cinema. I confronted a psychoanalysis directed at texts rather than patients by scholarly practitioners, who hotly contested truths received and unreceived of which I had never conceived, using a discourse even more arcane than the lingo of high-church analytic meetings. Tropes were valorized, metonymies privileged, and traces of dominant ideology excavated from forties Weepies and Cheapies that I had thought to be about as political as broiled flounder. Debate veered wildly from Charles Peirce to Mildred Pierce.

Although I counted myself in fortyish prime time, my own paper was greeted with the respectful spatter of applause reserved for a dense, if not doddering, elder statesman. Not too long afterward the same audience roared with delight over the explication of a twenty-second cut from *Rancho Notorious* (1952): Arthur Kennedy turns sharply on his own axis to draw and fire at a belt hung on a wall behind him—quick dissolve to a medium shot of the aggressive Marlene Dietrich heroine.

With the nimbleness of a mountain goat the presenter danced past Michelangelo's *Bound Slave* into a disquisition on the relationship in Flemish Renaissance landscapes of the wall to the Symbolic order. He concluded with the insight that Dietrich's placement in the sequence following the shooting contest was such that Kennedy, had his bullet "continued" across the dissolve, would have drilled her precisely in the crotch—a testament to the hero's castration anxiety. (I exaggerate but slightly.)

There were more dizzy exegeses—but also a paper by Laura Mulvey on the vicissitudes of feminine spectatorship that raised issues about Hollywood sexism, which, until then, I had but dimly sensed. Several other contributions were equally provocative.

It was evident that the brand of psychoanalysis I had been raised on was held in no great esteem here, whether due to its principles or practitioners, the latter being generally viewed, it seemed, as members of one great bourgeois, paternalistic cabal. I was certainly in no position to determine whether the brand to which these folks subscribed would ultimately yield fruitful or absurdist results. But I had rarely seen cinema taken so seriously or discussed so passionately by members of my own profession.

On the return flight, I mulled over my weekend in the wilds of movie academia by turns mystified, irritated, and fascinated. Back home, my wife, a psychoanalyst with a background in philosophy, diagnosed a case of severe intellectual overload complicated by mild ego bruising and prescribed a dose of concentrated scholarship.

Over the next few years, I jury-rigged my own graduate program in film studies, focusing upon the continental cinesemiologists, their American counterparts, and Jacques Lacan, as well as his critical and clinical interpreters, of whom, I quickly discovered, the former far exceed the latter, at least in English publications (I own no French). I also explored film industry history, artistic and economic practice in greater depth than the first time around; scanned relevant work in literary theory, philosophy, feminist and Marxist studies, popular culture, linguistics, so forth. Along the way various colleagues old and new provided guidance, curricula, and clarification of often daunting material.

I wrote my first article for an academic film journal in 1984; thereafter divided publishing essays on movies and media between film theory and psychoanalytic venues. In 1988 I became film and TV critic for *Psychiatric Times,* a monthly newspaper circulated mostly to American and Canadian psychiatrists. The responses to my reviews by nonpsychiatric readers encouraged me to address lay audiences directly. Meanwhile, I continued to receive requests for copies of *The Movies on Your Mind* from libraries, film theory programs, scholars both cinematic and analytic, and ordinary, stoned movie buffs.

This book is an assemblage of pieces from many of these sources, plus one new essay— "On the McMovie: Less is Less at the Simplex." Psychoanalytic film criticism by its nature is (or should be) an interdisciplinary enterprise. The current collection therefore pursues several agendas in aid of serving a mixed clientele with varying interests in literary or cinema studies and in psychoanalysis or the other mental health disciplines (pick any combination). If previous experience is any guide, it is not unlikely that lay cineasts will also find it useful.

Various attempts to reissue *The Movies on Your Mind* through the years have ultimately foundered in an increasingly cost-conscious publishing climate. With no reason to suppose the future would hold any different outcome, I have selected for this book chapters from the earlier book most cited by reviewers or scholars and most frequently requested by correspondents. These appear virtually unchanged, except for a few stylistic alterations. (I have taken more liberties with my other essays, but not many.) Since I have no illusions about having the final word on any subject, a few supplementary remarks are occasionally furnished, as well as references to subsequent significant work on the film or topic under discussion.

The material from *The Movies on Your Mind* contains considerable description and direct quotes from films now available on videotape. Nevertheless, I have refrained from extensive editing here because so many readers have told me they enjoyed the idiosyncratic weave of interpretation through the more leisurely close readings that marked my earlier criticism.

Despite greater bridge building between clinicians and the film academy, psychoanalytic critics may still be unaware of work in disciplines outside their own. Scholarship in this area can be exceptionally frustrating because the literature is scattered across such a diversity of discourses. Besides publications specifically devoted to film theory, significant work is often found in journals and books from the fields of psychoanalysis; general psychotherapy; psychiatry; psychology; psychiatric social work; family and group therapy; philosophy; aesthetics; literary theory and history; popular culture, so forth.

Parochial blindness, the resolute passion *not* to know what the Other is doing may also restrict one's critical vision. In hope of redressing such unwitting or willful ignorance, the next essay, "Reel Significations" (undertaken with the assistance of Professor Krin Gabbard) offers an unpolemical overview of analytically oriented cinema study from its inceptions to the present writing. References in this and other essays include many of the important publications in, or apposite to, the field. An additional bibliography is available upon writing to me through Columbia University Press.

Outside my elaboration of semiotic/suture theory in "Reel Significations," the reader will find little "Lacanalysis" in these pages. (I should also mention that the general reader who might be put off by the comparatively abstract discussion of "Reel Significations" can skip this essay without compromising his or her understanding of other essays in this collection.) I respect the scholarly commitment of the best Lacanian-influenced film theoreticians. This body of work has been vital to the surge of academic cinema study over the past several decades. It has sparked vigorous rereadings of Freud which deserve attention beyond the academy.

However, if no longer a skeptical neophyte, neither am I an unskeptical convert to the Lacanian mode. My original reservations over many points of Lacanian metapsychology and notions of child development persist. For instance, I remain dubious about Lacan's postulating an unconscious "language"—based on a Saussurean model which many linguists today believe to be simplistic and often inaccurate; about Lacan's assertion—absolutely unsupported by Piagetian or other psycholinguistic study—that the resolution of the Oedipus complex is hallmarked by the child's acquiescence to a magisterial, but anomalous "Law of the Father," with an attendant passage from the Imaginary into the Symbolic Order that somehow precipitates the acquisition of meaningful language (no substantive explanation or description of this momentous "entry" process is tendered; it seems to happen all at once, a developmental "big bang"). Moreover, I remain dubious about Lacan's "mirror stage," which is based on antique, faulted research unvindicated by the meticulous documentation of actual mirroring behavior in young children.

Norman Holland has forcefully spoken to these, and other deficiencies in the Lacanian project.[1] The specific dilemmas posed by unqualified acceptance of Lacan for film theorists have been cogently explored by David Bordwell and Noel Carroll. My current view (which I am not alone in holding) is that many fertile questions posed by poststructural and semiotic film theory need not be processed through Lacan's tortuous machine to prove their merit, but can be engaged by less convoluted discourses, psychoanalytic or otherwise. Among these concerns, I cite the inherent instability, uncanny absence/presence of the cinematic image; the skill with which the classic Hollywood "apparatus" enfolds the audience in its narrative net; and various issues related to visual pleasure, specularity, and subject construction (here, I am specifically partial to Gaylyn Studlar's elegant formulations).

My strongest cavil with Lacan may perhaps expose me in some quarters to charges of the very parochialism decried in "Reel Significations." Critical deciphering of books, poems, films only makes or mars textual meaning, or reputation, or tenure. But I have yet to be persuaded about the usefulness of Lacanalysis in deciphering the text of a patient's suffering toward the alleviation of psychic wounds. On the basis of a slim English literature, Lacanian therapy seems a twisty and rather bloodless affair indeed, best suited to an elitist clientele of brainy true believers with relatively few emotional scars.[2]

Of course, non-Lacanian Freudian psychoanalysis has drawn similar criticisms. Their validity is difficult to gauge. More to the point of my argument, it is still insufficiently appreciated outside the mental health profession that an extensive course of psychoanalytic therapy does *not* constitute the norm for the overwhelming number of patients in psychotherapy, who are neither wealthy malcontents nor philosophically inclined intellectuals with little to do but complain to a hired listener at exorbitant rates.

In the half-century since his death, Freud's original work—amplified and corrected by orthodox or heterodox inheritors (notably omitting, however, the Lacanians as far as I know)—has been applied to the treatment of quotidian psychological ills across every class and circumstances. Modified clinical Freudianism continues to command a substantial constituency despite the so-called biological revolution, and worries on the left or right about a stultified "therapeutic" society. Contemporary psychotherapy has pragmatically adapted the style, depth, and frequency of classic psychoanalysis to treat a vast client majority where the whole nine yards would be inappropriate, where it might prove frustrating or downright harmful.[3]

Freudian theory regularly grounds a variety of analytically oriented individual therapies, group and family approaches; it even articulates usefully with the prescription of medication and other "nontalking" modalities. I speak here, inter alia, of those core concepts on the phases of psychic development over the life cycle; on psychic mechanisms of defense; on transference and its origins within family life; on conscious and unconscious mental representation; on the complex interface between intrapsychic and external reality.

No unqualified panegyric to the Freudian (clinical) field, absent Lacan, is here intended. My thrust is only that, vis-à-vis these and many other issues vital to psychoanalytic practice, Lacan's project has frequently proven too cumbersome, too arcane, unsubstantiated by clinical observation, or simply too glacially unconcerned to be applied with any material benefit, compared with the "ordinary" Freud largely disdained by the Lacanians.[4]

As with life, so with art. Lacanian Freud has managed to find a purchase in literary and cinematic academia it has not so far achieved in the office—at least not in American offices and clinics.[5] (How long its sway over film theorists will endure is moot.) Nevertheless, after early promise the recognitions of Lacanalysis now seem to many film scholars increasingly barren, monocular, icily remote from the human realities played upon a screen its followers often view as such a fundamental paradigm for deception. Increasingly, one comes away from Lacanian film critiques with little if any sense that conflict, intrapsychic or interpersonal, has been vividly illuminated.

As a group, the Lacanian theorists certainly do not betray the ignorance of film art and craft that often characterized negligible work from other Freudian schools in the past; they are far more cinema literate than their predecessors. The problem resides not only with the aridity and tunnel vision of their peculiar discourse but with the failure from the first of Lacanian metapsychology/psychodynamics to provide a valid, vital account of why we do what we do.

Granted that no one has ever seen a superego lacuna under a microscope any more than an Imaginary. But the former construct does offer reasonably good grounds to explain, in terms a reasonably intelligent layperson can understand (or a patient could utilize), why a pillar of rectitude like the father in Woody Allen's *Crimes and Misdemeanors* (1989) should have fathered two worthless bums for sons. Working with teenagers, one often finds that the parent of a delinquent has unknowingly projected personal unconscious delinquent impulses upon the adolescent child; disavowing this moral gap, he or she primes the youth with subtle cues toward wrongdoing.

I submit that Lacanalysis is ridden with a shortfall of analogous means to clarify the psychodynamics of a movie character, let alone an office client, so lucidly and convincingly. Indeed, I have begun to wonder if many Lacanalysts are interested in movies at all, beyond ponderous ruminations upon why we watch them in the first place.

Well, well, I hear the true believers gibe, you are simply more at home in your own church, with your own lingo. You use it to ratify your received truths as we use ours; it encloses you as much in its privileged rationales as ours—only our ideas about the psyche are newer, stranger, not nearly as comforting, and threaten your establishment. Perhaps so. But my particular psychoanalytic background has allowed me to help many of my patients discover less symptomatic ways of enduring a distressing world. In contrast, the Lacanians would surely scoff at such "American" humanistic hopes for enhanced happiness in work, love, and play, or at least the semblance of content promoted by other analytic visions, as further fictions spun by an ego that quakes before acknowledging the fictitiousness of its own premises of existence.

This admittedly unobjective Chautauqua on Lacanalysis is meant to underscore how important the pragmatic association between what "works" in clinical and critical practice is for me. My word processor lies comfortably at hand near the chair from which I listen to clients. Working with them joins closely with my study of film, and vice versa. Both proceed from a base of reasonably nondogmatic Freudianism, idiosyncratically inflected by contemporary ego psychology, the English object relations school (Winnicott and company in particular), the interpersonal theory of Harry Stack Sullivan, and a number of Buddhist psychological teachings.

Since most people I treat are enthusiastic moviegoers, I often find it helpful to use film as a touchstone in therapy. When a movie moves a client, I ask him or her to free associate and regularly find that it has struck some poignant psychic chord, invoked some privileged or painful past experience. Mutatis mutandis, in analyzing a film I often turn to relevant clinical material (as in the dream of the obsessional young man from which I took the title of my chapter on Hitchcock's *Psycho*).[6]

My clinical concerns are intimately related to the group of patients followed at any given time. I've rarely been concerned, in and out of print, with broader metapsychological issues. Correspondingly, I have not much debated the large issues swirling around the cinematic apparatus, subject construction, the nature of genre; nor since the first book have I discussed the forces compelling us to cinema at any length.[7]

My critical focus usually begins (and often remains) with the personality, conflict, and motivation embedded in a current film, which is likely to be a mainstream movie playing at the local sixplex. Exploring its psychological motifs has intermittently provided a springboard for investigating broader thrusts within genre, issues of reception, pathobiography,[8] or some other aspect of filmmaking from an analytic perspective.

In *The Movies on Your Mind,* I cautioned analytic critics against our native literary bias. Nevertheless, my own exegeses still tend to probe the verbal content of the medium more than the visual, a predisposition rooted in training and personal physiology. I have ever been more of a wordsmith than an innate appreciator of images. Searching out the "declarations of camera" that foreground a film's psychological preoccupations does not come easy to me, compared to the acute visual intuitions of a critic like William Rothman.

From the first, my work has addressed the impact of social and cultural trends upon cinema (and vice versa). The earlier critiques were politically neutral, or faintly liberal. Since the early eighties, my ideology has shifted towards the noncombative socialist left, influenced to some measure by the political cast of various texts from my nonmatriculated course in film/cultural studies (inter alia, Althusser via Robert Ray, the Frankfurt School, and various inheritors thereof). Consequently, this book's recent material often cites the role of late twentieth-century capitalism in shaping the reception/production of cinema, as one quite special aspect of the corporate culture's complex impact upon modern consciousness.

My clinical and critical approaches are both centrally informed by modesty of intention. Freud cautioned against messianic expectations for his therapeutic enterprise. Analogously, the reader hoping for some overarching psychoanalytic theorum with which to hunt genre or spectatorship down to earth, or illuminate cinema's entire reach and grasp, will search these pages in vain. I wrote in 1975 and still affirm that "there is . . . more, infinitely more, to patients and pictures than the analysis thereof. . . . let the analyst be as humble in the halls of art as in the office; one has, after all, a limited provenance in either locale."[9]

My interpretations mainly strive for the validity and internal consistency recommended in the next chapter—no mean task in itself.

After "Reel Significations" comes an essay on *Casablanca* and cult cinema. In the happy confluence of circumstance that makes for the enduring popularity of such a film, cinematic craft rates as an inconstant factor. I speculate that the depth psychological theme in *Casablanca* promoting intense viewer identification is its flawed hero's Oedipal dilemma, the resolution of which cunningly articulates with patriotic fantasies of noble doing without to incite a frisson of redemptive renunciation in viewers of both sexes, incredibly potent now as in 1943.

Essays 3 through 6 are devoted to genre, analyzing films from the detective/*policier,* military, and "weird" canons. My genre work is much influenced by Thomas Schatz's seminal formulations on the tension between the individual psyche and the demands of the genre community (the latter frequently reflects some actual ideological thrust impacting upon the offscreen community).[10]

A great deal of my daily therapeutic endeavor involves adolescents, or clients struggling with adolescent issues in later life. While assembling this book I was struck by how often my genre pieces consider like-minded protagonists who wrestle with—or are frankly alienated from—the received values of their respective communities. Sometimes their estrangement is chosen deliberately (the hard-boiled detective); some times it is dictated by hurtful external circumstances (the Vietnam vet).

Adolescent-tinged alienation within genre pinpointed here and elsewhere isn't simply a function of my occupation, or personal preoccupation with the vicissitudes of puberty. Heroes/heroines contending with central pubertal issues—conformity versus nonconformity, fusion with group identity versus radical individuation—have frequently been valorized in a wide range of American narratives dating nearly from the republic's inception (e.g., Natty Bumppo, Huck Finn, Hester Prynne, Ishmael—for that matter, Ahab himself).

Much of my genre writing focuses upon "weird" cinema. The horror film has been widely perceived as an especially fertile playground for psychoanalytic interpretation because it processes such a panoply of unconscious material related to our uncertain origins and unquiet ends. The science-fiction movie deserves equal pride of place in this regard.

After long neglect, adaptation has become a hot topic for film scholars. Essay 7 critiques Ruth Prawer Jhabvala's heavy-handed, albeit instructive botch-up of Henry James's narrative and psychological intentions in the Ivory/Merchant version of *The Bostonians.*

Essay 8 interrogates the tendency toward monumentally big, bad filmmaking, cutting across genre, which has emerged over the past decade or two in Hollywood. The peculiar entity I classify as the "McMovie" is anatomized vis-à-vis style, content, and the notable narcissistic pathology of its hero. The McMovie's creation is ascribed to the relentless commodification of film industry practice, as well as other less obvious influences (television, cocaine, the alarming psychological/intellectual impoverishment that pervades American society). The final essays address developments in mainstream cinema since the McMovie reached its apogee at the height of the Reagan era.

A concluding word on the pleasure of the film theory text, or lack thereof. When he so chooses, Christian Metz can write as appealingly about the movies as any scholar I know. In *The Imaginary Signifier,* he warned about the dangers of loving cinema so uncritically as to become "its third machine . . . after the one that manufactures the films, and the one that consumes them, the one that *vaunts* them, that valorizes the product. Often, by unexpected paths, unperceived by those who have quite unintentionally taken them, writings on film become another form of cinema advertising."[11]

Thus, presumably, can an unwary critic be rendered blind to a film's effaced ideological work. But Metz also speaks feelingly of returning to one's first love "at the next bend in the spiral," so as "not [to] have forgotten what the cinephile one used to be was like . . . and yet no longer be invaded by him; not have lost sight of him, but be keeping an eye on him. Finally, be him and not be him. . . . This balance may seem a somewhat acrobatic one."[12]

My final argument with many contemporary theorists of whatever stripe is that, in the anhedonic rigor of their enterprise, they have eschewed the next bend in the spiral. All too often, they seem to view pleasure at the movies as a seduction away from clarity about the apparatus' more doubtful operations. As their joy in cinema has withered, so has their prose.

Like my first book, the current collection is unashamedly intended to entertain as well as instruct. I see no dichotomy between enjoyment and illumination about the psychology of the movies on our minds. I can only hope that my readers are as pleasured in the course of learning from these pages as have I in all the Bijous of my life.

Reel Significations: An Anatomy of Psychoanalytic Film Criticism

If the little brute were left to himself and kept in his native ignorance, combining the undeveloped mind of a child in the cradle with the violent passions of a man of thirty, he would wring his father's neck and sleep with his mother.

—Denis Diderot, *Rameau's Nephew*

Those who tread on the tiger's tail: the press corps of *King Kong* as homily on the limitations of psychoanalytic intrusions into the halls of art: "It is absurd to conceive that the shibboleths of a single, totalizing strategy will unlock any film or genre. Patient- and dream-texts regularly defy our illusion of absolute understanding. It is no less certain that the cinematic text . . . will endure past the present mode of criticism."

*T*wo and a half centuries before *The Interpretation of Dreams,* Diderot thus boldly anticipated Freud's meditations on the Oedipus complex. Our hidden motives and the heart's dark turnings were ever the artist's native territory. Freud was quick to acknowledge the groundwork art had already laid for psychoanalysis. In 1907 he wrote: "The portrayal of the psychic life of human beings is, of course [the artist's] most especial domain. He was . . . the precursor of science and scientific psychology."[1]

Throughout his career, Freud frequently cited artistic insights to ground his theories. He admired the uncompromising honesty of creators like Ibsen, discovering in their work a willingness to look passion in the eye absent from the psychology of the day. He very likely identified with the singular love of truth that compelled another of his favorite "cases," Leonardo.

The members of Freud's circle needed little encouragement to analyze art. They were people of culture, even considerable aesthetic erudition. Rank and Sachs brought to their apprenticeship with Freud independent backgrounds in the arts. It was as native as drawing breath to search out artistic resonances with the exciting discoveries of the consulting room, to probe art for clues to unravel the riddles of neurotic torment. Freud also encouraged members of the Viennese intelligentsia to join his circle, thus helping to spread variably accurate versions of analytic theory among respectable literati as well as the bohemian fringe.

By 1911 the profession's pervasive fascination with art encouraged Rank and Sachs to found *Imago,* a journal devoted to the psychoanalytic study of the arts and humanities. Over subsequent decades, the original *Imago* and its American version were joined by other journals across the world committed to publishing analytic explorations of art side by side with clinical contributions. The list of papers, monographs, and books in the field by practicing psychoanalysts is now substantial.

Studies of art by analytically influenced academics quickly succeeded work by practitioners. Initially, these met with a less than enthusiastic reception, but by the 1940s and 1950s analytic strategies had become highly regarded within the American critical establishment.

During the first half of the century, most analytic critics focused on literature, drama, and poetry. The "nonverbal" arts—painting, sculpture, architecture, music, and dance—commanded far less attention.[2] Cinema remained almost completely neglected until the last few decades—a puzzling lacuna given the evident "literariness" of most films.[3]

Can Freud's silence on the movies be implicated in the shortage of early analytic film criticism? By his death in 1939, many silent and talking masterpieces were already filmed. Yet cinema goes unmentioned in his papers on the arts, and is only discussed in his letters in passing, during an exchange with Karl Abraham quoted below. As far as is known, he stepped into a movie theater only once, when—appropriately enough—he viewed a Western during his visit to America.

Samuel Goldwyn offered Freud $100,000 to consult on a film about the great love affairs of history, commencing with Antony and Cleopatra's. Reading between the lines of Jones's account,[4] one senses Freud's urbane amusement at the ingenious (and ingenuous) exploitation of his work, combined with irritation at Goldwyn's hucksterism. He summarily rejected the proposal, declined to speak with Goldwyn, and became one of the few authors to turn a deaf ear to Hollywood's siren song. His telegram to the producer supposedly created a greater furor in America than the publication of *The Interpretation of Dreams*!

Did Freud, comparing cinema with loftier fare like *Crime and Punishment,* perceive the former as too base, popular, even too "American"? (He was not enamored of our nation long before the Goldwyn episode.) Was his disinterest related to the debilitating illness which greatly restricted his activity during his later years? (The conjecture does not account for his silence about film during much of the silent era—and before his jaw cancer.)

Throughout the Freudian project, one is struck by the lack of reference to telephones, automobiles, radios—the entire jangling paraphernalia of twentieth-century life. Freud's avoidance of cinema may ultimately reside in his identification with the comforting ethos of the preceding century, and an aversion to a medium identified with the rush and press, the avid technology of modern times, particularly after the debacle of World War I.

Abraham and Sachs were notable exceptions to the inattentiveness of the early Freudians to film (at least, in print). Abraham served as consultant to the director G. W. Pabst on *Secrets of a Soul* (1926), the first serious—if flawed—celluloid depiction of psychoanalytic theory and practice at the movies. Freud did not want his name connected with the project, and was openly skeptical about the participation of one of his staunchest supporters. His statements do seem to indicate misgivings about cinema's aesthetic power—at least its power to convey the nuances of psychoanalytic process. *"My chief objection is still that I do not believe satisfactory plastic representation of our abstractions is at all possible"* (italics Freud's).[5]

The Freud-Abraham correspondence on Pabst's project brackets Abraham's terminal illness. Responding to a circular Freud sent to his adherents complaining about Abraham's "harshness," the dying Abraham wondered mordantly if he wasn't being set up for the rejection previously meted out to Jung and Rank. Freud demurred in a not overly warm reply. Abraham's death shortly thereafter poignantly clipped off possibilities for a definitive reconciliation.

Sachs, a notable film-lover, took over as advisor to Pabst after Abraham's passing and became the director's close friend. He published an accessible monograph on psychoanalysis to accompany *Secrets of a Soul*.[6] He contributed several pieces to *Closeup,* a British magazine "devoted to the Art of Film," which appeared from 1927 through 1933, and which frequently published analytically oriented material.[7] Elsewhere, Sachs reviewed *Battleship Potemkin* (1925); discussed "kitsch" in relationship to psychoanalysis and aesthetics; described the animated cartoon as a hilarious excursion into the world of the id and an embodiment of childhood magical thinking.[8]

The most comprehensive early psychological study of cinema was *The Photoplay,* written by the Gestalt psychologist Hugo Münsterberg.[9] A German who emigrated to the United States, Münsterberg became a rabid fan of all things American. He briefly served as Kissinger-like

Albuquerque Academy Library
6400 Wyoming Blvd. NE
Albuquerque, NM 87109

doyen of the Harvard intellectual set, only to be shamefully discredited by his adopted land in the wave of anti-Teutonic sentiment that swept the United States during World War I.

Münsterberg's phenomenological bent made him acidly critical of the Freudian unconscious, but his insights into the psychophysiology and cognitive aspects of moviegoing sort well with current ego psychology. He astutely recognized that the camera's perceptions were arranged by filmmakers to mimic the intelligence behind the human lens and retina:

[Our] attention turns to detailed points in the outer world and ignores everything else; the photoplay [does] this when, in the close-up, a detail is enlarged and everything else disappears. . . . Memory breaks into present events by bringing up pictures of the past: the photoplay [does] this by its frequent cutbacks (flashbacks). . . . We think of events which run parallel in different places. The photoplay can show in intertwined scenes everything which our mind embraces. . . . *The photoplay tells us the human story by overcoming the forms of the outer world—namely space, time, and causality—and by adjusting the events to the forms of the inner world, namely attention, memory, imagination and emotion.*[10]

This happy correspondence between human and movie eye enables cinema uniquely to reflect back to us our mode of organizing experience, constantly depicting what it is like to be at once within the world, and within oneself.

Desultory interpretations of films occasionally appeared in the professional literature from the thirties through the fifties. All too often these betrayed ignorance both of the medium and nonanalytic critical practices, besides being marred by the naive reductionism of earlier depth psychological art study. Clinicians had yet to learn there was more—infinitely more—to the creator and creation of film than the analysis thereof.

Far too easily an untutored psychoanalysis renders down subtle creativity into a few dreary rubrics—penis envy, faulty bowel training, so forth. Art may evoke in the unwary analyst a kind of exegesic delirium, a madness to interpret solely according to our "mystery." Consequently, as Durgnat acerbicly observes, no work "is felt to be 'about' its subject matter. Its specificity, concreteness . . . richness of detail dissolve into a sort of spiritual soup [making] nonsense of all the differences between one culture and another, one person and another, one [work] and another"[11] . . . and one medium and another.

The authoritative study at mid-century was *The Movies* by Martha Wolfenstein and Nathan Leites,[12] which explored Hollywood and European releases during 1945 for their universal, as well as culture-specific psychological themes—e.g., the "good-bad" girl of Hollywood cinema. The authors found that movies are pervaded by "false appearances": a forbidden wish is portrayed, then denied under the disclaimer—"this never really happened, what *really* happened was . . ."

By ascertaining the "disavowed" plot element about which the film seeks to reassure the viewer, analytic criticism can unmask cleverly rationalized neurotic conflict—e.g., Ilse Lund's adulterous tendencies, based on an unconscious splitting of the masculine image, is "explained" in *Casablanca* (1943) by her "mistaken" assumption that the Nazis had murdered her husband shortly before she met Rick Blaine in Paris.[13]

While psychoanalysis had achieved a firm foothold in literary academia and belle-lettres by the fifties, analytically oriented film studies remained comparatively sparse because of the indifference of psychoanalysts, as well as the limited interest of academics or working critics in serious film scholarship of *any* persuasion. Early work like Parker Tyler's *The Hollywood Hallucination*[14] was often as unknowing about analytic theory as clinicians were about film technique and theory.[15]

More Recent Studies by Psychoanalysts

During the past twenty-five years, working psychoanalysts and academics have created an impressive body of sophisticated analytic film criticism. This reflects the general recognition accorded to cinema as a powerful art form with a remarkably various appeal to sensibilities high and low, with a unique aesthetic and history, with canons and conventions as worthy of the instruments of psychoanalysis as other art forms.

Unlike their Viennese predecessors, psychoanalysts now attend movies often and enthusiastically. Psychiatric residencies, psychotherapy training programs, and not a few analytic institutes use cinema to illustrate psychopathology or psychodynamics. Movies are regularly presented and discussed at analytic meetings. The number of cinema-related papers in journals, and larger studies published elsewhere has increased accordingly.

The majority of film studies by clinicians reflect the more or less orthodox Freudian viewpoint still prevailing at the average American psychoanalytic institute, leavened by ego psychology and object relations theory. A smaller body of Jungian film interpretation exists, but work from the schools of Klein, Sullivan, Horney, Kohut, et al. is difficult to find. Lacanian film studies by American psychoanalysts are virtually nonexistent—a marked difference from academic criticism here and abroad.

Contemporary psychoanalytic film study faces the same problems that have confronted practitioners of "applied psychoanalysis" from its beginnings. Clinical conclusions are intimately bound up with the patient's specific productions, a plenitude rarely if ever replicated in the analysis of art. Instead of the exhaustive documentation provided to the clinician, the analytically inclined literature or drama critic usually makes do with the artist's letters, diaries, and related *materiel*. Taken with the artwork, these are "treated" as one might interpret a patient's associations, transferences, resistances. The inherent limitations of this enterprise are considerable.

By analogy, analytic film criticism labors under the brute reality that "films last no longer than two or three analytic sessions, hence psychological conclusions about plot and character must be highly inferential, especially when certain crucial childhood events that are principal grist for the analytic mill are rarely furnished. We will never know how James Bond took to toilet training, or if Sam Spade sucked his thumb."[16] Probing material collateral to the film may prove even more problematic than in the case of other art. It constitutes a bewildering pastiche indeed—annotated shooting scripts; biographies of director or star, producer or writer; histories of studio and industry; posters, lobby cards, press books, so forth.

All things considered, the analytic film critic does best to heed Freud's modest justification for his method's intrusions into the halls of art, eschewing certainty that one's reading of a film will be definitive. It is most appropriate to provide skillful means for making sense of particular characters or particular films; for ascertaining how clinical psychoanalytic theory can best illuminate the text, characters, or subtext of a film; or for clarifying the viewer's psychological reception of the picture. *Ideally, these endeavors should aim primarily for psychoanalytic validity and internal consistency.*[17]

Psychoanalytic inquiries into cinema have proceeded along similar lines as studies of other art forms, subject to modifications dictated by the medium's peculiarities. Until recently, most studies have used movie scripts or characters to discuss symptoms and diagnosis, normal or pathological mental mechanisms, developmental parameters or psychological vicissitudes of the life stages, so forth.

Pathobiography—a staple of applied literary psychoanalysis—presents particularly thorny problems, since a film is a collaborative effort involving many disciplines. Auteur theory posits the director as the film's true author—hence the search for articulations between events, personalities, and conflictual themes in his/her life history and cinematic oeuvre. However, inquiry into actual industry practice often shows that authority supposedly exercised by directors over their films has actually been quite limited. Pathobiography owns greater currency in evaluating the career and work of auteurs like Fellini, Hitchcock, or Bergman, who have exerted considerable control over their pictures.[18]

The relationship between the biography and work of other key film figures—e.g., actor, producer, screenwriter—has elicited more attention from academic scholars than psychoanalysts. Stephen Weissman's lovely vignette on Chaplin's working through the angst of his orphaned childhood in *The Kid* (1920) illustrates the fertile possibilities for clinical study in this area.[19]

Psychoanalysts have occasionally addressed the obscure feedback process through which moviemakers translate the viewer's inchoate needs, fears, and fantasies into extravagant scenarios. But cinema aesthetics, audience response, and ideological manipulation of the viewer have been subjects pursued by analytic film scholars rather than clinicians. Likewise, the obsessive pull of genre pictures—a significant focus of academic film theory from its inception—has received little scrutiny by professional psychoanalysts.

Studies by Jungian analysts/critics search out cinema's archetypal configurations with results that can be as drably reductionistic as a simpleminded Freudianism. Happily, such is not the case with John Beebe's outstanding explorations into the "transcendent," "alchemical" function of film imagery.[20] Supreme artists like Hitchcock weave archetypal material out of the stuff of everyday reality. Beebe is convinced that viewers are helped in their personal quest for intrapsychic wholeness through identification with the Hitchcockian character's struggle toward transformation and healing.

Recent Developments in Academic Psychoanalytic Film Theory

Before the seventies, most analytically oriented academic cinema study mirrored the Freudianism of clinically trained critics—e.g., the work of

Norman Holland.[21] The Jungian-influenced myth criticism of North-rop Frey and his school, which achieved considerable influence in literary circles during the fifties and sixties, has never attained a similar position in film theory.[22] However, Don Frederickson elegantly speculates upon how a Jungian approach might supplement or even transcend other methodologies.[23] Clark Branson's tendentious interrogation of Howard Hawks's films typifies the pitfalls of a less sophisticated Jungian approach.[24]

Recent academic application of Freudian and post-Freudian thought has been profoundly influenced by the semiotic revolution. The rigorous theoretical emphasis of semiotic critics is a relatively recent development, especially for American film scholarship. Originally the study of "sign systems" that generate spoken and written language, the semiotic enterprise now embraces the production/play of meaning in many other communication fields—physical gestures, advertising, road signs, artwork, so forth.

Auteur theory preceded cinema semiotics, and was forged out of an exhaustive examination of film—notably American movies—undertaken in the fifties and sixties by critics at the influential French review, *Cahiers du cinema*.[25] In retrospect, auteurist reading emerges as another method of "centering" the decoding of film around a monistic creative vision—here, a director's, which implicitly confers upon a movie the aesthetic "legitimacy" of a Beethoven symphony or a Van Gogh painting.

The *Cahiers* group gradually began to incorporate concepts of theorists seeking to "decenter" critical study away from a single, "totalizing" authority. Italian semiotic research (Eco et al.) was appropriated, as well as the work of French-speaking theorists such as Ferdinand de Saussure, the founder of modern linguistics, and the structural anthropologist Claude Lévi-Strauss.

In the context of the 1968 student upheavals, the *Cahiers* writers turned to the politically charged (often leftist) philosophies of Louis Althusser, Roland Barthes, Michel Foucault, Julia Kristeva—and Jacques Derrida, preeminent philosophical opponent of centers, architect-in-chief of the deconstructionist movement. The post-Freudian metapsychology of Jacques Lacan also became increasingly attractive to the *Cahiers* group (Lacan's most influential interpreter for film theory has been Christian Metz).[26]

In one fashion or another the discourses of researchers from diverse disciplines spoke to the organizing "deep" structures embedded in cultural institution and practice. Film theorists became convinced that analogous configurations could be discovered at work in the movies. By the mid-1970s, a new generation of film critics with roots in French theory and semiotics was writing prolifically in England, America, and France. Journals like *Screen* in England, *Communications* in France, *Camera Obscura* and *Wide Angle* in America began publishing papers drawing heavily upon the *Cahiers* methodologies.

A fascinating feature of the semiotic enterprise over the past fifteen years or so has been the rediscovery of Freud by the critical academy. Although Lacanian psychoanalysis goes virtually unpracticed by American clinicians, Lacan's writings are quite fashionable in our universities. Lacanian Freud is a crucial ingredient of Metz's semiotics which, together with related work, is still taught as received truth in many cinema study programs at this writing.

Contemporary psychoanalytic film criticism has been marked (and frequently marred) by polemics directed by the semioticians and their detractors against each other. Some critics who privilege French theory charge that differing approaches, past or present, are hopelessly impressionistic, ideologically naive, lack methodological rigor, are ungrounded in the actual visual "language" of film, or borrow strategies haphazardly from other fields.

Mutatis mutandis, critics outside the charmed circle find the semiotic perspective so top-heavy with arid intellectualizing that it robs film study of specificity and vigor. Semiotic practice itself has been charged with imprecise generalizations; opponents perceive semioticians as hopelessly locked into one ideological regimen or another, tiresomely discovering the same signs in every film—e.g., an eternal return to motifs of castration and absence. Future critics may conclude that the signal contribution of French theoreticians and their disciples has been to foster an intellectual climate in which all are compelled to lay methodology (and ideology) squarely on the table, thereby undermining elitist assumptions that readers share the writers' unspoken judgments.

However, even with the dawn of critical *glasnost,* it can still be fiendishly difficult to locate the precise boundaries of current trends in psychoanalytic film theory, because so many critics thoroughly—and sometimes idiosyncratically—incorporate Freud's legacy into the larger semiotic project. Kaja Silverman even argues that Freudian psychoanalysis should be construed as a branch of semiotics.[27] Like many contemporaries, Silverman's thought conflates psychoanalysis with linguistics, feminism, the theories of kinship structures advanced by Lévi-Strauss, and Marxism.

Jacques Lacan, psychoanalytic doyen of the new criticism, presents problems for even the most knowledgeable analyst or film scholar. His prose is wildly daunting; his terminology seems to slide and shift meaning under the reader's perplexed eye. Silverman notes that it can be impossible to formulate a definitive version of Lacanian theory, because Lacan himself rarely agreed with his own commentators. For the purposes of this discussion, we shall only touch upon Lacan's theories of the mirror stage, the Imaginary, and the Symbolic—and the subsequent use of these constructs in the overarching concept of cinematic "suture."

Lacan's revision of Freudian developmental theory locates the core of the Imaginary in the newborn child's blissful "oceanic" sense of complete union with the mother. Somewhere between ages six and eighteen months the child perceives its image in a mirror, experiencing the reflection as the *anläge* of a unified self-concept. Lacan theorizes that the child then *misrecognizes* its image as more coordinated and focused than it actually is. The "misreflection" is next projected outside itself, and taken as an ego-ideal. Later, when this ego-ideal is introjected, the child begins to passionately desire identification with others. In due time, its desire will dictate the experience of pleasurably identifying with screen characters.

The important element for film theorists here *is the child's exclusive understanding of itself through projection, hence its inability to see itself except in terms of the Lacanian "Other."* Lacan asserts that the infant develops a dramatically ambivalent relationship with the reflected self, loving it (for its embodiment of the child's ideal image), but also hating it (because it resides unattainably outside the body). Consequently, the child acquires a facility that will later be called into play while watching movies—*an ability to identify binarily with exhibitionist and voyeur, master and slave, victim and victimizer.*

This ambivalent order, with its curious extremes of love and hate, is defined by Lacan as the Imaginary. In *The Imaginary Signifier*, Metz suggests that identifying with the visual images encountered in the cinematic "mirror" reconnects viewers with childhood identifications. *Thus, the irresistible appeal of movies resides in their intimate relationship with the mirror stage, with the moment in development when self and Other are first confused.*

With the acquisition of language the child enters the Lacanian Symbolic order. Images produced during the Imaginary stage persist; the Symbolic serves to control and derive meaning from them. Lacan posits a crucial association between the Symbolic order and Oedipal crisis. He proposes that the primordial law of the Oedipus complex centrally informs the order of language.

Language is the means by which we structure the world. In Western culture at least, the Oedipal crisis is resolved by assimilating a patriarchal value system which mediates this structuring. Along with the Symbolic order, the child acquires an acute awareness of sexual difference, ridden with phallocentrism. Lacanian discourse centrally privileges the concept of "lack," perceived in the narrower sense as the phallocentric key to sexual difference, symbolically, as a fulcrum for interpreting the world in terms of presences and absences.

Over the past several decades semiotics, articulated with Lacanian theory, has profoundly influenced diverse critical disciplines. Research has been deflected away from the meaning of the text, and directed toward the processes through which any assumed meaning is *generated*. Cinema semioticians focus on *how* the audience experiences a movie. Rather than psychoanalyzing characters or filmmakers, students of Lacan often explore the complex fashion in which the "cinematic apparatus" invokes the Imaginary and Symbolic orders of the viewer.

Recently, the concept of "suture" has become an important focus of cinema semiotics. It is a highly theoretical, controversial subject, still uncertain of empirical verification. Suture was first explored in Jean-Pierre Oudart's essays for *Cahiers du cinema,* later reprised in *Screen* magazine.[28] Oudart's original views have been variously, and sometimes incompletely appropriated elsewhere. Suture, in terms of the medical metaphor, is usually understood to imply that cinematic gaps created by cutting or editing are "sewn" shut by viewers to include themselves, through identification with some aspect of the "gaze" created by the camera.

According to suture theory, instead of asking "Who is watching this?" and "Who orders these images?" viewers tacitly accept what is seen on the screen as "natural" and "real," even when the camera's gaze shifts abruptly from one scene or character to another. Suture works because the cinematic coding makes each shot appear to be the object of the gaze of whoever appears in the shot that follows.

The most commonly cited example of suturing is the "shot/reverse shot," in which each of two characters is alternately viewed over the other's shoulder. We do not have to ask "Who is watching?" because each shot "answers" the "question" of the previous shot. The Israeli theoretician Daniel Dayan calls this process "the tutor code of classical cinema": "Unable to see the workings of the code, the spectator is at its mercy. His Imaginary is sealed into the film."[29]

Semioticians stress that the "tutor code" is but one device by which classic cinema seamlessly effaces the means of its operations, such that one appears somehow to create the movie within one's head as the projector unspools. The operation of suture in a particular movie dictates the unique fashion of experiencing it, especially determining how an audience is affected by its "subtexts." Viewers may be all too easily influenced by "hidden" ideological agendas, right or left. Conscious manipulation need not always be inferred here; filmmakers may be completely unconscious of the biases that influence them, as well as their craft's hidden powers of persuasion.

Some of the most original, provocative contributions to film theory over the past twenty years come from psychoanalytically oriented feminist critics. Members of this community have conducted rereadings of Freud as searching as any undertaken in psychoanalytic training institutes, albeit for different purposes. The feminist criticism widely disseminated throughout academia[30] is informed by the basic assumption that classical cinema's "apparatus" has historically served the interests of patriarchy (and, implicitly, capitalism). Mainstream movies overwhelmingly valorize the gaze of a male hero, and subordinate the heroine as its object:

In *Suddenly, Last Summer* (1959), Dr. Cukrowicz (Montgomery Clift) first meets the heroine, Catherine (Elizabeth Taylor), a hospitalized psychiatric patient, as she is being supervised by a sadistic nun. Clift is placed in the foreground of the shot. Taylor enters without seeing him. He drifts out of the frame, stationing himself behind a bookcase, and observes an exchange between the victimized Taylor and the victimizing nun. The tormented Taylor unintentionally burns the nun's hand with a cigarette; Clift emerges from left frame to save her from punishment. Later, when a corrupt hospital director demands that Taylor be lobotomized because of her "violent" behavior, Clift insists the burn was provoked. The audience can verify Clift's judgement, since the episode was seen from his viewpoint.[31]

One identifies with Clift because one has "become" him, watching from his compassionate perspective, projecting him into the action as one's surrogate to rescue the helpless, lovely heroine. The feminist critics, however, would perceive Clift—for all his compassion—as part of a system that dominates and regulates the woman's behavior, while simultaneously using her for voyeuristic pleasure.

Laura Mulvey created a revolution in film studies with her groundbreaking essay "Visual Pleasure and the Narrative Cinema."[32] Mulvey theorizes that the patriarchal narrative and camera style of classical Hollywood assuages castration anxiety in male viewers by submitting women to the masculine order, "fetishizing" the anxiety at its source—the woman's body. Hence, the voyeuristic abstraction of the feminine corpus throughout the history of American film, e.g., Busby Berkeley's bizarre eroticized choreography, or the lush display of film noir's dangerous ladies (uncertain heroines like the eponymous *Gilda* [1946], or malevolent antiheroines like Brigid O'Shaughnessy of *The Maltese Falcon* [1941], who must be safely married off or imprisoned so that the masculine status quo ante can be restored).

Psycho (1960) contains more complex examples of suture. Cinematic convention would have one believe that Hitchcock's movies are more "realistic" than Berkeley's production numbers. But in *Psycho* the camera seems to take on an independent life, performing feats which negate the possibility that it might "possess" or signify the gaze of any character: "Just after the famous shower murder, a close-up of the dead Marion (Janet Leigh) alone in her motel room is followed by a long tracking shot away from the bathroom, into the bedroom and across the bed. The camera pauses to "glance" at the newspaper containing the stolen money, then "looks" out the window to the house where Norman Bates (Anthony Perkins) is heard shouting, "Mother!! Oh God, Mother!!! Blood, blood!!!!"[33]

Silverman describes the sequence as essential to an intricate suture system which keeps the narrative going after the heroine has been catastrophically lost. We identified with Marion in the shower, even though the camera frequently threw us back into the Imaginary by letting us experience the murder from several viewpoints—of the victim, the victimizer, even the shower head.

The extent of viewer complicity in the murder becomes clear when the camera becomes the only "living" thing in the bathroom. The tracking shot which rests momentarily on the stolen money promises that the story will continue: "What sutures us at this juncture is the fear of being cut off from the narrative."[34]

To satisfy us the shot continues out the window to the house from

which Norman Bates emerges, the next person with whom we can identify. We are so hungry for suture that we do not rebel against a movie
which implicates us in murder and voyeurism, even exposes its own
"filmwork." What we finally get for our trouble is *Psycho*'s narrative
closure, the statements of a psychiatrist who would seem to comfortably
exorcise our terror with the authority of science.

The comfort is dubious—thinly masking persistent uneasiness about
the horrors into which we have permitted ourselves to be sutured. In the
final scene, Norman speaks eerily to us with the voice of his long dead
mother, once more compelling an identification with the missing Other.
Oudart suggests this Absent One is actually the same unattached, seductive Hitchcockian camera that has brought us into the terror of the Imaginary, and lurks outside the psychiatrist's facile discourse.[35]

Other critics disagree with suture theory's account of classical cinema's "construction" of the viewer. Robin Wood, for instance, denies
that Hitchcock's camera invariably instructs women to collude in the
punishment of transgressors against their sex, or to accept the dominant
male order. Citing the heroine of *Vertigo* (1961), he argues that "from the
moment when Hitchcock allows us access to the consciousness of
Judy/Kim Novak, the male identification position is undermined beyond all possibility of recuperation; no spectator of either sex, surely,
acquiesces in (her) death or perceives the male protagonist's treatment of
her as other than monstrous and pathological."[36]

Raymond Durgnat is even more skeptical about Lacanian analogizing
from the film spectator's mental operations to pathological psychological
conditions. He states that "Lacan's theoretical scoptophilia is fatal to the
study of film."[37]

In their analysis of suture, prominent semiotic theoreticians like
Dayan, *Screen* critic Stephen Heath,[38] and Colin MacCabe[39] notably in-
voke Marxist thought, e.g., Althusser's Marxist reading of Lacan.[40] Althusser argues that ideology represents the Imaginary relationship to
one's specific material conditions. In this context, the suture system is
interpreted as an exploitation of the worker's Imaginary; the product of
complex technology, manipulated by a major industry with an implicit
paternalistic, repressive bias, in order to "naturalize" an arbitrary corporate ethos.

The left-oriented semioticians claim to "demystify" Hollywood films
and their international clones, revealing—at least to their satisfaction—
how viewers can be bound outside of awareness to questionable ideologi-

cal regimens. Although the prose of these influential writers skirts inaccessibility (Heath's in particular), they have provided critics on both sides of the Atlantic with strategies for exceptionally thorough psychological and political readings of cinema.

Many of today's analytically oriented critics neither reject, nor exclusively depend upon Lacan, Metz, Althusser, et al. Stanley Cavell[41] and Robin Wood read Freud for quite different purposes, but both have worked psychoanalytic theory into worthy investigations. Cavell, a prominent philosopher and aesthetician, entertains an abiding interest in the impact of skepticism on modern thought, chiefly citing Freud, Wittgenstein, and Kierkegaard. He is perhaps best known for his study of the recuperation of the ordinary in classic thirties and forties Hollywood "comedies of remarriage." Wood has elegantly analyzed Hitchcock's oeuvre,[42] traced the emergence of conservative trends in popular cinema during the Reagan era, and described a subversive anticapitalist counterthrust in the contemporary horror film.

During the past decade, penetrating interrogations of the relationship between film and dream which cite the relevance of the "dream screen" to film theory have been undertaken by Bruce Kawin, Marcia Kinder, and Robert Eberwein.[43] Drawing on these sources, as well as the pioneering efforts of feminist psychoanalysts like Nancy Chodorow, Gaylyn Studlar has formulated a semiotically inflected theoretical position that rejects the Lacanian/Metzian model.[44] Studlar's study of von Sternberg emphasizes the role of pre-Oedipal dynamics and psychopathology in the evolution of an "aesthetic of masochism."[45]

Outside the feminist canon, but by no means hostile to it, other critics have assimilated psychoanalytic methodologies into ambitious projects that cut across the spectrum of film theory. The work of Robert B. Ray and Dana Polan is especially strong.[46] Ray transcends the parochialism of the *Screen* and *Cahiers* critics, undogmatically borrowing from their methods to illuminate the convenient happy endings and facile reconciliations pervading American cinema. His interpretations are notable for thoroughness and clarity. His approach is admirably flexible, citing Freud, Althusser, and Lévi-Strauss, sans the vague and cumbersome language that characterizes semiotic writing at its worst.

Polan's reading of American films of the forties discovers compelling "other scenes" which undermine what many critics have thought was that cinema's univalent, dominant ideological stance. Polan also assesses the variegated purposes that psychoanalysis serves in Hollywood—as plot device, simplistic explanation of behavior, so forth—in films un-likely as *Fighting Father Dunne* (1947) and *Young Man with a Horn* (1950). While the psychoanalytic study of cinema is achieving increasing importance for clinicians with the onset of the nineties, the prestige of analytic methodology in film academia would seem to be declining. Some critics have moved on to other strategies without comment. A few well-known investigators now proclaim that psychoanalysis has wielded a disproportionate, even unhelpful influence upon cinema studies. In perhaps the most dramatic defection, Ben Brewster—enthusiastic translator of Metz and Althusser, as well as an early member of the *Screen* collective—has publicly deserted that ideological fold for research into early cinema.

Formerly sacrosanct tenets of the semiotic/analytic project are coming under attack in this setting. Thus, film historian Ben Singer critiques Metz's influential concepts of disavowal and fetishism in film spectatorship.[47] Invoking Freud's attribution of fetishism to castration anxiety, Metz had equated the film viewer's experience of "lack" or "absence" in cinema with the child's first traumatizing experience of viewing the mother's "missing" penis. Singer underscores the gross imbalance between the catastrophic nature of the child's castration anxiety, and the substantially less powerful distress (if, indeed, such is present at all) the film viewer might feel upon perceiving the lack of real bodies behind cinema's projected images.

David Bordwell's *Making Meaning: Inference and Rhetoric in the Interpretation of Cinema* is an ambitious metacritical treatise on film theory, which takes aim at virtually every movie scholar who has ever appropriated the psychoanalytic enterprise.[48] A preeminent worker in the field, Bordwell appears to have read everything ever written in film study. He provides a thorough history of the discipline, fleshed out by an extensive *Who's Who*.

He argues that academic film criticism has responded to institutional forces by creating an arcane jargon and methodology excluding all but a small in-group. He asserts that psychoanalysis—notably its French incarnation—has been adopted by the American/English academy as a means of discovering "symptomatic" meanings hidden beneath a movie's smooth narrative surface. These are usually unpacked in a Barthesian demystifying discourse; the film's bourgeois ideology is inevitably "read" as passing itself off *de rerum naturae*. Symptomatic critics justify their privileged status by explicating what "really" is happening to the hapless psyches of the naive audience as the seductive images flash by. Bordwell implies this endless cine-detection may serve little valid purpose beyond providing film theorists with tenure and book contracts.

After discussing a wide spectrum of difficulties in the current criticism's hermeneutic armamentarium, Bordwell endorses a "historical poetics," based upon empirical study as a creative alternative to the endless cycle of "———ian" decoding. Although his vision may not stampede scholars into the archives, it does come at a moment when academics are increasingly studying the art and business of cinema during its first three decades.

In *Mystifying Movies: Fads and Fallacies in Contemporary Film Theory,* Noel Carroll expresses similar reservations about the dogged search for occulted meanings and hidden ideological agendas, going so far as to call for the complete repudiation of the Althusserian/Lacanian paradigm.[49] He focuses upon refuting a handful of influential theorists whose formulations he believes are the most questionable.

Carroll especially labors to expose the false metaphors of "subject positioning," the crucial concept that binds an ideological reading of cinema to a psychoanalytic understanding of spectatorship. He nimbly plumbs the texts of Metz, Braudy, and Heath, inter alia, rejecting their specific arguments point for point—often brilliantly—with the kind of commonsense ratiocination favored by Anglo-American empiricist philosophy. Unfortunately, Carroll's overwhelming contempt for the semiotic/analytic enterprise eventually precipitates dogmatic overkill. He states flatly that

not all beliefs, not all emotional, social, aesthetic, and cognitive responses are candidates for psychoanalytic investigation. Insofar as psychoanalysis is designed to conceptualize irrational behavior, which is only identifiable as a deviation from rational behavior, there is no work for psychoanalysis to do where the behavior is of an unmistakable rational sort. That is, where adequate rationalistic explanations are available, we do not require psychoanalysis.[50]

Carroll resolutely chooses to dismiss—or is ignorant of—inquiries by modern psychoanalysis into the conflict-free sphere of ego functioning, where emphasis is often placed upon cognition untainted by neurosis and, more specifically, upon the healthy artistic ego's successful integration of conflictual material from earlier developmental epochs, via the "artwork."

Carroll's attempts elsewhere to explain away the enormous power of popular cinema on the simple basis of its accessibility, pictoriality, and question-and-answer narration also ignores a large body of scholarship already alluded to, much of which does not call upon Althusserian or Lacanian theory. His assumption that the viewer comes to the movies with ideology firmly in place, incapable of being swayed, appears naive in the extreme.

Psychoanalytic methodology remains a vital force in feminist film theory, especially for those critics who continue to respond to Mulvey's model of spectatorship. In recent studies by Silverman, Penley, Doane, Flitterman-Lewis, and Kaplan, the feminist appropriation of psychoanalysis produces further trenchant readings across a wide variety of film texts.[51]

An exhaustive survey of current concerns in feminist film theory appears in the special issue of *Camera Obscura* entitled "The Spectatrix," accompanied by a valuable bibliography.[52] Fifty-nine critics briefly summarize their perspectives on the problematic of the female spectator. Many contributions express ambivalence or downright dissatisfaction with the portrayal of feminine spectatorship as an ahistorical phenomenon resisting differences of culture, race, ethnicity, and film genre.

The significance of the pre-Oedipal stage in relationship to spectatorial pleasure is also controversial. Studlar's previously noted discussion of a "masochistric aesthetic"—rooted in pre-Oedipal experience, its gratifications potentially available to both sexes—contains the most significant counterstatement yet to Mulvey's insistence that the camera's gaze in dominant cinema is largely shaped by masculine, Oedipally inflected castration anxiety. Studlar's view offers a convincing alternative to what Miriam Hansen has called the "Manichean stance on visual pleasure" which seems integral to Mulvey's initial position.[53]

The bisexual basis for cinematic pleasure is further explored in Tania Modleski's work on Hitchcock, and Linda Williams's studies of pornography.[54] Both authors foreground the fluidity of viewer identification regardless of gender, noting "previously overlooked passive-identifying-masochistic pleasures of male viewers, and . . . active-objectifying-sadistic pleasures of female viewers."[55]

The feminist theorists have not been completely immune to the institutional shift in methodology that parallels the backlash against psychoanalysis. Feminists who formerly made signal contributions to psychoanalytic film theory are now involved with different modes of research (including archival scholarship). Though by no means abandoning her model of masochistic pleasure, Studlar is writing about female reception of 1920s cinema, particularly in fan magazines. Penley, one of the founders of *Camera Obscura* and an assiduous student of psychoanalysis' heuristic potential for avant-garde and mainstream film is lately interested in the "underground" writing practiced by female devotees of the *Star Trek* series.

While feminists may not be as engaged in explicit discussion of theory, many obviously still valorize psychoanalysis as a fundamental ground for larger interpretive projects. Maureen Turim's investigation of the flashback is exemplary for its psychoanalytic elucidations of that complex phenomenon, and for an undogmatic articulation of psychoanalytic theory with other conceptual grids—formalism, structuralism, theories of ideology, philosophies of memory and consciousness, so forth.[56] In her supple approach,

one theory will come to the foreground temporarily, while another recedes. This ebb and flow of points is in part a response to the historical shifts that the flashback undergoes, but it is also a product of my desire not to fix on a single theoretical vantage point that ignores others. Rather than seek to hold on to all perspectives simultaneously throughout this analysis, an impossible and immobilizing task, it is better, I believe, to allow the vantages to shift and comment on one another self-consciously.[57]

This passage could also characterize recent research such as Susan White's overview of Hollywood Orientalism vis-à-vis *Full Metal Jacket* (1988),[58] Ilsa Bick's study of time-travel romance films,[59] essays by Thomas Elsaesser and Patrice Petro on Weimar cinema,[60] and much else that is best in cinema studies today.

Psychoanalysis in Cinema

Hollywood served up idiosyncratic visions of emotional illness and its healing well before Goldwyn's futile attempt to hire Freud. Cinema and psychoanalysis grew up together. From the earliest days of both practices, movies have irrationally idealized or degraded the mental health profession, by turn viewing therapists as objects of admiration, dread, or contempt.

Schneider notes the appearance of three distinct therapeutic "types" at the beginning of the silent era—Dr. Dippy, Dr. Evil, and Dr. Wonderful.[61] They are regularly reincarnated to this day. Gabbard and Gabbard indicate that psychotherapists have been used by filmmakers to fulfill the expectations of virtually every traditional genre, as well as to legitimize the conformist ideology of many a classic screen drama. The therapist often functions as an exemplary narrative facilitator, a faceless *"ficelle"* (Henry James's felicitous use of the term: the *ficelle* is the system of strings controlling a handpuppet), empowering exposition, flashback, dramatic revelation, explaining motivation, so forth.

The Gabbards speculate on the historical basis for Schneider's types. Until the forties, Hollywood favored Dr. Evils and Dr. Dippies. The exposure of military physicians and their patients to new psychiatric techniques derived from psychoanalysis helped demystify the mental health field, contributing to an increasingly positive attitude toward psychotherapy in the postwar period.

Gradually, Hollywood's scales began tipping toward Dr. Wonderful, culminating in a "golden age" of protherapy films which appeared between 1957 and 1963 (e.g., *David and Lisa* [1962], and *Splendor in the Grass* [1961]). The abrupt termination of this era correlates with decline in government-sponsored research (and perhaps a dawning public recognition that psychotherapy offered no instant cures). After another period of disparagement, American movies seemed to be moving toward a more realistic view of the psychoanalyst/psychotherapist, albeit tinctured by a mild resurgence of Dr. Wonderful–ish comfort-cum-hugs (e.g., Judd Hirsch's Dr. Berger in *Ordinary People* [1980]). However, 1991 witnessed the resurfacing with a vengeance of Dr. Evil (*Silence of the Lambs*) and Dr. Dippy (*What About Bob?*). Dr. Wonderful was also reincarnated as the dedicated, unhappy Dr. Susan Lowenstein in *The Prince of Tides*. Lowenstein's increasingly flagrant therapeutic boundary violations culminated in an affair with her fragile patient's twin brother (*The Prince of Tides*). At this writing, successive cineanalysts have been having similar problems keeping their hands off clients and relatives (*Basic Instinct* [1992], *Final Analysis* [1992], inter alia).

In the main, Hollywood has given little back to the profession compared to what it has taken. The Gabbards demonstrate that the mite of therapeutic process displayed at the Bijou is either distorted or trivialized beyond redemption. Cine-therapeutics still largely privileges the quick fix over the boredom and sweat of therapy. Celluloid practitioners continue to push catharsis without insight, the occasional shot of hypnosis, commonsense advice one could get across the garden fence, and a prerequisite amount of parent-bashing (leavened with forgiveness and reconciliation with one's callous progenitors, who presumably would have done better if *they* could have logged in more couch time).

The Future

Psychoanalytic clinicians interested in cinema studies still have much to learn about the realities of filmmaking and the richness of other critical strategies. Mutatis mutandis, many analytically inclined film scholars could profit from acquiring greater depth in metapsychology, or at least a better appreciation of the clinical subtleties which flesh out dry theory.

Not a few film theorists, whatever their persuasion, would do well to be less dismissive of other analytic projects than the orthodox Freudian and Lacanian schema they have staked out as their peculiar corner, into which they often seem to have painted themselves with no easy exit. Polemics by film scholars no less than psychoanalysts leave one with the uneasy impression that, were it possible, their authors would gladly consign dissenters to rack, thumbscrew, and flame.

The worker in the field today, inheritor of postmodern variety, confronts a cornucopia (or Pandora's box!) of multiple methodologies spawned by a host of disciplines. Increasingly, informed analytic criticism is based on knowledge of actual industry history, and of economic and technical practice. In this diverse setting, it is absurd to conceive that the shibboleths of a single, totalizing strategy will unlock any film or genre. Patient- and dream-texts regularly defy our illusion of absolute understanding. It is no less certain that the cinematic text, like its literary counterpart, will endure past the present mode of its criticism. Today's Lacanians may be tomorrow's Kohutians, or else devoted to another as yet unknown practice.

Thus, modest tolerance for a plurality of approaches would seem encumbent upon the contemporary analytic film critic. Happily, flexibility and crossfertilization is finally beginning to occur within our still-fledgling profession. After a half century of naive borrowing, working psychoanalysts with an interest in aesthetics and film theoreticians are finally beginning to learn substantively about each other's work.

Professor Roy Huss's pioneering efforts in this direction were cut off by his untimely death. A prominent educator and film scholar, as well as an adept clinician, Huss wrote brilliantly,[62] and briefly edited *Film and Psychology Review,* inheritor of *Psychocultural Review.* In the pages of that journal, he hoped to build significant bridges between clinicians and academics of different psychoanalytic persuasions. The *Review* did not survive his tragic passing. But Huss's generous vision lives on in the ecumenical spirit emerging within many publications and institutions today.

Cult Cinema: *Casablanca*—If It's So Schmaltzy, Why Am I Weeping?

Any way we go, baby, one or the other
You'll look prettier than me
When we're laid out in the last scene,
You in pink or blue with the angels
Me in the same scar I was born with.
                              —Norman Rosten, "Nobody Dies
                                     Like Humphrey Bogart"

Casablanca: The quintessential Bogart
alienated hero confronts his most hurtful
justification for armoring against
intimacy. Rick wants neither Ilsa's
sympathy nor her rationales for her
supposed faithlessness— "only to punish
her until his pain is driven away."
Courtesy of Museum of Modern
Art/Film Stills Archive.

*C*ritic after critic has come away from *Casablanca* puzzled, almost vaguely ashamed of enjoying the film as if one should somehow have known better. Much has been made of the discrepancy between the picture's aesthetic shortcomings and the intense gut response it invariably provokes. Pauline Kael calls *Casablanca* "the result of the teamwork of talented, highly paid professional hacks . . . a movie that demonstrates how entertaining a bad movie can be."[1] For Andrew Sarris the film is "the happiest of happy accidents," an inexplicable pop masterpiece that eludes auteurist theory.[2]

Certainly, *Casablanca*'s creators had no pretenses that they were worshipping in the temple of high art. The director, Michael Curtiz, was an old war-horse of the Warner stable, with an impressive roster of bread-and-butter pictures to his credit (*Adventures of Robin Hood* [1938], *The Charge of the Light Brigade* [1936], etc.) and no particular cinematic philosophy other than giving his audience one hell of a good time. Howard Koch supposedly assumed the mantle of chief writer by default when a shaky collaboration with Philip and Julius Epstein broke down.[3]

The brothers Epstein left for greener pastures once they sensed the picture was in trouble (or so Koch claims), forcing him to improvise madly from a play by Murray Burnett and Joan Alison that never made the Broadway boards—*Everyone Comes to Rick's.* A tight production schedule supposedly threatened to outrace the hapless author's inventive powers—the legend goes that right down to the wire no one was sure who would wind up on the Lisbon flight as Curtiz, cast members, colleagues, and kibitzers assailed Koch's sensibilities with contradictory advice.

Small wonder that on paper the screenplay rarely heaves itself above the pedestrian. One grants Koch a certain pithy irony, but nevertheless many of his lines read monumentally hokey, or merely graceless[4]— "Victor, please don't go to the underground meeting tonight!" "Was that cannon fire, or is it my heart pounding?" Improbable device and unlikely coincidence abound, but—"Don't worry what's logical," instructed the amiable Curtiz, "I make it go so fast, no one notices!"[5]

In the best Hollywood fairy tale tradition, Koch's flawed scenario underwent a remarkable metamorphosis before the camera. The lines were now utterly convincing, acted by a superb cast against Max Steiner's lovely, slightly overripe score. Bergman and Bogart—the first and last time they played together—lit up the screen. The film went on to garner three Oscars—picture, direction, and, rather incredibly, screenplay.

During the three decades since its release, *Casablanca* has acquired an ineluctable shimmer of nostalgia. Yet it still speaks powerfully to young people born after World War II who are only marginally acquainted with the politics of its day. "*Casablanca* succeeds as allegory, popular myth, clinical psychology . . . and as a superb romantic melodrama," writes Richard Corliss.[6] The secret of the film's perennial appeal continues to elude easy definition. But to a large measure it is the extraordinary attractiveness of the Bogart hero that has made *Casablanca* into the stuff of legend.

I have elsewhere pinpointed the paranoia of characters like Fred C. Dobbs[7] and Sam Spade[8]—blatant paranoia in the former, latent and better compensated in the latter (an excellent case could be made that Dobbs is Spade decompensated, in a more advanced, delusional stage of psychological deterioration!). Throughout his career, Humphrey Bogart was exceptionally successful as the outsider, the dweller in marginal and dangerous milieus, exiled from affection. Typically, the Bogart protagonist has thrust closeness away, exercising eternal vigilance to survive in a hostile world. Men savagely compete with him, women seek to ensnare and exploit him. Inevitably, his deepest allegiance must be to his own embattled self if he is to keep his tenuous balance on the precipice.

But if the essence of the Bogart persona were pure paranoia, nothing truer or finer, I do not think we would still be drawn to his mystique. Paranoids of whatever stripe are rarely notable for their endearing qualities. Dobbs and Spade are unadmirable, unlikable men. In their icy denial of the heart, they resemble the ruthless gangsters of earlier Bogart movies. Yet it is unlikely we would have been given the later disillusioned romantics and cynical humanists, were it not for the melancholy hoodlums Bogart portrayed with increasing subtlety and depth. In Bogie's criminals taken at their best, the potential for violence could be tempered by an unexpected softness and sadness. One remembers Roy Earle, the inarticulate bank robber of *High Sierra* (1941), who spent his ill-gotten gain healing a faithless crippled girl, and whose affection for a raggedy mutt precipitated his bloody death.

As Bogart grew in talent and stature, the troubled idealist behind the callous facade became more accessible. One discerned an authentic decency shining through the uncaring mask the traumatizing past had forced upon the protagonist. Surely the prototype of these embittered gentlemen is Rick Blaine, exiled champion of lost causes come to uneasy rest in pro-Vichy Casablanca, owner and sole proprietor of the nightclub where the silver screen's headiest blending of patriotic and erotic fantasy is acted out.

Casablanca was filmed in 1942, while the United States still preserved ties with the Vichy regime in France and its North African colonies. This allegiance provoked sharp censure of President Roosevelt by increasingly vocal antifascist Americans. In retrospect, Roosevelt's tangled Vichy policy was never dictated by sympathy for the Nazis or their minions. Rather, his advisors failed to grasp the charisma of Charles De Gaulle, and Roosevelt himself apparently had taken a dislike toward the ascetic, inflexible colonel who was exiled in England and heavily touted by Winston Churchill.

Roosevelt sought to woo better-known French military figures thought friendlier to American interests. Unfortunately, some of them were frank collaborators, such as the notoriously corrupt Admiral Jean Darlan, while others owned divided loyalties—like General Henri Giraud, a personal friend of Petain, but an avowed anti-Nazi. Roosevelt hoped that Giraud and Darlan could persuade a conservative, Anglophobic colonial French army elite not to resist a combined English-American invasion of North Africa.

Casablanca was first released in November of 1942. By then, the reactionary French officers ruling the colonies with our tacit consent had proven as repressive and unfriendly to the Allies as the Nazis. American troops had been killed by Vichy gunfire on North African soil. Despite his opposition to the Gaullists, Roosevelt significantly elected to show *Casablanca* at the White House on New Year's Eve, December 31, 1942. The president may very well have been telegraphing a change in strategy, for soon afterward the controversial connection with Vichy was severed. Two weeks later, on January 14, 1943, Roosevelt traveled to Casablanca to confer with Churchill, De Gaulle, and Giraud. Giraud was discarded not long after the Casablanca conference, and Roosevelt, however unhappily, accepted De Gaulle as unquestioned commander of the Free French forces. My summary does scant justice to the Byzantine complexity of U.S.–Vichy–Free French–Allied relations.[9]

Warner Brothers sounded the alarm over Hitler several years before America's formal entry into the European theater. The studio already had produced strong antifascist pictures in the late thirties and early forties—*Confessions of a Nazi Spy* (1939), *The Great Dictator* (1940), so forth. One guesses that the makers of *Casablanca* were either ignorant or scornful of Roosevelt's devious games.[10] Hence, Rick Blaine's refusal to take up the sword, at a time when Hollywood had become a haven for talented emigrés fleeing Nazi persecution, may well have been intentionally symbolic of the Roosevelt administration's vacillation in North Africa. By the same token, Rick's change of heart at the end would forcibly point out to our equivocating leaders the path of honor.

The cinematic Casablanca actually captures the essence of the city during those turbulent days, however perceived through Hollywood's distorting prism.[11] Espionage flourished. One reason Roosevelt insisted upon keeping a legitimate American presence throughout Vichy territory was to provide cover for the efforts of an impressive intelligence network. For example, a dozen "vice-consuls" dispatched to North Africa in aid of studying "social and economic conditions" were actually OSS operatives on the payroll of "Wild Bill" Donovan. They frequented haunts very much like Rick's café—sleazy hotbeds of intrigue where "German and Italian officers, spies, double agents, genuine diplomats and elegantly coiffured prostitutes" rubbed elbows.[12]

Thousands of refugees from the blitzkrieg swelled the city's population. Many were Jewish, and at least fairly well off. They arrived by tortuous routes; then, unless they owned wealth or influence enough to promote a quick exit, they were entangled by the corruption and prejudice of the Vichy bureaucracy. Victimized by pitiless predators who fattened upon their suffering, their hope and cash dwindling each day, the refugee presence lent Casablanca the air of a bourgeois concentration camp, a kind of festering Brighton.

The film's opening quickly sketches in this hectic ambience. Columns of dispossessed trudge wearily forward, superimposed upon a revolving globe. The camera pans down from a mosque into the teeming streets of Casablanca. To the ominous strains of "Deutschland über Alles" a police official intones over the radio: "Two German couriers carrying important official documents murdered on train from Oran . . . round up all suspicious characters." A man in the crowd is seized by police. He breaks away, is shot down before a poster of Marshal Petain, in his wallet documents bearing the Cross of Lorraine. Suspects are herded into the station house, under the tarnished motto "Liberté, Egalité, Fraternité."

An airplane drones overhead, followed by the hungry gaze of the refugees. But the plane is not the daily flight to Lisbon, gateway to freedom in the Americas. It displays the swastika, and carries Major Heinrich Strasser (Conrad Veidt; earlier in his career a German matinee idol, as well as the somnambulist of *The Cabinet of Dr. Caligari* [1919]), a Gestapo official complete with monocle, disdainful smile, and a thoroughly nasty disposition. Strasser is met by the Vichy prefect of police, Captain Louis Renault (Claude Rains). The two are perfect foils—Strasser, apotheosis of the Hollywood Nazi; Renault, a stock company Parisian, urbane, witty, an inveterate womanizer. Renault regards the corrupted world and his own lack of scruples with equally amused detachment. He is outwardly deferential, but his *politesse* has a derisive edge that is lost upon the arrogant Nazi:

> RENAULT: *Unoccupied* France welcomes you . . . you may find the climate of Casablanca a trifle warm, Major.

> STRASSER: Oh, we Germans must get used to all climates, from Russia to the Sahara.

Renault assures Strasser that the courier's murderer will be taken tonight at Rick's nightclub—"Everyone comes to Rick's!"

Dissolve to the Café Americain at the edge of the airport. Throughout the film, a finger of light from the airport beacon sweeps intermittently across the club, evoking intimations of escape or confinement. The camera ushers us inside where the decor is ersatz Moorish, and a jaunty Negro, Sam (Dooley Wilson), entertains a receptive crowd from his piano. We drift from table to table, through shady deals and the exchange of dubious information in diverse accents: "Waiting, waiting, waiting, I'll never get out of here, I'll die in Casablanca . . . Sorry, Madam, but diamonds are a drug on the market, everybody sells diamonds . . . The fishing smack, *Santiago*. It leaves at one tomorrow night. Bring fifteen thousand francs, *in cash*."

The clientele embraces nearly every race and condition, dressed elegantly or humbly, faces reflecting feverish gaiety, furtive greed, blind hope, dumb resignation. Everyone *does* come to Rick's. The club is a ship of fools, a frenetic microcosm of Casablanca and the world beyond the airstrip, a world in chaos, where tradition and class distinction have been turned upside down.

In the gaming room, affluent guests ask a genial waiter, Carl (S. Z. "Cuddles" Sakall), a former mathematics professor, to invite the owner to their table. Carl refuses—Rick never drinks with the customers. Perhaps, insists a gentleman, if Rick knew he ran the second largest banking house in Amsterdam? Carl responds: "That wouldn't interest Rick. The leading banker in Amsterdam is now the pastry chef—and his father is the bellboy!"

Close-up: an empty glass, a smoldering cigarette, a hand scribbles across a check— "OK—RICK." The camera pulls back, revealing Richard Blaine staring expressionlessly at a chessboard, perennial loner in a crowd. Commotion at the door. He rises, peremptorily disposes of a bumptious German trying to bull his way in. An unctuous little exporter of refugees, Ugarte (Peter Lorre), approaches him. Rick pointedly evades questions about his origins and disparages Ugarte's hypocritical expression of sympathy for the murdered couriers: "They got a break. Yesterday they were just two German clerks. Today, they're the Honored Dead." Ugarte insinuates that he killed the couriers to obtain "Letters of Transit, signed by General Weygand. They cannot be rescinded, not even questioned."[13] He is going to sell the letters tonight for a fortune, and quit Casablanca. Precisely because he knows Rick despises him, Ugarte thinks the American can be trusted. He hands him the letters, and Rick surreptitiously slips them under the top of Sam's piano to the tune of "Who's Got Trouble?" (Sam's songs cleverly furnish a running commentary on the action throughout the film.)

Signor Ferrari (Sydney Greenstreet), the bloated proprietor of the rival Blue Parrot and head of the thriving black market, importunes Rick to sell him the café—an offer, one senses, tendered many other times and ritually rejected once again. As Rick passes by the bar, a young woman drunkenly reproaches him.

YVONNE: Where were you last night?

RICK: That's so long ago, I don't remember.

YVONNE: Will I see you tonight?

RICK: I never make plans that far ahead.

Before she can make any more trouble Rick hustles her out, and directs his mad Russian bartender, Sascha (Leonid Kinskey) to take her home. "What a fool I was to fall in love with a man like you!" she cries after him.

Renault, who has observed the scene, joins Rick on the terrace. He wonders wryly if his chances with Yvonne will improve now that Rick has thrown her over. He, too, attempts to probe Rick's past.

RENAULT: I have often speculated on why you don't return to America. Did you abscond with the church funds? Did you run off with a senator's wife? I should like to think you killed a man!

RICK: It was a combination of all three.

RENAULT: And what in heaven's name brought you to Casablanca?

RICK: My health. I came . . . for the waters.

RENAULT: The waters? We are in the desert!

RICK: I was misinformed.

When Renault advises him not to interfere in an arrest at the club tonight, Rick counters sharply—"I stick my neck out for nobody!" The film has deftly established him as the morose master of a unique private kingdom. He has indeed come to Casablanca for his health—his spiritual health, in a misguided quest to cure melancholy with solitude. Within the perimeter of the Café Americain, Rich has reinvented himself. Like Sam Spade, his paramount concern is the preservation of his privacy. Outsiders, whatever their purposes, are treated as unwelcome intruders—the customers who want him to join them, the obstreperous German, Ugarte, Ferrari, Yvonne—even Louis Renault.

Sam Spade enjoys thwarting intruders, but there is little zest in Rick and much grimness. His waning energy has been consumed constructing a sanctuary run by a cadre of devoted followers, requiring a minimum of personal engagement. Defended against human contact and comfort beyond the ritual camaraderie of his staff, Rick exudes an air of haughty withdrawal enormously attractive to customers. But his attention is inextricably turned inward. Depressed and dispirited, he prowls his borders, a brooding enigma cloaked in inviolable sadness. Unlike Fred C. Dobbs and Spade, Rick still evokes warm responses and concern from others. His paranoia is not yet confirmed, although given sufficient time it might yet prevail.

Of those seeking to penetrate his cover, Rick seems most sympathetic to Louis Renault. Renault seeks Rick's friendship, but his questionable politics and competitiveness stand in the way. Renault envies and resents Rick's easy success with women—note his fantasy of taking up Rick's discarded mistress. Rick shares Renault's mistrust of altruistic motive. However, Renault's opportunism is worn gaily; he's still very much a social being, while Rick has come to serve himself alone out of the extremity of his despair.

Renault reveals that a famous Czech freedom frighter, Victor Laszlo, has escaped from the Gestapo and arrived in Casablanca. A mysterious beauty travels with him, and it's rumored he has the cash to purchase the letters of transit. Renault observes that Rick is impressed by mention of Laszlo, the first time he's ever seen him impressed by anyone. Rick bets the prefect ten thousand francs that Laszlo will succeed in escaping Casablanca, but wonders why Renault thinks he would help the Czech. Renault suspects the secretive American is a closet idealist; he knows Rick ran guns in Ethiopia and fought against Franco in Spain. Rick becomes obviously uncomfortable, implies he's always acted purely for profit, but fails to convince the wily policeman.

Meanwhile, Strasser and his party have been ushered to a choice table ("I have . . . given him the best," says Carl, "knowing he is German and would take it anyway!"). On cue, Renault's men arrest Ugarte at the roulette wheel. He flees through the club to Rick, who coldly refuses to lift a finger as the little man is dragged off, still screaming for help. "I stick my neck out for *nobody!*" repeats Rick to an offended bystander.

Renault introduces Rick to Strasser. It becomes evident that the Gestapo has a file on him, too: "Richard Blaine, age 37—cannot return to his country—the reason is a little vague." Like Renault, Strasser thinks Rick might help Laszlo. His interrogation yields only bland evasions and Rick's assurance of absolute neutrality—"You'll excuse me, gentlemen. Your business is politics, mine is running a saloon!"

Strasser's dossier compounds rather than clarifies Rick's mystery. Noble and base motives are commingled in this "saloonkeeper." He has fought on the right sides, but always (he would have us believe) for the worst reasons, strictly as an entrepreneur. Rick is an exile; much is made of this, but the film never explains exactly why he can't go home again.

He might have been scapegoated for a Red-lover: there were witchhunts in the thirties. But the exile of a native American for political reasons is usually self-imposed. Although it's not impossible his actions in behalf of leftist causes may have put him on the wrong side of the law (notably as a gunrunner), *I* should like to think that Rick has never committed a deportable or indictable offense. His banishment is *symbolic.* Very likely *Casablanca*'s creators meant it as a metaphor for the bitter estrangement the Committed Left felt from the majority of their countrymen who remained indifferent to the ravages of fascism. I submit that at a deeper level Rick is exiled from *himself,* and theorize that a crime is indeed involved, or—more accurately—disturbing fantasies attendant upon one of the first crimes a male child ever contemplates, particularly in the nuclear family of bourgeois Western culture.

Oedipus, king of Thebes, was condemned to wander blindly through alien lands because he slew his father and wedded his mother. Louis Renault jokes that Rick cannot return to *his* homeland because he is guilty of stealing sacred property (church funds), absconding with a high official's wife (the *president's* wife in an earlier script, later amended to a senator's wife), or murdering someone. Equally in jest, Rick confesses to "a combination" of all three offenses.

The psychoanalyst, accustomed to searching out hidden truth in such banter, interprets the sacrosanct stolen treasure as the wife of a preeminent older man, and her husband as the murder victim. Renault, Rick's alter ego, meditates upon Oedipal struggle in his mock charges against the man he would have as friend. Deadly intent toward a beloved father, a crucial motivator for the little boy's anxiety and remorse during the Oedipal stage, still appears to trouble Rick's adult sensibilities. Sam Spade bedded his partner's wife, and was indirectly responsible for his death (see essay 3). One may only speculate how Rick's Oedipal fantasies were acted out on home ground. The scenario will provide him with ample opportunity to confront them in Casablanca.

Victor Laszlo enters the club, clad in immaculate white, lean, elegant, and self-assured; on his arm is a woman of extraordinary loveliness, also in white (the underground appears to be taking good care of its own). The couple is an instant cynosure. Sam, glancing up from his piano, recognizes the lady with yearning and intimations of catastrophe; shortly thereafter, he launches into "Love For Sale"! Renault goes to their table, and she asks him about "the boy who is playing the piano." Renault tells her that Sam came from Paris with Rick, and that "Rick is, well, Mademoiselle, he is the kind of man that . . . if I were a woman . . . and *I* were not around, I would be in love with Rick!" The prefect unwittingly betrays repressed homosexual longing for the very man he's been competing with. In the therapy of committed "straights," the psychoanalyst often discovers unconscious sexual attraction toward an idealized and envied rival.

Strasser attempts to speak with Laszlo. When the Czech is deliberately offensive, the major superciliously orders him in for interrogation at Renault's office the next morning and stalks off. Laszlo goes to the bar, learns to his dismay from an underground contact that Ugarte has been taken. Meanwhile, the woman in white has bidden Sam and his piano to her side, setting in motion the mainspring of the plot.

Sam is deferential, wary: he well remembers how this Circe can enchant, then hurt. We, too, have been moved by her powerful blend of innocence and sensuality. The camera eye catches Bergman in a series of breathtaking close-ups, as she tempts every man who sets his eye upon her, the more enticing for her disarming lack of seductiveness.

She asks Sam to play "some of the old songs"; he tries "Avalon," but it is not what she wants to hear. He evades her questions about Rick with the feigned imbecility of a black man who dares not confront a white woman head-on with deeply disapproving feeling. When she persists, he drops his handkerchief-head routine with a gentle admonition: "Leave him alone, Miss Ilsa. You're bad luck to him." Still she presses him: "Play it once for old time's sake. . . . Play it, Sam. Play—'As Time Goes By'!"

Against his better judgment, Sam is swept away by her allure, by their shared nostalgia for happier days. He sings of the timeless rituals of lovers, and Ilsa's eyes brim with tears. Rick comes tearing out of the casino, furious at hearing the forbidden song. The music stops for a few heartbeats, as Rick gazes at her across the months of anguished, now aborted, mourning.

Renault and Laszlo, returning from the bar, discover them thus. Before Renault can introduce them, they greet quietly. Renault tries to present Laszlo to Rick, but Ilsa firmly takes over—she *wants* the two men to meet, and at her direction! To Renault's surprise, Rick breaks a standing rule and accepts Laszlo's invitation to join them for a drink. They exchange compliments. It is evident Rick considers himself the Czech's inferior:

LASZLO: This is a very interesting café. I congratulate you.

RICK: And I congratulate you.

LASZLO: Thank you. I try.

RICK: We all try. *You* succeed.

At Renault's instigation, Rick and Ilsa speak about their last meeting—in Paris, the day the Germans occupied the city. "I remember every detail," says Rick. "The Germans wore gray. You wore blue." Their recollections skirt the edge of indiscretion. Lazslo, unperturbed, rises to leave and Rick takes the check. "Another precedent broken," Renault exclaims with relish.

Throughout the scene, Rick has addressed Ilsa evenly, as if there were nothing between them. After she goes, his poise crumbles. A few hours later find him hunched numbly over a half-empty bottle as the airport beacon intermittently probes the darkened, empty café. Sam tries to cozen Rick into fishing, drinking, some other worthy masculine pursuit. But Rick is obstinate—"I'm waiting for a lady"—so Sam remains on to watch over his employer.

How deeply rooted were our prejudices that, in a film of such liberal pretentions, the slighting reference to "the boy at the piano" falls so trippingly from a white heroine's lips (and an antifascist to boot). Sam stands on much more equal footing with Rick than most blacks with whites in cinema of the forties, but his character is nonetheless warped by racist convention. He owns enough native dignity to escape total caricature. But if he is no Stepin Fetchit, there is still a great deal of Uncle Tom in him—in his self-effacing servicibility toward "Mr. Rick," and his humble demeanor toward "Miss Ilsa."

Sam's music provides the key that unlocks the lovers' longing. But Sam himself, like his songs, is only a touchstone, lacking substance or sexuality, a gelded servant. He loves Rick, yet isn't even permitted the limited prerogatives of the white hero's "sidekick" in the western or adventure genres. Note that he is not allowed to fight beside Rick with the Free French at the film's end. One concludes Sam is a slightly liberalized edition of that old Hollywood favorite, the faithful family retainer of the antebellum plantation house, Uncle Remus in *Song of the South* (1948),

Mammy in *Gone with the Wind*—the surrogate "darky" parent who hovers anxiously over the fortunes of his or her adoptive white children and respects, indeed treasures, a lower place in the order of things.

"It's December 1941 in Casablanca," muses Rick. "What time is it in New York? . . . I bet they're asleep in New York—I bet they're asleep all over America! . . . of all the gin joints, in all the towns, in all the world, she walks into mine!" He free-associates America's unwillingness to recognize the rise of fascism with Ilsa's reappearance. The connection is not accidental: Rick projects upon the remiss homeland his own ideological dereliction, for he has let his commitment to the cause of liberty slumber since a disastrous affair with her. Now he asks Sam to "play it again," and the camera slips away from his face, bleak with the memories stirred by the music, into a flashback. . . .

Paris, before the German invasion. Rick and Ilsa meet and fall in love. Presaging the lovers of *Last Tango in Paris* (1972), they promise not to question each other's past. But Rick, like Brando, cannot keep to the bargain. Why should someone like himself be lucky enough to find her unattached? (Even the happier Rick is faintly self-minimizing.) Ilsa admits there was another man, but he is dead and Rick her only beloved. Cut to newsclips of the *Anschlüss*. Now it isn't safe for Rick—he has a "record," a Gestapo price on his head (no reason given, vide supra).

At the bar of their favorite bistro, Sam playing in the background, Rick toasts Ilsa with the last of the proprietor's champagne—"Here's looking at you, kid!" Ilsa pleads with him to flee. Chuckling at the thought, he suggests they marry on the train from Paris. She doesn't share his joy, but he's oblivious to her suffering. She promises to leave with him later in the day, and asks to be kissed "as though it were the last time."

Dissolve to Rick, waiting at the station. Sam brings him word that Ilsa checked out of her hotel, leaving a cryptic message that she can never see him again . . . "You must not ask why. Just believe I love you." Rain blurs the page, Ilsa's cruel farewell seems to dissolve in tears. Rick throws the fatal letter away and stares, utterly devastated, down the platform.

Dissolve back to the present. Ilsa stands at the door; she says she would not have visited the café had she realized he was *the* Rick, but this only exacerbates his smouldering resentment. He wants neither her sympathy nor her explanations, only to punish her until his pain is driven away. She belatedly tries to tell him something of her history, about a young girl from Oslo, freshly arrived in Paris, who met "a very great and very good man." He opened her eyes to a new world of ideas and ideals—"and she looked up to him, worshiped him with a feeling she supposed was love."

Rick rudely stops her. He's heard it all before, to the tune of "a tinny piano in the parlor downstairs." Ridden with self-disgust, he plunges on nevertheless, driven to soil irreparably what he once held so dear. "Who was it you left me for? Was it Laszlo—or were there others in between? Or—aren't you the kind that tells?!?" She refuses to honor his spite with an answer, leaving silently. Rick's head slumps forward, and we do not see, but rather sense, his tears.

Degrading her into every man's slut will, he hopes, redeem his loss, for if she is a whore then it is of meager consequence to have lost a whore's affections. Yet, listening with the third ear, one hears the strangled scream of pain over his beloved's betrayal in the arms of a more desirable lover. The Bogart protagonist rarely speaks openly of these abrasions upon his spirit. Instead, one is more likely to encounter the precipitate of pain: a protective shell of paranoia, flawlessly articulated against the peril of further involvement—"Nobody takes advantage of Fred C. Dobbs!"

Rick dismisses Ilsa's account of a schoolgirl infatuation with Laszlo as a cheap rationale for her promiscuity. His accusation contains a kernel of psychological truth, for she is not quite the innocent she seems (or believes herself to be). She has actually been unfaithful to Rick *and* to Lazslo, although *Casablanca* will go to great lengths to justify her infidelity. She would have us believe she would never have come to the Café Americain, had she known Rick was in Casablanca. If the club's name wasn't sufficient tip-off, Sam's presence should have alerted her. For, knowing *his* fidelity, she could have guessed that whither Rick went, there surely followed Sam. Nevertheless, she stays and compels Sam to play the song that must bring Rick back into her life.

In my interpretation of *The Maltese Falcon* (see essay 3) I describe the "madonna-whore" complex, wherein a man cannot endure one woman satisfying both sexual and nonsexual needs because of anxiety over unconscious incestuous feelings toward his mother. The feminine image in this case has been split, so woman is viewed either as an all-good source of nurture and support, or an all-bad object of sexual desire. The typical madonna-whore type goes unaroused or frankly impotent with his spouse, for the wife unconsciously represents the forbidden mother. But sex will be highly enjoyable away from the marriage bed, often with women chosen from a lower social class, or from a denigrated ethnic/religious background—as different from the idealized, nonsexual mother as night from day.

The madonna-whore complex is but one of many symptomatic outcomes of the male Oedipal configuration. If a little girl cannot work through the vicissitudes of the corresponding Electra complex, she too may experience a radical "good/bad" split in her unconscious image of the male. Such may be the outcome when a father has behaved seductively toward his daughter, escalating the erotic fantasies of the Electra phase, intensifying her wish to supplant the mother, as well as fear of her mother's punishment for harboring "reprehensible" longings.

In the flush of her youth, the daughter may find herself unaccountably drawn to an older man—frequently a widower!—who wakens the noblest sentiments in her bosom, yet fails to inspire passion, for passion would complete the dreaded equation between suitor and father. Eventually she becomes physically attracted to another man, usually younger and—in the more troubled variations on this theme—from a baser or frankly debased background (e.g., the heroine of *The Barefoot Contessa* [1954], whose yen for assorted loutish types the film ascribes to her Gypsy origins, rather than incestuous anxiety).

The woman in question may opt for marriage to the older man, drawn to his wisdom, kindness, or prestige, then keep a troubled relationship afloat by a succession of affairs, inevitably returning to the father substitute. (The "Contessa" weds a gentle, castrated nobleman, but still can't keep her mitts off the gardener inter alia.) She may eventually work through her neurotic splitting with or without therapy, leave her husband with the recognition that her marriage is a bloodless fiction, or discover she truly loves him and make a decisive commitment.

Ilsa Lund has been incapable of commitment to one man, neither to Laszlo, who we will discover is her husband, nor to Rick. Her vacillation makes her a teasing riddle to both her lovers, indeed to every man who comes within her magnetic field and imagines she can be his, for in fact she can be no one's. Laszlo constitutes an idealized, asexual father figure: he inspires heroic thoughts, but leaves her frigid below the neckline. I suggest that Rick, this mysterious man of questionable background, lacked Laszlo's ethical purpose even before Ilsa left him, his idealism compromised by self-doubt, and perhaps a tinge of venality. For Rick, a dethroned, humanized Laszlo, for flawed and fallible Rick, Ilsa may burn. Relative to the Czech's implacable righteousness, Rick is made of baser metal; but he is also inherently more attractive, as Milton's bloodless God pales in comparison to Lucifer.

At Renault's office the next morning, Strasser offers Laszlo freedom in return for betraying the underground leadership. Laszlo predictably denounces the Nazi. Renault, ever amused by any excess of zeal, takes the wind out of his sails with the news that Ugarte has died during the night, presumably from Gestapo foul play.

Rick visits the Blue Parrot to allow the police to search the Café Americain. Ferrari, suspecting he has the letters, offers to dispose of them at an enormous profit, but Rick plays dumb. Laszlo and Ilsa arrive; while Laszlo goes off to confer with Ferrari, Rick fumbles an apology. It is Ilsa's turn to play the rejector. Soon she will quit Casablanca, never see him again, it is better that way. Rick let his guard down tentatively, now it goes up, instantly. He says she will lie to Laszlo as she lied to him, and then he'll be waiting for her—"up a flight." Never, she rejoins, Laszlo is her husband, and was at the time of their affair! Having delivered the coup de grace, and incidentally vindicating his paranoid certainty of her faithlessness, she leaves him speechless.

Ferrari has told Laszlo he cannot secure him a visa—even though "as leader of all illegal activities in Casablanca I am an influential and respected man." It would be possible to smuggle Ilsa out. But she refuses—she stands by her husband, just as he has never abandoned her. Ferrari is transformed, another cynic converted to altruism against his better judgment (the film is full of them!), and counsels Laszlo to see Rick about the letters.

Later that evening, the same cast of characters reassembles at the café. Rick gloomily mulls over Ilsa's revelation. Annina, a comely Bulgarian refugee, interrupts his drinking, and pleads for guidance. Her husband is trying unsuccessfully to raise money for visas at the tables. Captain Renault has promised to waive his usual bribe if she will give herself to him. Can he be trusted? She asks Rick for absolution in advance of sinning:

ANNINA: If someone loved you—so that your happiness was the
        only thing that she wanted in the world . . . and she

did a bad thing to make certain of it . . . could you forgive her?

RICK: Nobody ever loved me that much.

Rick dismisses her as harshly as he did Ilsa the previous night. But a moment later, after greeting Laszlo and Ilsa courteously, he fixes his own roulette wheel, letting Annina's husband win to her overwhelming gratitude, his staff's admiration, and Renault's chagrin. Then, when Laszlo asks him in the name of the dignity of man—or for several hundred thousand francs—to part with the letters, Rick refuses: "I'm not interested in politics. The problems of the world are not my department. I'm a saloonkeeper." Rick positively glories in the title, masochistically savoring his downfall. He tells Laszlo his wife knows why he will not yield.

Annina's dilemma has struck uncomfortably close to home. Like Ilsa, she seems the soul of innocence, yet she is ready to betray her beloved and sell herself, for the purest reasons, of course. Pity for her plight and rage at her perfidy struggle for mastery in Rick's divided heart. By letting her husband win, Rick affirms his basic decency, but also cheats the prefect of his prize.

Renault is more than Rick's competitor—he is an extension of Rick's persona as well. His principles also lie in hopeless disrepair. He, too, has excluded himself from the lists of love—he indulges in casual liaisons with women who value his power over his person. Tellingly, he asks Rick: "Why do you interfere with my little romances? When it comes to women, you have charm, I have only visas." At this point, Rick has only the letters with which to vanquish Laszlo and win back Ilsa—how shoddy a victory!

Strasser leads his party in a thumping rendition of "Die Wacht am Rhine." Hearing the hated anthem, Laszlo strides decisively over to the orchestra, and demands the "Marseillaise." The bandleader looks uncertainly to Rick, who having just stated his disinterest in crusades, once again reverses field and nods permission. On one side of the café, Strasser urges his men into the harmonic fray, while on the other Laszlo shakes his fist at the despoilers of liberty, while Ilsa watches admiringly. The scales shift—the majority take up the "Marseillaise" with mounting exhilaration as the Nazis subside and sit glumly by. Tears stream down the cheeks of patriot and erstwhile collaborator alike. The die is cast. At Rick's behest, a line has been drawn between good and evil, in a place where moral ambiguity has been the order of the day—also at Rick's behest.

The "Marseillaise" concludes to wild applause. Outraged, Strasser commands Renault to close down the cafe on any pretext. "I'm shocked!" cries the prefect, "*shocked* to find that gambling is going on here!" as a croupier surreptitiously hands him his winnings. Strasser threatens Ilsa with Laszlo's death unless both come back with him to occupied France on a dubious safe conduct. From his goatish look, it's only too clear he would enjoy having her for himself, with Laszlo out of the way.

Back at their hotel, Laszlo tells Ilsa about Rick's intransigence, asks about her life in Paris during his internment. She evades the question, her words echoing her last message to Rick—"Victor, whatever I do, will you believe that I . . ." Aware he's standing on delicate ground, Laszlo kisses her tenderly, without much passion, and goes off to an Underground meeting.

Dissolve to the café. Rick enters his apartment to find Ilsa waiting, as he predicted. She begs him to put his jealousy aside and remember the "Cause." He counters sardonically that "I'm the only Cause I'm interested in!" She invokes an unshared secret that will explain her apparent betrayal, but his mistrust remains adamant. She reproaches him for a self-pitying coward, then breaks down sobbing. He is their last hope—without the letters, Laszlo will die in Casablanca.

> RICK: What of it? I'm going to die in Casablanca. It's a good spot for it!

He turns away to light a cigarette, and back, to see her level a gun at his heart. With an oddly pleased smile, he denies her the letters again:

> RICK: If Laszlo and the Cause mean so much to you, you won't stop at anything. . . . Go ahead and shoot—you'll be doing me a favor!

The gun wavers, drops. She cannot kill him, she has never ceased loving him. Resigned to whatever fate attends the surrender of her responsibility to her husband, she comes into Rick's arms.

Later, Ilsa reveals the secret which will exonerate her. Shortly after her marriage, Laszlo went to Prague and was arrested. After months of anxious waiting, news came of his death. Then she met Rick. Laszlo had sworn her to silence about their marriage because she knew so much about his work that he didn't want her endangered—hence her lack of candor to Rick. (A premise as absurd as the letters of transit: Why would the Gestapo be less prone to interrogate a single woman than a married one, since they already knew of her close relationship to Laszlo?)

Just as she resolved to leave Paris with Rick, Ilsa found out Laszlo was alive, grievously ill nearby. She could not tell Rick, because she knew he would have stayed, to his peril. She will not leave him again, but lacks the strength to deal with Laszlo—Rick must think for both of them, arrange her husband's passage from Casablanca so he can carry on his work. Then he will have everything he's lived for.

> RICK (*heavily*): All except one . . . he won't have you.

Here is the film's psychological fulcrum. Until now, Ilsa has divided her commitment. Her splitting of the male image, her predisposition toward infidelity are explained away by the classic dream-factory practice of rendering an unacceptable wish acceptable, legitimizing psychological conflict by invoking the demands of reality or a twist of fate—Hollywood reality, Hollywood fate. The fortunes of war and the Nazi evil have forced two lovers upon this pitiable woman, not the vagaries of her psyche. Thus is she kept worthy, pure and guiltless, exciting admiration rather than censure.

If Laszlo and Rick are unconscious reflections of a father for Ilsa, she in turn possesses profound maternal resonances for his unconscious. His anguish since Paris reads as a reinvention of the little boy's suffering during the Oedipal stage, when he realizes that his beloved mother belongs irrevocably to another, and that he can never make the same claims upon her affection as his father. It is fashionable today to mock Freud for a naive reductionist, but the analyst who breaks down the walls of repression still stands as amazed as that wise man of Vienna at the timeless agony of the Oedipal child, raging at the "faithless" mother.

Bested by an unknown rival, Rick sinks into boozy depression and rages at Ilsa as a faithless slut. The discovery that his adversary is Laszlo consolidates the Czech patriot's position in Rick's psyche as a revered and envied father-surrogate. For Laszlo, unswervingly committed to his ideals, represents an ideal toward which Rick once aspired and then fell away. The core of the Oedipal dilemma is the blend of murderous and loving feelings toward the father. Freud believed this essential ambivalence was resolved when the boy ceased competing with his father, identifying with him instead (an analogous but somewhat more intricate process is said by Freud to take place with the little girl vis-à-vis her mother). The boy affirms that when he grows up he will be like his father, achieving the prerogatives of adulthood, including a sustaining relationship with a woman, as the father had with *his* wife. This is not to be misread as the child's being constructed into a conformist simulacrum of the father, finding the mother's clone in the process. We spend the rest of our lives forging and refining the instruments of identity: assimilating what makes sense about parental values, discarding what does not.

The blow that destroyed Rick's trust in a woman's love has also soured his dedication to the "Cause," a dedication one senses never rested on as firm a foundation as Laszlo's. The film will not clarify whether Rick worked for the Underground in Paris, and leaves more than a shadow of a doubt concerning his motives in Ethiopia and Spain. We know little about Rick's past, his parents or family, childhood or adolescence. Against this disclaimer, all signs indicate he was not as whole or centered a personality as Laszlo even before Paris, quite possibly because of his inability to work through the Oedipal dilemma and identify effectively with his father. When Laszlo pops up with Ilsa in Casablanca, Rick's long repressed Oedipal ambivalence resurfaces with a vengeance. He respects, admires Laszlo, but will send him to most certain death by withholding the letters unless he can get Ilsa back, regaining the lost mother, and healing the Oedipal trauma.

Ilsa Lund, like Brigid O'Shaughnessy in *The Maltese Falcon* (see essay 3), metamorphoses into the Bogart hero's death, a death Richard Blaine would gladly meet, for he has nothing to lose except his pain if Ilsa pulls the trigger. Her hand falters, the balance shifts back to the side of life. The epiphany is complex: Ilsa finds the commitment that has eluded her, as she perceives how deeply she has hurt Rick, how much she has deluded herself into believing she loves Laszlo. But Rick, winning the Oedipal victory, holding all the cards, immediately is overcome with guilt, as he realizes what her loss will mean to the valiant Czech. His remorse indicates his mask of selfish cynicism is dropping away, and his authentic, moral self is now being reborn.

Carl returns to the café with Laszlo, who has been wounded when the Gestapo broke up the Underground meeting. The original triangle of Paris is recapitulated. Hearing the commotion, Rick comes out upon the balcony, sees Laszlo below. He asks Carl to join him and, out of Laszlo's line of vision, tells the avuncular waiter—a Jewish Sam!—to take Ilsa home. Then he goes downstairs and pours Laszlo a drink:

RICK: Don't you sometimes wonder if it's worth all this?

LASZLO: Do you know you how sound? Like a man trying to convince himself of something he doesn't believe. . . . I wonder if you know that you're trying to escape from yourself, and that you'll never succeed.

Laszlo reveals he knows Rick loves his wife. Since no one is to blame, he demands no explanation, seeks no revenge. He asks only that Rick use the letters to save Ilsa. Then the police crash in and take him away.

Rick's conscience, already troubled by Ilsa's capitulation, is burdened further when Laszlo nearly catches him *in flagrante delicto*. He discerns Laszlo's unwavering political convictions, his selfless devotion to Ilsa, his complete lack of vindictiveness toward *his* rival (once again, the fortunes of war defuse conflict, allowing Laszlo to disavow anger toward the man who stole his wife while he languished in a concentration camp, just as Ilsa was allowed to take two lovers!). Rick is forcibly reminded that where he has been inconstant, selfish, and spiteful; the Czech has proven almost inhumanly virtuous, beyond petty narcissism.

As noted, classical psychoanalytic theory holds that the Oedipal crisis passes as the boy gives up his claims for exclusive possession of the mother, and makes common cause with his father. After Laszlo is seized, it would have been only too easy for Rick to let the Nazis execute his own murderous designs, then keep Ilsa for himself. But no child ever really wants to win the Oedipal struggle; the boy would rather go down fighting, secure in the knowledge that the bond between his parents will be preserved against his jealous manipulations. Now certain that Ilsa loves him, Rick chooses to renounce her and take up the cherished Cause, vindicating Laszlo's faith in him, and consolidating his identification with Laszlo. Rick has found the cure he sought in the spiritual wasteland of Casablanca.

His apathy dissipates, and he commences shuffling and baffling his adversaries as adroitly as Sam Spade in *The Maltese Falcon,* but without Spade's narrow ends of protecting an embattled, paranoid self. At police headquarters, Rick persuades Renault to free Laszlo by appealing to the Frenchman's greed, his need to placate Strasser, and his delight in scandal. He admits having the letters, says he intends to use them this evening. He wants to take Ilsa out of Casablanca without Gestapo interference.

He proposes to trap Laszlo by handing the letters to him at the Café

Americain. Renault will then arrest Laszlo on the spot as an accessory to the courier's deaths, a crime weighty enough to send the Czech back to a concentration camp. Rick and Ilsa will depart unimpeded, Renault will profit by Strasser's goodwill and the ten-thousand-franc bet. Plotwise, Rick's plan has about the same credibility as the letters of transit. But Curtiz, true to his promise, accelerates the last scenes to such a clip that the leaky strategies of the screenplay are hardly noticed, while audience attention is riveted to the issue of who will wind up with the lady on the Lisbon flight.

Rick sells his business to Signor Ferrari, securing the lion's share of the profits for Sam, also leaving the rest of his staff liberally provided for. Back at the café he conceals Renault, then greets Ilsa and Laszlo. Ilsa is worried because Laszlo still thinks he is leaving with her. Rick promises her to tell him the truth at the airport—"the less time to think, the easier for all of us!"

Rick brushes aside Laszlo's gratitude, refuses to accept any payment. As he hands him the letters, Renault steps in, pistol drawn—exactly what would have happened had Rick decided to finesse his rival. But instead he turns his gun on Renault, forcing him to notify the airport that two more passengers will be boarding the Lisbon plane. Renault relays Rick's instructions—directly to Strasser, who calls out the troops.

Dissolve to the airport, shrouded in mist and rain, *Casablanca*'s characteristic weather for conflicted departures. While Laszlo puts the luggage aboard, Rick commands Renault to fill out the letters in the name of—*Mr. and Mrs. Victor Laszlo!* Rick thus announces to the world that Ilsa is wedded to another. He overrides her tearful protests, a hypnotic urgency rising in his voice as the theme song plays for the last time:

> RICK: You said I was to do the thinking for both of us. Well, I've done a lot of it since then, and it all adds up to one thing. You're getting on that plane with Victor, where you belong . . . inside of us, we both know you belong with Victor. You're part of his work . . . the thing that keeps him going. We'll always have Paris. We didn't have . . . we'd lost it until you came back to Casablanca. We got it back last night.

> ILSA (*ruefully*): And I said I would never leave you!

> RICK: And you never will. I've got a job to do. Where I'm

going, you can't follow. What I've got to do, you can't
be any part of . . . (*touching her chin*) . . . Here's
looking at you, kid.

Over Laszlo's objections, Rick reveals that Ilsa visited him last night,
but only for the letters. She tried to convince him that she still loved
him—"but that was long ago." Laszlo welcomes Rick back—"This
time I know our side will win!"

"Goodbye, Rick—God bless you!" Ilsa murmurs. Numb, drained,
she turns away and walks toward the plane with her husband. Laszlo regards her with a quizzical, yet sympathetic expression. From their vantage point Rick is framed, standing alone. He has both foresworn and
affirmed his love. Giving Ilsa back to Laszlo, he has metaphorically returned his mother to his father, yet enshrined Ilsa in memory as perpetual reassurance of his worth.

His last speech is meant to undo the competition with Laszlo, to al-
leviate Rick's still unquiet conscience, and to redeem Ilsa from adulterous taint. Rick would have the Czech believe she came to him to protect
her marriage, rather than to destroy it. The reality, of course, is precisely
the reverse. But Laszlo remains remarkably tolerant, totally accepting
Rick's explanation. Laszlo implicitly commends Rick's sacrifice like a
benevolent father, welcoming his prodigal son back to the fold.

I've always felt Ilsa gets short shrift while the menfolk go about solv-
ing their problems; the film seems to hint obliquely that she deserves
what she gets. Rick's arguments cannot hold much validity for her. Why
can she not go where he must go, since she has repeatedly followed Laszlo
into the very jaws of death? When all's said and done, she goes with her
husband out of love for Rick!

Once she nominates Rick as her final choice, he turns the tables on
her, reversing the abandonment at the Paris train station. He hustles her
forever out of his life, back into an unfulfilled marriage in which nobility
serves as a tepid substitute for passion. Rick disposes of Ilsa with something of Sam Spade's fierce purpose in "sending over" the chronically
treacherous Brigid O'Shaughnessy. Indeed, Bergman's blasted appearance as she boards the plane is uncannily reminiscent of Mary Astor's
blank mask as she descends in the elevator at the conclusion of *The Maltese Falcon*. Rick *sends over* Ilsa to an analogous imprisonment—empty
wedlock—not only to make peace with the Oedipal father, but also to
disentangle himself from the possibility of future trauma at the hands of
a woman he can never completely trust again.

Rick's murderous impulses toward Lazslo do find an acceptable displacement in the person of Major Strasser. I have remarked upon Laszlo's striking absence of ill will toward Rick. Strasser, on the other hand, is perfectly cast for the part of hated rival/baleful avenger. The film has implied that Strasser, too, desires Ilsa for more than her politics. He obviously detests Rick, and just as obviously deserves to perish. When the Gestapo chief arrives and tries calling the control tower to halt the flight, Rick coldly guns him down.

Renault has witnessed everything, correctly gauging that Ilsa left unwillingly. In the face of Rick's rejoined commitment, the prefect's gibes ring hollowly in his own ears, and he can no longer maintain his ironic detachment at the expense of honor. Ever Rick's mirror, Renault suddenly executes an ideological about-face, recuperating *his* lost self-respect, and orders his men to "round up the usual suspects" rather than arrest Rick. He drops a bottle of Vichy water into the wastebasket, kicks it away distastefully. He and Rick gaze up at the Lisbon plane, climbing to freedom. Renault suggests he can be induced to arrange passage for Rick to the Free French garrison in Brazzaville, and Rick reminds him of their bet.

RENAULT: . . . that ten thousand francs should pay our expenses.

RICK: *Our* expenses? Louis, I think this is the beginning of a beautiful friendship!

The camera cranes over them, as they turn and walk into the mist bordering the airstrip to the triumphant strains of the "Marseillaise." The union of these patriots manqué brings *Casablanca* to a smashing finale—it is hard to look upon this felicitous conclusion without a moist eye or fast pulse. Rick's newly cemented friendship with Renault follows hard upon his relinquishment of Ilsa, and a camp interpretation would have us believe it is fitting that Rick and Renault should stride together into the night, because it is Renault who Rick has secretly loved all along.

The idea that Rick has been a closet queen is lunatic (and, to members of the Bogart cult, heretical). But his rejection of Ilsa in favor of a friendship that will thrive in the sacrifice of combat is certainly informed by Rick's fear of women, and his attendant misogyny. In many Bogart classics, indeed in many adventure films throughout the history of cinema, one repeatedly discovers the chauvinism and the strong antifeminine bias characteristic of the typical gang of preadolescent boys.

These movies suggest that in war, in the mining camp, or the detection of crime, men function at their natural best, without feminine intrusion. If a woman does manage to invade the male community, her sexuality renders her suspect unless she proves herself as loyal and tough as a reliable buddy. Howard Hawks was a director particularly partisan to the spartan virtues of male bonding (Lauren Bacall's part in Hawks's *To Have and Have Not* [1944] is a notable example of the feminine "buddy"). In this regard, Sam Spade's remark to his secretary, "You're a good man, sister!" is perhaps the ultimate compliment that can be bestowed upon a woman by a hard-boiled forties hero.

I've inferred that Rick is exquisitely sensitized to Ilsa's potential for further harm. Far better to fight on, in the fellowship of comrades, sustained by the remembrance of Paris, before the fall of innocence. It is a fate less lonely than Sam Spade's, who ends the dirty business of *The Maltese Falcon* with neither friend nor love, in fact or in memory. Rick purchases his redemption at a poignant price, one urged upon him by the limitations of his character, for we may speculate that the intimacy of an extended relationship with a woman would ultimately be unendurable for him. And yet, the victory and tragedy attendant upon his renunciation continue to move us profoundly, for in losing his beloved, he has won back the better part of himself.

Woody Allen's *Play It Again, Sam* (1972) provides an amusing commentary on the central Oedipal dynamic in *Casablanca*. Allen's *nebbish* hero bolsters his sagging ego by hallucinating Humphrey Bogart as a sexual mentor. With Bogie's assistance, he seduces his best friend's wife. The friend is everything that Allen is not—rich, attractive, as supremely confident as Laszlo. The wife turns to Allen because her husband seems more absorbed in his business affairs than their relationship, echoing Laszlo's political commitment at the expense of his marriage. Having vindicated his desirability, Allen persuades the wife to return to her husband in a lovely airport scene, lifted directly from the source.

Other reasonably sound interpretations of *Casablanca* which, in my obviously biased opinion, still suffer from the failure to account for its Oedipal theme, have been offered by Barbara Deming and Richard Corliss.[14]

Afterword

Casablanca's renewed popularity with succeeding generations of fans has been matched by a continued flow of scholarly and popular writing about the film. The most comprehensive recent psychoanalytically oriented study is "Play It Again, Sigmund" by Krin and Glen Gabbard.[15] Consonant with the pluralistic approach of their previous work, it offers elegant multiple readings.

The Gabbards amplify my analysis of Rick and Laszlo's Oedipal triangulation, using classical Freudian paradigms. Rick's ownership of the camera's "gaze" is then explored from a Lacanian viewpoint. With the Nazis' entry into Paris and Ilsa's inexplicable disappearance, Rick's previous omniscient perspective is radically disrupted. The putative hero dwindles into an object in someone else's plot. The Oedipally inflected rapprochement, ratified by Rick's engineering Ilsa's return to the valiant Czech, symbolically restores Rick to a sense of origin/identification embodied by this just father and his honorable Law. Committing himself anew to the Cause, Rick also regains control over the narrative trajectory.

The Gabbards call upon Mulvey's well-known theories in an account of Ilsa's fetishization by the camera eye (underscored by Bergman's luminous visage), and her ultimate suppression by the screenplay, as dangerous, transgressive object of desire (vide supra, my remarks on Ilsa's resonances with Brigid O'Shaughnessy in *The Maltese Falcon*). Unlike the majority of her noir counterparts, Ilsa's sins are those of omission rather than commission. Significantly, after deeding power of choice over to Rick, she is rendered virtually voiceless (see Silverman's remarks on the repression of feminine "voice" in classic cinema).[16]

The Gabbards cite Robert B. Ray's work to further unpack *Casablanca*'s political agenda.[17] Ray, who used the film as a tutor text for his theories, described Hollywood cinema's tendency to displace complex or controversial ideological issues into melodramatic struggles between individual characters "where familiar emotions overwhelm ideas."[18] Resolution through tidy reconciliation is then likely to be the order of the day. The Gabbards elucidate the potent visual and narrative strategies which compel the viewer to identify with Rick. His romantic dilemma cleverly captures in "softer," more acceptable fashion his central conflict between remaining an alienated "outsider" (thus a symbol of intense American prewar isolationism), versus becoming a self-sacrificing member of the antifascist team.

The Gabbards conclude that *Casablanca*'s cult status resides in a unique blend of star presence, artfully deployed nostalgic music, a satisfying resolution of Oedipal conflict,[19] and "the reassuring message that the American outlaw hero (and by extension all Americans) can be true to his instincts, even in a world war"—or presumably a Star War:

This last message may seem specific to the 1943 audience, but movies have been quite successful in keeping old myths alive, and when configured for the Era of Reagan and Bush, these myths can be more vital than ever. . . . Just as "As Time Goes By" eased the 1943 viewer into a nostalgic imaginary, the film itself now grants the viewer benign regression to a lost moment when right and wrong were clear cut, and going off to war could be a deeply romantic gesture.[20]

3

The Detective Film: *The Maltese Falcon*—
Even Paranoids Have Enemies

The only effective kind of love interest is that which
creates a personal hazard for the detective. . . . A really
good detective never gets married.
——Raymond Chandler

"I guess somebody lost a dream," the intern said. He
bent over and closed her eyes.   ——Raymond Chandler

The detective's homoerotic ploy in *The Maltese Falcon:* "To get the better of the Fat Man, Spade must seem *conspiratorial* and *seduceable.*"

$\mathcal{T}$he grip of the detective mythos upon the collective imagination is as acute now as in the forties—the golden era of the Hollywood hard-boiled private eye, when tough shamuses like Sam Spade and Philip Marlowe ruled the screen and the airwaves, sidestepping danger with a wisecrack, an adoring secretary ever poised with pencil ready to take "the notes from my last caper, sweetheart."

Psychoanalytic inquiry into this immensely popular genre has been sparse and highly conjectural. The orthodox Freudian party line on the detective was advanced by Pederson-Krag.[1] She suggested the private eye symbolizes the curious child ferreting out the secrets of grown-up sexuality. The "crime" he seeks to unravel is actually the Freudian primal scene—parental intercourse—which psychoanalysts believe can be imprinted upon the untutored mind of the young as an act of summary violence, with the partners misperceived as locked in mortal combat. Like many analytic intrusions into aesthetics, Pederson-Krag's views are singularly hard to prove or disprove, since she offers no supporting evidence either from detective literature or the therapy of detectophiles.

I find the observations of Dr. Leo Bellak much more congenial.[2] Bellak, who at least sounds like an aficianado, believes the detective story satisfies enthusiasts at multiple levels. One identifies with criminal *and* sleuth—with the criminal via the Id, that vast reservoir of primitive aggressive and sexual impulses which recognizes no social restraint and would stop at nothing, mayhem included, to have its wishes fulfilled;

alternately with the sleuth as an embodiment of the Dr. Jekyll/Superego side of one's personality. In his Superego guise, the detective represents the inner voice of conscience; he is an idealized figure of superhuman intelligence, implacably allied with the forces of law and order. (By the by, the English psychoanalyst Edmund Berlger postulated that one could even identify with the *victim,* if one were masochistic enough!)

Bellak states that detective fiction gratifies an inherent pleasure in having tension skillfully manipulated; increased, then suddenly reduced following the elucidation of the mystery and capture of the criminal. In an uncertain life brimming with unpredictable trauma, it is uniquely entertaining to undergo carefully constructed anxiety, with the certainty of relief when the book is finished or the movie ends. Mystery buffs confront danger selectively, not willy-nilly—and it is, after all, someone else's peril. Since we're inherently problem-solving creatures, we also enjoy what Bellak terms "closure satisfaction" at the riddle's resolution, savoring the gestalt of the crime.

With few exceptions, psychoanalysts have addressed the British school of detection—wherein the sleuth is often upper class by origin or lifestyle (Sherlock Holmes, Lord Peter Wimsey); victim and criminal are likely to share an identical Church of England background; the action unfolds in a setting of implacable gentility, replete with rose gardens, high tea, and humble servitors; motivation is likely to be less important than the elegant Chinese puzzlebox of the murder. Sleuthing follows conventions as strict as Robert's Rules of Order, and even the perpetrator owns at least the outward show of gentility.

I sing of another school of detection, one with its own unique, far less elegant conventions. It grew out of American pulp fiction in the twenties and thirties—notably *Black Mask* magazine—in a crisis-ridden postbellum era of prohibition and economic depression. It thrived not on decorum, but on the sheer will of its protagonist to endure and prevail in the end, with his skin and precarious integrity intact, and a desperate truth revealed.

All but a few of the writers who created the tough American private eye are unsung and forgotten now. Their tabloid style left much to be desired, but what they lacked in technique was redeemed by acute perceptions into the shadow side of a ruthlessly competitive, materialistic culture. Ernest Hemingway and John O'Hara owed them much, and out of their ranks came a few truly great innovators—e.g., Dashiell Hammett, the ex-Pinkerton operative who transformed the mystery novel from a pallid teatime affair into a social document of brutal power. Now the "how" of killing was subordinated to the "why" residing in the dark turnings of the heart and the unquiet past. Raymond Chandler, Hammett's equally famous inheritor, wrote that Hammett "gave murder back to the kind of people that commit it for reasons, not just to provide a corpse, and with the means at hand, not hand-wrought dueling pistols, curare, and tropical fish."[3]

Hammett's 1929 masterpiece *The Maltese Falcon* perfectly captured the essence of the private eye's peculiar, seamy milieu.[4] Two imperfect versions of the novel were filmed, one in 1931 under the original title, and another in 1936 as *Satan Met a Lady*. In 1941, a fledgling director named John Huston assembled a memorable cast, and undertook a third remake. George Raft is said to have turned down the starring role, objecting to Huston's lack of experience. Humphrey Bogart was chosen instead, and played Sam Spade to the hilt. A remarkable success financially and artistically, Huston's movie took the American shamus off the printed page, and launched him on an odyssey that elevated his persona to the status of existential hero, cousin to Camus's *Stranger*.

I find it oddly appropriate to use another brand of sleuthing—psychoanalysis—to follow Spade as he goes about the intricate business of digging up the human wreckage left in the Maltese Falcon's wake. The private eye as analyst manqué—the analyst as shamus manqué! Both professionals keep their personalities anonymous, enigmatic. Both prize truth above all else—but truth is never easily known, it hides beneath the surface of ambiguous reality, where character and event never merely signify themselves, and no one is who or what he or she claims to be. For the analyst, the truth is concealed by the chimera of unconscious defense and resistance, by repression and amnesia forged over a lifetime, persisting against a patient's better judgment, keeping him or her ill. For the detective, the truth is buried out of conscious malice, greed, or guilt, and he traces it out to *his* direst peril.

The Maltese Falcon begins with a low pan over the Golden Gate Bridge, across a gray San Francisco skyline. The classic American detective is an urban animal, a facile manipulator of the lackluster paraphernalia of city life—taxicabs, telephones, desk clerks. The action typically unfolds in California, at the furthest perimeter of the barely civilized frontier. The brief opening pan is as much as we shall see of the metropolis's exterior rush and glamor; instead, we will move amidst the traumatizing rawness of the underground city, descend into a claustrophobic world of alleys and seedy hotel rooms inhabited by permanent transients, where no blade of grass or bit of uncluttered sky relieves the blight cast by the overweaning lust for profit and power.

The offices of "Spade and Archer, Private Investigators" are furnished spartanly. In his living and working quarters, the shamus invariably eschews the decorative for the (barely) functional; indeed, he positively revels in the dilapidation of his environs. Spade is alone, self-possessed even at rest, competently rolling a cigarette. Enter Effie Perine (Lee Patrick), his secretary—a wholesome, direct young woman as much a part of the iconography as revolver and trench coat. She ushers in a new client, "Miss Wonderly" (Mary Astor), a fur-clad brunette radiating desperation and teasing insincerity. Spade, like the analyst, is a good listener and draws her out easily.

Wonderly is trying to find her younger sister Corinne, who ran away with a man named Floyd Thursby while her parents were in Honolulu. Corinne vanished after writing she had come to San Francisco. She left only "General Delivery" as her address. Wonderly followed her, hoping to retrieve her before her parent's return. She met Thursby at the post office, picking up her last letter to Corinne. He refused to take her to her prodigal sister, but made an appointment to meet her that evening at her hotel.

While she spins this unlikely yarn, Spade's partner, Miles Archer (Jerome Cowan) enters and gives a silent whistle of appreciation. A gigolo about ten years older than Spade, Archer has a certain coarse cunning, but is clearly not the brains of the outfit. Spade briefs him, tells Wonderly they'll trail Thursby back to Corinne and "if she doesn't want to leave him . . . well, there are ways of arranging that." Eyelashes aflutter, Wonderly emphasizes Thursby's violent tendencies. Archer gallantly volunteers his personal services, to Spade's amusement.

Wonderly gives them two hundred dollars—a stiff retainer in 1941— and exits. Her convoluted tale would make any unthoughtful red-blooded American male salivate like one of Pavlov's dogs—an innocent girl duped by an evil seducer, a glamorous, helpless rescuer, presumably well-to-do parents and the promise of a fat fee. But Spade's intelligence races ahead of this damsel's too obvious distress, probing for hidden purpose. Archer, on the other hand, has been thoroughly gulled,

ARCHER: Oh, she's sweet! Maybe you saw her first, Sam, but I
spoke first!

SPADE (*ironically*): You've got brains—yes *you* have! . . .

Dissolve to a terse shot of Miles approaching the camera. His expectant smile gives way to disbelief, a shot roars out, he staggers back.

Dissolve: a call from the police jangles Spade awake in his apartment. His reaction to Miles's death is remarkably even. Blinking the sleep from his eyes, he phones Effie with the news, tells her to notify Iva, Miles's wife and—"Keep her away from me!"

Dissolve: the scene of the crime. Spade glances over a broken fence at his partner, sprawled brokenly below on rocks beetling over surf. Detective Tom Polhaus (Ward Bond) greets him. Cop and shamus are old acquaintances and adversaries. They rehearse the details of Archer's death, Spade holding rigorously to professional detachment. Miles was shot at the end of a blind alley, fronting on the ocean. He fell over the fence—his coat was burned by the blast, his gun still on his hip, unfired.

Spade curtly refuses to view the remains, and won't tell Polhaus more than that Miles was tailing Thursby. The decent policeman pronounces Miles's epitaph gruffly, as one city-dweller trying to puzzle out meaning in the random, savage passage of another stranger: "It's tough him getting it like that, ain't it. Miles had his faults, just like any of the rest of us, but I guess he must have had some strong points too, huh?" Spade grunts ambiguously. Wonderly's hotel tells him she has left without a forwarding address. Back home, he's visited by Polhaus and his superior, Lieutenant Dundy. The cops run a standard Mutt-and-Jeff routine, Polhaus awkwardly amiable, Dundy oozing suspicion from every pore. They reveal Thursby has just been gunned down. Spade is now involved in *two* murders! Dundy taps Spade's chest with a thick finger, and Spade uncharacteristically blows his cool—"*Keep . . . your . . . paws . . . off . . . me*!!!"—then quickly recovers, sidesteps the grilling and eases them out.

Next morning in his office Spade is accosted by Iva Archer, an overripe woman slightly past her prime, who he has obviously been bedding for some time with waning enthusiasm. She collapses into his arms, weeping and asks if he murdered Miles—"Be kind to me, Sam!" He laughs harshly; she's using him, half-hoping he's the killer, and he'll have none of it.

Turning mock-solicitous, he dismisses Iva with a dubious promise to see her later. Effie is distressed, but unsurprised to hear her boss is under suspicion, not—one guesses—for the first time. His disordered life holds few secrets from her, but he evades her concern. One senses the scene has been played out between them on many occasions: he accepts her technical assistance, treats her as the obedient extension of his expertise, but he will not tolerate her—or anyone—invading his territory, questioning the risks he insists upon taking.

The migratory Miss Wonderly resurfaces, phoning Spade to meet her at another hotel, under another name—LeBlanc. She blames herself ostentatiously for Miles's death, admits her previous story was a lie, and that her two identities are lies, too. She is neither Wonderly nor LeBlanc, but plain Brigid O'Shaughnessy. Spade greets this news coolly: "We didn't exactly believe your story—we believed your two hundred dollars." As for Archer, Spade says he had a large life insurance policy, and a wife who didn't like him—no need for remorse.

Brigid throws herself on his mercy; Thursby betrayed her after she engaged him in the Orient to protect her—from some obscure danger that still threatens her. When he tries to pin her down, she's as slippery with him as he was with the police. "You won't need much of anybody's help," he says admiringly. "You're good—chiefly your eyes, I think, and that throb you get in your voice when you say, 'Be—*generous, Mr. Spade.'*" Then, curiously, he relents. He takes three hundred dollars—most of her cash—over her protests, and leaves with the warning to admit no one until he returns.

What draws him to her, since he clearly pegs her for an artful schemer from the first? Not simply her physical charm. There are certain men who cannot accept a woman as nurturer and bed partner both. It's inconceivable to them that a "good" woman can have "bad" sexual feelings; therefore, they split the feminine image in two. The intrapsychic basis for this cleavage is the unconscious wish to negate the incestuous desire of childhood for the mother, the boy's first beloved—for if mother is denied her native sexuality, it becomes easier to deny a sensual claim upon her.

Clinically, one discovers that a sufferer from the "madonna-whore" complex may have been particularly imbued with the bias of a patriarchal culture which overtly or covertly denies sexual pleasure to a "good" married woman. Often he has been exposed to a mother who has also bought into that prohibition and puritanically discouraged healthy displays of sexuality in her male child. Typically such a boy, grown into neurotic adulthood, is unaroused or frankly impotent with his wife—she now represents a newer version of his mother—but will become a sexual quarterback with prostitutes, or a mistress from a different, usually lower social class.

Effie is Spade's madonna!—a permanent fixture in his turbulent life, self-sacrificing, devoted to his welfare. She could almost be his wife, were it not for the fact that she holds about as much attraction for him as her typewriter. But shady ladies of uncertain reputation *do* turn him on, especially when their criminal tendencies come candy-coated in cloying helplessness. Iva Archer is a lesser example of the breed; Brigid is a nonpareil. And, beyond her allure as a degraded love-object, she holds the key to two murders of which Spade himself now stands as prime suspect, as a direct result of his entanglement with her. He must bind himself to her devious cause so that the work of detection—*and* his ultimate liberation—can be accomplished. The way in, as the Zen saying goes, is the way out.

Back at the office, Effie hands Spade a card reeking of gardenias—another client, one Joel Cairo (Peter Lorre), a fulsome Levantine. Effie calls him "queer" outright in the novel; typical of the film's unreflective spin here and elsewhere Spade's bemused reaction to the scented card, Lorre's mincing portrayal leave no doubt as to Cairo's inversion.

He offers Spade five thousand dollars "on behalf of the rightful owner" to recover "an ornament that . . . shall we say . . . has been mislaid, a statuette, the black figure of—er—a bird. . . . I am prepared to promise that—what is the phrase? (*a knowing roll of the eyes*)—'No questions will be asked!'" Then when Spade's back is turned, the little man pulls a gun and demands to search the office. The detective easily disarms him and punches him out. A search through his pockets reveals multiple passports, a perfumed handkerchief that elicits another quizzical glance—but no five thousand dollars.

Cairo awakens and makes straight for a mirror: "Look what you did to my shirt!" he whines absurdly, then resumes negotiations as if nothing has happened. Spade allows Cairo to believe he can get the statuette—like a good analyst, he practices silence when ignorant, under the assumption that one rarely gets into trouble by keeping one's mouth shut, when the other party is under considerable pressure to keep his open.

Cairo thinks he has outsmarted Spade, since he has divulged little about the "bird," and nothing about the "rightful owner"—unaware that the detective has never heard of the Falcon until his new "client" spilled the beans. Cairo maintains his first offer was in good faith. He will put down a retainer, the rest to follow later:

CAIRO: You will take, say, one hundred dollars.

SPADE: No—I will take, say, *two* hundred dollars!

He returns the gun, and breaks up with genuine amusement when Cairo once again aims the weapon at his chest and proposes to search the office: "Sure, g . . . go ahead, I won't stop ya!!!"

Spade loses nothing here. He who sought to manipulate the shamus has been himself cannily exploited. In his last match with Brigid, Spade knew he was being fiddled, and left her convinced she had engaged his sympathy (she *has*, a little, but Spade is aware of *this*, too!). Cairo, has also been lulled into assuming Spade is on his side—purely for profit. From both, Spade takes more money than they were willing to part with, not from greed, but to underscore that he owns the competitive edge. They have started the game, but he will most certainly play it out to his satisfaction, and by his own rules.

Spade leaves the office, and shakes a clumsy tail by a diminutive, pinched-face young thug, Wilmer (Elisha Cook, Jr.). At Brigid's, Spade casually reveals he has met Cairo. She reacts with equally studied nonchalance until he mentions the "Black Bird," and the sum Cairo was ready to pay. Bitterly, she says she can't raise that kind of money—"if I have to bid for your loyalty . . . what else is there I can buy you with?" He takes her face in his hands, kisses her with a curious expression close to despair—as if he were giving in, or giving up.

Brigid has admitted she is base—"bad, worse than you could know!" She seems the least likely candidate to deserve what little good faith remains in Spade—and it is damned little. Yet she continues to tantalize him, a diamond on a dustheap. From the start, Spade has kept a curious set of double-entry mental books on Brigid. He senses her treachery, yet cherishes the illusion that she's as helpless, vulnerable, as she would have him and the world believe. He knows better, but at the same time hopes to redeem a sour expectation of betrayal against his better judgment.

Brigid begs again for his patience, asks him to set up an interview with Cairo at Spade's apartment, for she is apparently terrified of the Levantine. They leave, and Spade is doubly shadowed. Iva Archer watches furtively from her car as he and Brigid enter his lobby. Inside Spade peers through the curtains at Wilmer, standing idly under a streetlamp. Cairo arrives, and greets Brigid with too elaborate courtesy. Brigid promises the Falcon back within a week—Thursby hid it, she is anxious now to dispose of it because of his violent end. Their elliptical conversation is studded with references to "the Fat Man" and "the boy outside."

BRIGID: But you might be able to get around him, Joel, as you did that one in Istanbul, what was his name?

CAIRO: You mean the one you couldn't get to—!!!

Uproar, pandemonium!!! Brigid swings on Cairo, he slaps her back, Cairo draws a gun, Spade belts him, Cairo howls—"That is the *second* time you've laid hands on me tonight!!" It is never explained what sets Brigid and the Levantine going at each other like bargain-basement shoppers fighting over the last girdle. I suspect the anonymous boy from Istanbul was somehow involved in hunting down the Falcon; Cairo mixed business with pleasure, developed sexual designs on the boy, and Brigid came between them.

Dundy and Polhaus return in the midst of this bizarre squabble. Spade blocks them at the door, blandly denying Dundy's accusation that he murdered Miles to marry Iva. Cairo screams for help, Spade smoothly ushers them in—to find Brigid and the Levantine still brawling. Cairo accuses Spade and Brigid of entrapping and brutally interrogating him. Dundy, delighted by the mayhem, now has an excuse to book them all. Spade quickly explains that Brigid is an operative—they were indeed questioning Cairo—and says enough about the little conspirator to make it obvious to Cairo that involving the police will compromise his freedom.

Cairo, befuddled, now balks at pressing charges, and Spade abruptly shifts gears yet again. He tells the cops they've been flummoxed—he put his "friends" up to staging a fracas to give the law a hard time for bugging him. The wily shamus dances around Dundy's ponderous rectitude like a picador jabbing a particularly dense bull. Goaded past endurance, Dundy slugs him. Spade's objectivity seems to fracture, just as when Dundy previously touched him. Aware he's gone too far, Dundy departs grumpily with Polhaus in tow, Cairo slithering out between them.

BRIGID: You're absolutely the wildest, most unpredictable person I've ever known. Do you always carry on so high-handed?

Spade's performance *was* high-handed, but *never* wild. An icy lucidity reigns over his pranks and storms. Cairo has been intimidated, the police thoroughly bewildered, Brigid impressed. His outrage at Dundy was an artful sham; Spade deliberately provoked the lieutenant into striking him, guessing he would wilt after taking a mindless swing.

When Spade tries to elicit more about the Falcon from Brigid, she fobs him off with another one of her tangled histories. She says was promised a large sum to steal the bird in Turkey. Cairo and Thursby were in on the heist. She and Thursby discovered that Cairo meant to keep the Falcon for himself, so they absconded with it instead. Then she found Thursby had no intention of sharing the profits.

> SPADE   (*half-smiling*): You *are* a liar—was there any truth in that yarn?
>
> BRIGID   (*smiling*): Some . . . not very much. Oh, I'm so tired . . . of lying and making up lies, and not knowing what is a lie and what is the truth.

It is possibly the one and only time Brigid *is* being truthful. Like the pathological confabulator suffering from the entity known as Münchausen syndrome, she lives poised on the edge of reality and fantasy. Her success as a schemer resides exactly in the vividness her daydreams possess *for her*. She almost believes she *is* Wonderly or LeBlanc, haut monde instead of demimonde. She chronically presents herself a victim of scheming men. Her lie to Spade about a wealthy sister seduced and menaced by Thursby is another edition of a central fantasy; Corinne is a projected image of an imaginary, exploited self, which we shall see is quite at variance with her real exploitative, criminal self.

Brigid stretches out languorously on the couch. Spade bends over her, his expression a curious riddle of pain, anger, tenderness. The camera drifts away, through the open window. Rustling curtains frame the young gunman, loitering in a pool of lamplight, the period implicit in Brigid's sensual promise. This confrontation, like the last, ends with Spade accepting her body in lieu of the truth. The acceptance is provisional.

In the novel, Spade spends the night with her. For the sake of the Hays office, Huston omitted a sequence of Spade tiptoeing out of her apartment the next morning. Instead, the action shifts directly to Cairo's hotel. The deletion, although a sop to the censor, tellingly reinforces the subtle blurring of time that has occurred with the thickening texture of intrigue. One has lost track of the hours or days elapsed since Spade awakened to the news of his partner's murder. It has become increasingly difficult to separate day from night, especially since most scenes in the film take place indoors, and are shot in thin, artificial light. As the case gathers momentum, the detective characteristically neither slumbers nor takes more substantial food than black coffee and cigarettes. He is completely immersed in, nourished by the ugly business at hand. It is in this prolonged sleepless night that he comes authentically alive.

Spade spots Wilmer in the lobby of Cairo's hotel. Guessing a connection between Wilmer and "the Fat Man" from Brigid's enigmatic conversation with Cairo, he tells the boy he wants to see his boss, then has the hotel dick roust out the little gunsel. Wilmer cuts a comically sinister figure. Dressed in an overcoat two sizes too large, pockets abulge with gats, he's incapable of uttering a line that hasn't been cribbed from a "B" gangster flick: "Keep askin' for it, and you're goin' to get it—*plenty!*" Spade insults him openly, just as he incited Dundy.

Cairo enters the lobby, much the worse for wear. The police booked him after he left Spade's apartment, grilled him thoroughly, but he adhered to Spade's bizarre story. Now he wants no further dealings with the detective, since their dealings wind up with consistent disrepair to his haberdashery and person.

At his office, Spade finds Brigid, distraught as usual; her apartment has been ransacked while she was away. He packs her off to Effie's place for safekeeping, then sets up appointments with two callers—the district attorney, and a Mr. Gutman, who says he received Spade's message from "the young man." Wretched Iva interrupts, begging forgiveness for dispatching the police last night in a paroxysm of jealousy. Miles's widow is now completely peripheral to Spade's interest, either as a lover or a significant piece of the mystery—he's already rejected the possibility that *she* murdered Archer. He dismisses her and goes off to test his mettle against the mysterious Fat Man.

Kasper Gutman (Sydney Greenstreet), a vast penguin in cutaway coat and striped trousers, greets Spade at his hotel suite with effusive bonhomie, placing his hands familiarly on the detective as he guides him to a chair, a drink, and a cigar. Gutman sets the tone of a business conference between two straight-shooting men of the world surrounded by masculine accoutrements. But he is patently criminal, and a little less obviously homosexual; a degenerate old queen of ambiguous nationality.

(In the novel, he travels with a daughter, Rhea, who the screenplay eliminates, thus emphasizing Gutman's inversion.)

We have seen that Spade places the highest premium on his physical and emotional inviolability. He cannot abide being touched, *man-*handled. He would not suffer Dundy to lay a finger upon him, yet permits Gutman impressive liberties with his person. But he had clearly defined a habitual stance of noncooperation with the policeman, and felt secure defying Dundy's clumsy intrusions. Gutman's attack is parried differently. To get the better of the Fat Man, Spade must seem *conspiratorial* and *seduceable.*

Gutman's approach is informed by the subtly eroticized competitiveness of a seedy gay bar. He will not cease trying to swindle and outfox Spade. Ostensibly, his chicanery is aimed at acquiring the Falcon, but unconsciously Gutman craves a sensual victory. He wants to *screw* Spade literally and figuratively, and if the detective dies as a result, why that will give an added climactic pleasure!

The Fat Man speaks in orotund Wildean aphorisms, savoring his words as if each were a taste of Iranian caviar:

GUTMAN: Well, sir, here's to plain speaking and clear understanding. . . . I distrust a close-mouthed man. He generally picks the wrong time to talk and says the wrong thing . . . talking's something you can't do judiciously unless you keep in practice. . . . I'll tell you right out, I'm a man who likes to talk to a man who likes to talk!

Spade affirms that he acts for himself, not for those who sought to hire him. He infers that neither he nor anyone else can determine the nature and value of the bird except Gutman himself. The Fat Man chuckles voluptuously; thinking he holds trump cards, he refuses further information unless Spade reveals the Falcon's whereabouts.

Spade throws a tantrum worthy of a drag queen in high pique, smashes a glass, his voice cracking with hysteria. He gives Gutman a deadline to reveal what he knows—"You've got 'til five o'clock, then you're either in or out, for keeps!!"—and storms out. In the hall, he grins faintly as he regards a trembling hand. Murder surely waited inside, amidst the cigars and suave speech. He goes down one elevator, just as Cairo steps out of the other, neither seeing the other.

Bryan, the district attorney, next tries to back Dundy's muscle with the power of his office. A bespectacled, iron-jawed type, Bryan is easily foiled. He can't grasp Spade's unwillingness to cooperate if he's got nothing to conceal. Spade answers with the essence of his Weltanschauung: "*Everybody has something to conceal*!" He maintains insolently that he can only clear himself by finding the killers on his own, free from the bungling law. He exits abruptly with the D.A. choking on his words, much as he left Gutman. It's integral to Spade's style to provoke an opponent into breaking his rhythm with some mercurial piece of behavior. He consistently leaves turmoil behind him as he takes the next turn in the maze.

Wilmer waits for Spade outside his office: the Fat Man wants to see him again. As they go down the hotel corridor, Spade slips behind the youth and immobilizes him. He hands Gutman Wilmer's brace of pistols as he enters the room—"A crippled newsie took them away from him, but I made him give them back!" Gutman roars appreciatively, then sits Spade down and relates the Falcon's past with the eloquence of a natural actor, pausing only to replenish the detective's glass several times.

The bird is a sinister metaphor of rapacity, fashioned in 1539 from purest gold and rare jewels in the coffers of the crusading Knights of Malta—"We all know that the Holy Wars to them were largely a matter of loot." Intended as a gift for Charles V of Spain, it fell into the hands of pirates, then disappeared and reappeared in various locales, acquiring a coat of black enamel during its bloody passage. After a seventeen-year odyssey, Gutman traced it to one Kemidov, a Russian general living in Istanbul. When he refused to sell it, "I sent some—ah—agents to get it. Well, sir, they got it—and I haven't got it—heh, heh—*but I'm going to get it*!"

The Fat Man offers Spade $50,000, or a quarter of the Falcon's sale price, for his help. His flabby hand fondles the detective's knee, as he reverently speculates on the bird's real value—a quarter million—a million—who can say? Spade's speech thickens; he lurches to his feet, takes a few unsteady steps. Wilmer enters at Gutman's bidding, trips the detective and kicks viciously at his prostrate body. Cairo emerges from the bedroom, and the conspirators hurry out.

Several hours later: Spade heaves himself into painful consciousness—an obligatory sequence in the genre, the unexpected knockout, followed by fuzzy-headed, blurred-focus recovery. He calls Effie, finds that Brigid never arrived at her house. He searches the suite, comes up with a newspaper shipping page with a circled notice: "5:30 P.M.—LA PALOMA—from Hong Kong." For once, he has been bluffed—Gutman brought him back to the hotel only to neutralize him!

Spade rushes to the docks where the *La Paloma* lies in flames, no one aboard. He returns to his office, and starts to brief Effie when a gaunt seafarer staggers in, clutching a crudely wrapped parcel: Captain Jacoby, the master of the *La Paloma* (Walter Huston, conferring his blessing on his son's first picture in this cameo role). Jacoby groans, "The bird . . . ," and dies. "We've got it, angel, we've got it!" exults Spade, utterly unmoved by Jacoby's bloody demise. He has parlayed a few scraps of information into possession of the Falcon, and potential mastery of all who pursue it.

The phone rings—Brigid crying for help, then her muffled scream! In no great hurry, Spade gathers up the package and tells Effie to call in the police without mentioning the Falcon. He checks the package at a bus terminal baggage office, mails the stub to himself, then cabs to the address Brigid gave him—a vacant lot, more "hooey" thrown in his path. When he returns to his apartment, Brigid glides breathlessly into his arms (she's chronically out of breath; Huston is said to have gotten the effect by making Mary Astor race around the set between takes).

Spade opens the door; the light flicks on, revealing Wilmer behind him, guns drawn, Gutman and Cairo seated. "Well," says Spade without missing a beat, "are you ready to make the first payment and take the Falcon off my hands?" Gutman gives him $10,000—less than the original fee, but "genuine coin of the realm; with a dollar of this, you can buy ten dollars of talk!"

More important than cash, Spade says he needs a fall guy. Unless there is a believable suspect in the murders his neck is as good as in the noose. "Let's give them the gunsel," he says blandly—"He actually did shoot Thursby and Jacoby, didn't he?" Wilmer blanches with rage. Gutman assures him the idea is utterly repugnant, Wilmer is like a son to him (a concubine more likely). But he is obviously intrigued by Spade's guarantee that the police won't listen to Wilmer in their eagerness to nail down a conviction. (By this point, Spade has made a shrewd guess about Wilmer's guilt.)

If the Fat Man won't part with his minion, Spade nominates Cairo. Incensed, the Levantine suggests they frame Brigid. Gazing dispassionately at the quaking woman, Spade says he's open to *that* possibility, too. When Gutman affably threatens to torture the Falcon's location out of him, Spade studies his alternatives with the same detached pragmatism:

SPADE: If you start something, I'll make it a matter of your
having to kill me—or call it off. . . . the trick from

> my angle is to make my plan strong enough to tie you
> up, but not make you mad enough to bump me off
> against your better judgment.
>
> GUTMAN (*amazed*): By *Gad,* sir, you *are* a character!

Spade is willing to stake his pain threshold, even life itself. The risks are too high for the Fat Man to risk the gamble. Gutman and Cairo withdraw behind the Levantine's jeweled fingers to assess Spade's first suggestion. "Two to one they're selling you out, sonny," Spade sneers. Wilmer rises, rigid with fury, and Spade knocks him cold. Then he promises to have the bird delivered in the morning, but only if Gutman fills him in on the details of the killings— "so I can be sure the parts that don't fit are covered up." Gutman, unaware he's playing right into Spade's hands, spills the whole dirty business.

Brigid left the Falcon with Jacoby in Hong Kong, and came to San Francisco with Thursby. When Gutman couldn't win Thursby because of his unswerving loyalty, he was murdered by Wilmer to intimidate Brigid. Cairo pursued his treacherous confederates from Turkey to Hong Kong, thence to America. After he fell afoul of Spade, he decided to throw his lot back in with Gutman, establishing a precise alignment of homosexuals on one side of the "dizzy affair" and straights on the other.

Cairo discovered the *La Paloma* docking notice after Spade had met the Fat Man, remembered that Brigid and Jacoby had been seen together in Hong Kong. The detective was called back and drugged to keep him out of the way, so Gutman could surprise Brigid with Jacoby. The *La Paloma* was fired accidentally by Wilmer's inept search— "no doubt he was careless with matches." Brigid agreed to give up the Falcon at Gutman's hotel, was released, and never showed up. The gang then dashed to Brigid's apartment. Wilmer plugged the captain as he went down the fire escape, the rugged seaman still managed to escape. Brigid was "persuaded" to confess she had sent Jacoby with the package to Spade. She was forced to lure Spade away with a phony SOS, but by that time Spade already had the goods. So the gang returned to Spade's place.

Gutman fancies himself a Machiavellian master of intrigue, but in fact he and his companions are a sorry bunch of second-rate chiselers. Wilmer's inadvertent arson of the ship—a bad little boy playing with matches—is a ludicrous paradigm of their inveterate bungling. It's *Brigid* who emerges as the Dragon Lady of the piece: Brigid who deceived Gutman and Cairo in Istanbul, and thereafter has had every man connected with the caper dancing to her tune, every step of the way, with the possible—just barely possible—exception of Sam Spade.

Gutman looks down at Wilmer endearingly: "I want you to know I couldn't be any fonder of you if you were my own son. . . . Well, if you lose a son, it's possible to get another—there's only *one* Maltese Falcon." Brigid has been holding the envelope containing the $10,000. Gutman takes it from her and counts only nine bills! Spade, after brief consideration, says, "You palmed it!" and threatens to search the Fat Man if he doesn't own up. "Yes, sir, that I did," replies the latter merrily, "I must have my little joke now and then. And I was curious to know what you'd do in a situation of this sort!"

Spade has separated Gutman from his paramour, Wilmer. The Fat Man's "childish" prank has actually been motivated by pure spite: an attempt to drive a wedge between Spade and his (apparent) girlfriend to repair a humiliating loss, despite Gutman's airy disclaimer. Spade, although he completely mistrusts Brigid by now, will not give Gutman the satisfaction of thinking *he* can be divorced so easily from her.

Effie delivers the package, leaves. Spade places it on a table. The conspirators cluster around it like vultures at feeding time. Gutman, eyes moist, undoes the cord: "Now—*after seventeen years . . .*"—extracts the black bird from its wrappings, and fondles it almost lasciviously. He unclasps a knife, peels back a shaving from the Falcon's ebony surface, then another, and another. His face suffused, he hacks robotlike at the statue, his glazed vision fixed upon a terrible recognition—the Falcoln is a leaden forgery!

"You and your *stupid* attempt to buy it," howls Cairo. "Kemidov found out how valuable it was. . . . You—*imbecile!* You—*bloated idiot!!! You fat—,*" and collapses, blubbering. Gutman tugs at his collar, then quickly recovers his composure. He has spent seventeen years in the quest; another year is an additional investment of only "five and fifteen-seventeenths percent." On to Istanbul! Cairo, despite his imprecations, is instantly ready to follow, but Wilmer has glided out behind them.

Gutman demands the $10,000 back at gunpoint. Spade coolly extracts a single bill—"time and expenses"—and hands him the rest. Gutman tries unsuccessfully to cozen the detective into joining the Turkish expedition—"You're a man of nice judgment, and many resources!" He toddles out, bequeathing to Brigid "the *rara avis* on the table there, as a little—heh, heh—memento!"

Directly Spade is on the phone to Polhaus, turning in the whole murderous lot. Then he addresses Brigid with convincing urgency. Once caught, Gutman is sure to talk and they'll be implicated if he doesn't have *all* the answers. By turns pleading and bullying, he leads her through a labybrinth of lies to the last pieces of the mystery.

Brigid wanted Thursby out of the way before the *La Paloma* docked. So she hired Spade and Archer, then told Thursby he was being shadowed. She hoped that Thursby, fearing for his life, would kill or be killed by Miles. If the former happened, she would tip off the police and have Thursby arrested, rendering him *hors de Falcon.* But Thursby balked— apparently he was never the paragon of violence she painted. Spade reasons she decided to borrow Thursby's gun and lured the lecherous Archer to his death:

SPADE: Miles hadn't many brains, but he had too many years experience to be caught like that . . . up a blind alley with his gun on his hip, and his overcoat buttoned . . . but he would have gone up there with you, angel.

This was to have concluded her business with Spade and Archer. But when Thursby was murdered independently, she knew Gutman was on her trail again.

SPADE: You needed another protector, somebody to fill Thursby's boots . . . so you came back to me.

Brigid sobs wildly; she would have come back anyway, for from the first she loved him.

SPADE (*flatly*): Well, if you get a good break, you'll be out of Tehachapi in twenty years—and you can come back to me then. I hope they don't hang you, precious, by that sweet neck. . . . *I'm sending you over*!

Brigid tries to laugh away his chilling intention, but her face darkens as she grasps his cruel resolve:

SPADE: You're taking the fall—*I won't play the sap for you!* (*He shouts; his reserve finally snapped*) I don't care who loves who!!! . . . I won't walk in Thursby's—and I don't know how many others'—footsteps. You killed Miles,

and you're going over for it. . . . When a man's partner
is killed, he supposed to do something about it . . .
when one of your organization is killed, it's bad
business to let the killer get away with it . . . bad for
every detective, everywhere.

Finally, he can't let her off the hook:

SPADE: All of me wants to, regardless of consequence . . . and
because you counted on that, the same as you counted
on that with all the others.

A strange note of desolating triumph trembles in his voice. To her venal
insinuation that he would never have betrayed her had the Falcon been
real, and he had received full fee, he retorts:

SPADE: Don't be too sure I'm as crooked as I'm supposed to be.
That kind of reputation might be good business,
bringing high-priced jobs, and making it easier to deal
with the enemy.

Polhaus arrives with Dundy—Gutman and his accomplices have been
taken. Spade gives them Brigid, the weapons Wilmer and Cairo left behind, and the thousand-dollar bill. One realizes money has little intrinsic interest for Spade. He will very likely be required to yield up the
retainers Cairo and Brigid paid him. Even if he were allowed to keep the
few hundred dollars, the sum hardly justifies the risks he has taken.

Dundy escorts Brigid out the door. Polhaus looks down at the statuette, trying to fathom this ancient signet of greed.

POLHAUS: What is it?

SPADE (*with grim satisfaction*): The stuff that dreams are made
of.

He picks up the Falcon and walks into the hall. Brigid, manacled to
Dundy, stares fixedly ahead, her face drained of emotion as the elevator
gate closes upon her—a harsh portent of heavier captivity. It slowly descends as Spade, too, goes down the stairs, the fatal bird cradled in his
hands.

Spade's entrapment of Brigid causes him exceptional agony, despite his
disclaimer that it will cost him only a few nights' sleep. In the language

of psychoanalytic theory, Brigid represents a "narcissistic object choice"; much of what Spade prizes in himself is mirrored in her—her lucidity, her steely self-control (despite a phony fragile facade), her knack for gauging character and using her soundings to best advantage.

Above all, she reflects Spade's *criminality*—raised exponentially.

Leo Bellak speculated that the compulsive mystery buff is drawn to the genre to gratify unconscious criminal impulses. Frequently in the hard-boiled detective novel, the shamus *himself* must engage in shady practice to prove he is on the side of right (because the police themselves are too corrupt, or too inefficient to do their job). Thus, he often becomes the chief suspect, and his employer classically is the actual perpetrator.

Spade's explanation that he dissembles a crooked reputation to deceive an innominate "enemy" is a masterpiece of self-deception. Every brigand he brings to justice proves to him that he's not a rogue. If a man derives such kicks from tweaking the law by the nose, if he freely chooses to spend so many days and nights consorting with knaves and rascals, one must be highly suspect of the knavery within him. Brigid has long since passed permanently over the line Spade dares cross but provisionally, to grapple with malefactors and affirm his ambiguous morality. Brigid would have wedded him forever to her culpability had he not brought her low. But ultimately it is Miles's murder that sticks in his craw, makes him send her "over."

Archer's death has the primal resonance of Oedipal crime—the murder of the father/rival to enjoy the mother's favors. Although by indicting Brigid Spade shows himself innocent to the blaming world, he must stand half-convicted in his own psyche. For all his brave talk invoking a sacred code of detective honor, he bedded Iva Archer, violating the partnership's integrity—an impressive indicator that the fantasy of eliminating Miles one way or another was never far from his mind.

The psychoanalyst regularly finds in analyzing men who lust after a colleague's wife that, whatever the inherent charms of the lady in question, she also has come to symbolize the forbidden mother; the colleague is a substitute for a father the patient still seeks to displace. The obligations of partnership or professional association easily become equated in the unconscious with the incest barrier the child once longed and dreaded to penetrate.

I submit that an unacknowledged struggle for stud supremacy existed between Spade and Archer even before Spade bedded Iva. Miles smugly believes he has stolen away a glamorous, wealthy new client. While it could be argued that Spade could not have actually foreseen Miles's murder, his intuition—razor-sharp—surely made him suspect Brigid meant trouble. Yet, without warning Archer, he allowed him the illusion of victory, permitting him to take over Brigid's "case." Spade won—he always wins—but for once he got more than he bargained for, and Miles went to his doom!

Spade loses interest in Iva immediately after Miles dies. Admittedly, he may have been tiring of her before. Admittedly, Brigid has piqued his curiosity and lust. But his estrangement from the widow can also be inferred as a function of guilty anxiety over having "won" the Oedipal combat. One notes that with Miles out of the way, Spade becomes sole owner of the agency. The corpse is hardly cold before Spade dispassionately orders the office signs altered to show his name alone. Then he sets out on the new firm's first business—tracking down his partner's killer, and thereby denying/undoing a nagging sense of complicity.

Ernest Jones theorized that Hamlet procrastinates avenging his father's murder because in his heart he knows himself capable of the deed, an incest-ridden parricide in fantasy.[5] The inner perception of guilt that dictates Hamlet's delay is replaced in *The Maltese Falcon* by the maze of reality, the twists and turns of external circumstances that prevent the hero from identifying the murderer and exacting retribution.

Archer isn't just his partner's secret *victim:* he is his *stand-in,* in a sense his *patsy.* He *bought* Spade's death, an account which must be settled not only to assuage Spade's guilty conscience, but also to test the detective's skill at cheating the reaper. Barbara Deming asserts that the tough-guy hero of forties' cinema endures the assaults upon his person to demonstrate he can survive where others have been annihilated: "The hero takes the hopeless case, enters the deadly embrace, to prove to himself that he can emerge intact. . . . until [the] self is tried, the hero is no one, is nowhere."[6]

Repeatedly, Spade signifies that death shall have no dominion over him. He affects a studied indifference to Miles's killing, does not want to see the body, brushes aside expressions of sympathy—he strives to blot out the essence of Miles's *deadness* by displacing concentration upon the *puzzle* of his death. After Jacoby expires on his rug, Spade says resentfully, "Why couldn't he have stayed alive long enough to tell us something?" The cadaver could be just so much meat!

Spade's need to assert mastery over danger and death motivate his outrageous provocations of Dundy, the D.A., Wilmer, and the Fat Man. He regards his shaking hand outside Gutman's door with a mixture of admiration and numb relief, for he has unbalanced an adversary and kept death at bay. His "setups" of Gutman very nearly succeed in getting him killed. Gutman could easily have had Wilmer dispose of him after he was drugged. But one may speculate that he wanted Spade alive as a possible source of help if the *La Paloma* did not yield up the Falcon. Later, Spade will assent to torture rather than yield up the bird, outfacing Gutman, again denying death holds any terror.

With the Falcon's recovery, Gutman again could have elected to murder Spade before opening the package, thus retrieving the $10,000 retainer, and ensuring Spade's silence. He could just as easily have killed him *after* the bird was revealed a fake. That Gutman lets Spade survive is evidence of the fear and respect the detective has inspired (as well as Gutman's conviction that Spade is implicated too deeply to incriminate him).

Throughout the caper, Spade confronts adversaries bent on putting something over on him or getting something out of him. His antennae exquisitely sensitized to the possibility of exploitation, Spade always succeeds in turning the tables, putting something over or getting something out of his foe. The enemy may be overt or disguised, upright and uptight or down and dirty, on one side of the law or the other, but is always dedicated to sending him to the death he owes, whether by due process or hoodlum violence. Spade deals deftly with each opponent, changing style chameleonlike to match the man and the moment, relishing the competitive game for its own sake, as much as the actual work of detection.

But finally Spade's most formidable adversary in the "dizzy affair" is a woman. After Brigid hires him, he wards off repeated onslaughts of masculine aggression to seize the Falcon and embrace her at the mystery's core. Brigid and the Falcon are sinister equivalents: glittering birds of prey who have passed through the hands of one man after another, promising each successive owner supreme power, but bringing only ruin and destruction. Brigid is as lethal as the Sphinx, that other half-woman /half-monster who tore men apart unless they could solve her riddle.

I've noted that Brigid's attraction for Spade is compounded out of her beauty, out of his identification with her, out of the aura of sticky helplessness she radiates which he professes to scorn, and out of his itch to master her guile and bring her to heel. Brigid succeeds where all others have failed. She has engaged what passes for tender feeling in Spade, awakened something akin to love in his cold spirit—but then he perceives the skull-smile mocking him behind those imploring lips. Knowing how she served Miles, Jacoby, and Thursby, he sees she will certainly be *his* death unless he can disengage himself. Vindication of his faith in her duplicity provides a hollow victory. He has lain with his death, half-surrendered to the lure of oblivion, then freed himself on the precipice to take up his alienated existence. Analysis of the thanatophobe often uncovers the secret desire to die, to rejoin the mother in blissful union, returning to the womb of life to lie unborn and forever fulfilled.

In sum: Spade contends successfully with a series of hostile males who may be read as father-surrogates, gains the mother in Brigid, then recoils from her clutches. One finds in certain paranoids that the father, whose image is prefigured by various imaginary persecutors, has paradoxically posed less of a threat to the patient's integrity in childhood than an earlier source of woe—a mother intensely intrusive, suffocating, subversive of her child's bids for autonomy and independence (or so viewed, because of some poorly understood constitutional vulnerability in the child).

This type of patient tells us—often in a bizarre, psychotic way—that he or she stands a better chance of survival slugging it out with the father than confronting the desperately needed/feared Witch-Mother, the death-goddess of myth and nightmare—Medusa, the Harpy, Kali, the Furies, the Sphinx are her adumbrations. Prolonged dependency upon the mother in the earliest stages of development carries such a horrific threat of self-sundering that closeness with every person thereafter—father, siblings, friends, lovers—is fraught with humiliation and manipulation at best, utter extinction at worst. Protection of the damaged self against the wounding inherent in human contact becomes of paramount importance, so that the trauma of that first, frightening intimacy will never be repeated.

One need not be frankly delusional to be paranoid. There are milder forms of paranoia, quite compatible with the outward appearance of normality, especially in a dangerous environment. It is enough to be chronically suspicious, to aver that things are never what they seem on the interpersonal scene, to keep eternally vigilant for the hidden message, the double meaning, the iron fist concealed in the velvet glove and, armored against closeness, to treat each newcomer as ill-intentioned until proven otherwise.

We know next to nothing about Spade's past and forebears, so we can only speculate that his early life experience would conform to the model described above. Spade has chosen work in which *he* plays the role of perpetual intruder, yet keeps his own privacy sacrosanct. He lives alone, has nodding acquaintances connected with his work, but no evident binding male companionship. Hammett implies previous sexual liaisons: none has been durable, and although he has been capable of suffering with their loss—"a few nights' sleep"—it has evidently been more important for him to keep free from encumbrance.

Women find him attractive: his brand of elusiveness has particularly been known to stir up more than a few masochistic types. And—let's face it—the man has style! He's physically prepossessing, and has an attentive, courtly veneer replete with sexist "darlings," "sweethearts," and "angels"—which he well knows how to use to keep his distance intact. His most substantial relationship is with his secretary. As inferred, Effie plays a dependable, asexual wife-mother, an office Penelope to Brigid's evil Circe. Spade returns from adventures and infidelities to Effie for a touch of warmth, but ultimately denies her any profound participation in his life. Both in the novel and in the omitted last scene of Huston's script, it's tragically evident that she is sickening of his appalling coldness.

In our eagerness to romanticize the private eye, in our vicarious identification with his toughness, shrewdness, his peculiarly American self-sufficient loneliness, we have denied the barrenness of the marginal self that articulates with the very qualities we admire. During his quest for the Falcon, Spade eschews friendship, flirts with and rejects both homosexual and heterosexual entanglements. His career is his sole sustenance, a profession which validates his mistrust, withdrawal, and misanthropy. Poignantly, he invokes the lonely brotherhood of detectives arrayed against a faceless confederacy of criminal "enemies," to grant himself a meager semblance of communion with others. The circle comes full round, and with his next case he will resume the bootless struggle against his inevitable mortality.

Afterword

Of subsequent work on *The Maltese Falcon,* I particularly admire William Luhr's recent close reading, which uses shot-by-shot analysis not available when my essay was written.[7] Perceiving the film as a model of genre within the classic Hollywood tradition, he elucidates the formal means employed by Huston with great precision and further illuminates some of the psychodynamics I have mentioned (Spade's counterphobic "performances," inter alia).

Luhr notes that "the narrative progression of the film is developed largely around befuddlement, around the trying out and discarding of one potential narrative linkage for another."[8] The *Falcon*'s "gaze" is limited to Spade's viewpoint as perennial watcher. The detective (and, with him, the viewer) must "constantly process, question, and reformulate the often deceptive information he receives. . . . the sinister characters he encounters are developed with reference to deviations from cultural norms only hinted at in the dialogue."[9] The recurrent motif of a curtained window is one of the key visual icons pursued by Luhr, potently symbolic of the dangers Spade encounters as he treads the perilous labyrinth toward the deadly center of the Falcon's mystery. Huston's "subtextual implications of foreignness and deviant sexuality" are also artfully explored.

My study does not directly refer to *The Maltese Falcon*'s thematic and stylistic connections with film noir. The noirish aspects of the detective film have been discussed at length by Jon Tuska and J. P. Telotte.[10] Contrary to my pessimistic take on Spade's permanently hardened heart, Telotte perceives a ray of hope in his ability to speak haltingly about ethical commitment, during his final dialogue with Brigid O'Shaughnessy.

"Listen. This won't do any good. You'll never understand me, but I'll try once and then give it up." The remark sounds despairing, but it is nevertheless an effort at speech, at making something dark and obscure understandable. . . . Appropriately, it . . . leads into the film's most forthright assertion of ethics, of what one *must* do, simply because it is "right." That effort to speak, as well as the ethic prompting it, is central to the *film noir*. . . . it points to a persistent, driving, and finally *human* force that qualifies the form's otherwise fatalistic bent, and that can help us understand why such a dark form would have proved so popular.[11]

Telotte's argument is generically valid. It clearly applies to Philip Marlowe, questing down Chandler's famous mean streets toward finer ends than the shabby business of the shamus' hire.

But Spade's character is cut from a different cloth. Were I to classify him today, I would emphasize his narcissism as much as his paranoia.[12] His explanation to Brigid still rings false, pitched at persuading himself as much as she about the probity of his intentions. He may chiefly be motivated by the dangerous game of survival rather than sordid gain, but his ethics are no less questionable, his ungiving, guileful persona no less repugnant.

4

War Movies: Dangerous Recuperations—
Red Dawn, *Rambo*, and
the New Decaturism

The girl by the whirlpool's lookin' for a new fool . . .
—Bob Dylan

The Vietnamese-cum-"Jap" gets the
World War II death he deserves in
Missing in Action 2.

*W*hile American troops were being savaged on South Pacific beaches, I debated how many "Japs" were worth one marine with other bloody-minded seven-year-olds standing in the lobby of Philadelphia's Renel Theater. Then we went inside to watch square-jawed types like Robert Montgomery and Ward Bond fight hordes of Japanese for a few acres of atoll. Neither lack of ammo, malaria, nor the enemy's treachery deterred our side. Afterward, we realized how shamefully we had shortchanged American valor. The movies had artfully inscribed Hollywood's vision of the foe upon our small imaginations: no doubt about it, one marine was worth at least ten craven little sadists!

The War Genre Since World War II

Hollywood's militancy faded as World War II slipped into history, to be replaced by an emerging thoughtfulness. The movies began presenting former enemies in a more favorable, even forgiving light. The standard Nazi nasty like Major Strasser of *Casablanca* (1943) gave way to the "good German," epitomized by Brando's Hamletlike displays of troubled conscience in *The Young Lions* (1958). White racism delayed a friendlier depiction of the Japanese, but eventually the Eastern foe would also wear a human face at the Bijou. First nisei troops fought as bravely as white Americans (*Go for Broke!* [1951]). Then indigenous Japanese were partitioned from their wicked rulers and portrayed as innocent, even pitiable dupes (*Bridge to the Sun* [1961]).

Stylized gore, undamaging mortal wounds, and terminal oratory bowdlerized battle in the typical World War II film. The bloodiest deaths were reserved for Japanese soldiers who tortured prisoners, machine-gunned parachuting aviators, or pretended to surrender, then mowed down their captors with hidden weapons. White men were coded to die clean on screen because they fought cleanly in a virtuous cause. The antiseptic demise of an American soldier encouraged revenge rather than revulsion toward war. But the "Jap," fighting dirty in a dirty cause, deserved his disgusting end, blood spurting between the fingers that covered his macerated face. Western civilians were invited to relish such a death with no identification beyond a shudder.

After the war, movies gradually undertook a more realistic portrayal of the ravages wrought by ordinance upon vulnerable flesh, whether of friend or foe (*Hell Is for Heroes* [1962]; *Beach Red* [1967]). Paradoxically, the unsparing depiction of wartime carnage toward pacifist ends articulated with, and to some extent was enabled by, the increasingly permissive attitude toward violence in other genres: the western, as in Peckinpah's oeuvre, and horror cinema, e.g., *Psycho* (1960) and its cruel successors. The fortunes of the war film declined after the Cold War. The ambiguities of the Korean conflict failed to capture public and producers' interests compared to the epic polarities of World War II. With no real wars to fight, the old, "good" war was rejoined in blockbusters like *The Longest Day* (1962), *Tora! Tora! Tora!* (1970), *Patton* (1970), and *A Bridge Too Far* (1977). These pictures frequently presented the enemy as a worthy adversary. Politics was often deemphasized in favor of tactics— the chessboard of war. All told, war movies accounted for a decreasing fraction of Hollywood's output after Korea.

Vietnam at first seemed unlikely to revive the genre. *The Green Berets'* (1968) saber rattling even elicited frank ridicule. John Wayne's presence was curiously antique, more apt to *The Sands of Iwo Jima* (1949) than the rice paddies of Indochina. Films produced after the war's conclusion reflected widespread civilian disaffection. The popularity of *Apocalypse Now* (1979) and, most particularly, *Coming Home* (1978) appeared to vindicate antimilitarist sentiment.

The enemy wasn't much in evidence in these pictures. The Vietcong *were* actually America's least visible foe, and it was ineluctably more difficult to identify with Vietnamese appearance and culture than with the now Westernized Japanese. But a liberalized Hollywood seemed to be saying that even if one couldn't personally relate to this enemy, one could at least empathize with his wish to keep his turf to himself.

The Deer Hunter (1978) was applauded in some quarters as the summary peace picture, an erroneous if understandable reading. The film actually contains the first reactive groundswell of populist patriotism, tempered by a sense of the veteran's trauma. Racist images of friend and foe alike are resurrected. The Vietcong appear strange and barbarous. In the paradigmatic Russian roulette sequences, the Vietnamese are inscribed as Orientalist caricatures—venal, disrespectful of life, thoroughly inscrutable. Director Michael Cimino implies that here was no place nor ideals worthy enough for a white man to lay down his life. A small, wounded "God Bless America," raised by the returnees and their families at the end, signals latent readiness to sally forth again in a better cause.

In the years following *The Deer Hunter*, the disasters ushered in by Vietnamese defeat and the Watergate scandal seemed to compound themselves. The nation's plunging fortunes were foregrounded by the emerging wealth of former enemies. Wildfire inflation devoured livelihoods at home, while embassy personnel were held hostage abroad. A frustrated electorate finally swept Jimmy Carter from office. The times turned rightish, and apparently more propitious. The economy cycled into a semblance of recovery. Yippies became Yuppies. Grenada fell. The country's pride stirred. Ronald Reagan was reelected, as oil prices plummeted and the stock market soared.

A generation later, the rationales for entering Vietnam appear even more tangled and, to right-thinking revisionists, curiously negligible. Focus has gradually shifted from the war's causes, from actual compromises by our leadership in its conduct, to imaginary failures of nerve, the shameful treatment of veterans, or the fate of MIAs. Whether the United States should have become bogged down in an Asian land conflict seems beside the point.[1] Admiral Decatur's famous sentiments resound anew: *"My country, may she always be in the right, but right or wrong, my country!"*

A resurgence in the war genre parallels ideological repositioning toward Vietnam, and the overall conservative swing in American political life. One views the latest batch of war movies—from *Uncommon Valor* (1982) through *Top Gun* (1986)—with nostalgia and alarm. Their Decaturish philosophy, fondness for John Wayne heroics and patriotic gore often uncannily reprise the most flamboyant World War II agitprop.

This essay considers the strategies deployed by two pivotal "New Decaturist" films, *Red Dawn* (1984) and *Rambo: First Blood Part II* (1985), to recuperate the narcissistic injuries sustained by America in its Indochinese experience. *First Blood* (1982) will also be analyzed as a transitional piece; however melodramatically, it does capture many of the per-

sonal and ideological dilemmas raised by Vietnamese conflict—
particularly the veteran's return—which movies like *Red Dawn*
and *Rambo* attempt to resolve chiefly through bellicose patriotic fantasy.

Red Dawn: "Next Week, with Swords . . ."

Red Dawn posits a sneak attack upon the United States by a Cuban-Nic-
araguan strike force, backed by sixty Soviet divisions. Invasion is precipitated by a massive Soviet crop failure and the breakup of NATO. The
enemy keeps the use of atomic weapons minimal, so that U.S. grain will
escape radioactive contamination. The film shows the war's impact upon
the typical "heartland" town of Calumet, Colorado, specifically upon adolescents who escape to the mountains and form a partisan band, the
"Wolverines," named after their high school football team.

Red Dawn redeems Vietnam by identifying its teenage heroes with the
former enemy. The Vietcong, many of whom were no older, mounted
one of the most historically effective guerilla campaigns against a vastly
superior force. The Wolverines endure every vicissitude experienced by a
partisan group like the Cong: life on the run, ridden with fear and fatigue; chronic undersupply of arms and food; collaboration from without; doubt, dissension, even treachery from within.

The Russian/Latin invaders visit upon the citizens of Calumet, Colorado every indignity and crime of occupation. My Lai—and other less
publicized outrages—demonstrated that American troops could be
quite as cruel, although thankfully not as systematic in oppression. Such
atrocities arise from the loosening of conscience in an exotic clime, as
well as the enemy's no less brutal practice. Murder and rape of dear
ones harden the Wolverines' resolve that not one foreign soldier will
remain on American soil. (Frequent allusions are made to the mis-
treatment of American women in the film, recalling the lurid descrip-
tions of German rape used to mobilize the United States into World
War I.) Our presence, like the French before us, was equally repugnant to the Vietnamese foe (and many supposed friends).

Red Dawn acknowledges that well-intentioned or coercive methods
can never win the hearts and minds of a populace determined enough to
resist them. A Cuban airborne officer patterned after Che Guevara comes
to view the invasion as an expansionist subversion of socialist ideals. In
the end, he allows the two brothers who lead the Wolverines to die peace-

fully after they destroy Calumet's garrison. He may be read as a congenial symbol of ideological defeat, the picture's "good German."

But *Red Dawn* does not draw a rather obvious parallel between the Russian failure to gauge the depth of the Wolverines' resolve and American misprision of Vietcong commitment, noted by General Bruce J. Palmer, Jr. and many others. Having projected Vietnamese resistance on American youth, the film projects American misbehavior onto the bloodthirsty Russians and their Latino stooges. It is, after all, always the awful Other who harbors dark impulses, while we live in the light of our own good opinions.

Red Dawn's patriotism uneasily depends upon a dank, survivalist account of the human condition. The Russians need our grain to survive, and invade when our allies meanly abandon us. A downed U.S. flier reflects:

Who knows, next week it'll be swords. . . . The two toughest kids on the block started it. . . . Sooner or later they're goin' to fight. . . . I guess they forgot what it was like.

War is thus deemed inevitable because of our inability to learn from the past and, more fundamentally, because of mankind's congenitally predatory nature.

John Milius, writer and director of *Red Dawn*, owns an adolescent affection for combat. His heroes—*Conan the Barbarian* (1982), and the Barbary pirate of *The Wind and the Lion* (1974)—are types especially favored by American teenage boys: bold adventurers on the frontier between civilization and savagery. In *Red Dawn*, Milius's staunch conservatism is wedded to his pubertal enthusiasm for manly contention. War is hell, the script asserts, but his young men (and women) have one hell of a good time waging it.

In a concentration camp at the local drive-in where the invaders have interned him, the father of the two brothers asserts that they can now understand why he was always so tough on them—to help them endure and prevail in times like these. His sentiments go down smoothly, purveyed by a classically seamless style which cleverly effaces the film's hawkish politics, dissolving ideology in compelling action. But stop the camera, and *Red Dawn* deconstructs into an ominous Freudian fable, rife with paternal paranoia.

Although the father appears briefly, his role is central to the film's New Decaturism. The script approves his courage and frontier values.

He is executed singing "God Bless America": the anthem that sounded uncertainly at *Deer Hunter*'s end would appear to have finally found a cause worthy of its utterance. However, his patriotism has a darker cast.

A well-known analyst once wondered, only half in jest, whether wars might be brought on by old men unconsciously bent on eliminating a younger generation which threatens their waning potency. Along these lines, conceive that the father, unconsciously fearing the challenge to his authority posed by his sons' majority, oppresses and minimizes them during their formative years. Just so, let us suppose, his father minimized him. It is a common clinical picture.

The father assures the boys that he withholds tenderness in their best interests, that he punishes them so they can grow sturdy, self-reliant. He instructs them in the arts of survival; ever recommends eternal vigilance against the barbarous aggressor (projection of his own unconscious jealousy and rage) who somewhere rankles over their plenty, waiting for soft times to seize their land and women.

Conceive that the father is after all not a thorough monster; that he possesses genuinely loving qualities; that many of his sons' peers are raised in the same "tough" style, live in the same distressing Oedipal tangle; that their leaders trumpet similar "manly" beliefs. Eventually the sons identify with what they both admire and fear, taking their father's paranoia and xenophobia for their own.

Shortly after fleeing to the mountains, they kill a deer. They urge a companion who has never hunted to drink its blood as their father had them do, to incorporate its spirit. He does, and directly experiences a mystical bonding with his comrades. The scene reads as an idealization of the father's ruthlessness into "animal" courage. In effect, the sons have totemized the father as angry resident deity of their small tribe, Nemesis incarnate.

Conceive that with sufficient social, economic, or political pressure, with the tidal accumulation of greed, anger, and ignorance, a "Red Dawn" would inevitably fall when these true believers—or their children, or children's children—would lead others into battle against their opposite global numbers, as invaders or defenders or both.

Conceive finally that such a dynamic could constitute a regular casus belli in real life, not merely cinematic reality . . .

Admittedly, this is an oversimplified explanation of our complex impulses to war—although hardly less simplistic a rationale than Milius's decerebrate Darwinism. Years after my training, I still am drawn to the gloomy Freud of *Civilization and Its Discontents*.[2] Therein he speculated that war might be a periodic result of collective projected aggression, the dark price paid to keep society safe from the savage impulses of its members (particularly, one infers, from the savagery of intergenerational male rivalry).

No stranger to personal Oedipal struggle, Freud was an ardent nationalist in his youth. By the time he wrote his epic monograph, his naive patriotism had long since given way to an ironic fatalism about the consequences of humanity's entrenched aggression.

First Blood: "You Want a War You Can't Win?"

Relatively few films about the Vietnam veteran were produced prior to the rise of the New Decaturism. In these pictures, sympathy for the vet's suffering was tempered by fear about his mental instability and his potential for violence as a civilian.

One category of the veteran movie obscurely grasped his wrongs, then undertook an "acceptable" resolution which raised few questions about the origin of his violence. Typically, the veteran, his family, or friends were viciously attacked by criminals (*Rolling Thunder* [1977], *The Exterminator* [1981]). He retaliated, using his military training to exact bloody retribution. Perfunctory criticism might be leveled at society or its leadership. But the obvious focus of hatred was the unsocialized element, the small-time punks or big-time crime bosses threatening every decent citizen. The veteran's aggression was safely channeled by transforming him into that familiar hero of the postmodern western, the urban vigilante.

Less frequently, Hollywood constructed the veteran into a repellent, if pitiable, condensation of the entire Vietnam experience. A fantasied justification was thus offered for the shunning of returned veterans, the process by which the public symbolically killed the messengers bearing the bad news. Several bizarre exploitation films made more telling statements on this score than "reformist" movies like *Coming Home*.

In *Fiend with the Electronic Brain* (1971), criminals implant an electronic device in the brain of a veteran in aid of making him a zombie responsive to their will. The veteran villain of *Don't Answer the Phone* (1980) is an obese sadist who performs serial murders crazily pitched at "measuring up" to his father. The soldier of *Deathdream* (1972) comes back from Nam to his small-town home in response to his mother's long-ings. A "Monkey's Paw" conclusion reveals he has been killed in combat, then resurrected as a vampire.

Deathdream embodies the nagging suspicion that Vietnam would re-turn to haunt the public conscience despite massive denial of our sol-diery's very existence. Its zombie trooper eerily condenses horror about the veteran's deeds with an uneasy sense of complicity in his torment. The Vietnam returnee is reimagined as a psychotic "haunt," cousin to the spectral lunatics who stalk through "slice and dice" classics like *Hal-loween* (1978) and *Friday the 13th* (1979).

First Blood was produced during the first flush of economic revival and reawakened patriotism. As noted, it is a "bridge" film, central to subse-quent developments in the genre; deriving strategies both from the melodramatic and fantastic veteran movies. The text shuttles ambigu-ously between perceptions of its ex–Special Forces hero, John Rambo, as heroic vigilante or crazy avenger.

Rambo wanders into a small Oregon town after discovering that the only other survivor of his Vietnam outfit is dead from Agent Orange can-cer. The indignities heaped upon him by the local police cry out for punishment. We cheer to see them fall like ninepins when he finally erupts out of near-catatonic helplessness, during a brutal shower which provokes flashbacks to his torture by the Vietcong. But the film also re-frains from portraying most of the lawmen as unregenerate sadists. One of the younger cops senses that Rambo is off-balance, and tries to stop his harassment. Any of them could have served with their prisoner in Nam, and probably would have admired him.

Nor is their leader, Sheriff Will Teasle, the stock-company redneck. Although unintrospectively authoritarian, he is also a man of decent enough instincts when uncrossed. He is honest enough to be troubled by the intensity of his vengeance, even if he cannot restrain himself from pursuing it. In a quiet sort of way, he is also a patriot. He initially greets Rambo:

> TEASLE: Wearin' that flag on that jacket, lookin' the way you do . . . you're askin' for trouble around here, friend.

Yet he displays the same flag on his uniform, and is as profoundly com-mitted to defend the values his peaceful hamlet lives by as Rambo was when he stood tall for his country in Nam. These erstwhile adversaries are actually *mirrors*, reflecting each other's assets and liabilities: stubborn courage, adolescent competitiveness, rugged individualism combined with conformity. They could be father and son, at odds because of their similarities. Or Teasle could be a forty-five-year-old Rambo, sans war neurosis. A few years down the line might find them sitting together, listening to grateful speeches on the dais of a small-town Memorial Day tribute. But the time is out of joint for them now. Ignominious defeat wants burial, not remembrance.

The hard-headedness—and hard-heartedness—of Teasle and most of his force affords a harsh example of official callousness toward the veteran. Teasle's insensitivity also mirrors the failure in high places to gauge the depth of the Vietcong's commitment or skills. Rambo returns to the American heartland, bearing the scars of his leader's errors, trained only for violent confrontation. His service neglected, even despised, he's a time bomb waiting to go off.

He reinvents the conflict on home ground, turning the guerilla tactics of the enemy against his countrymen to devastating effect. Sam Trautman, the Green Beret colonel who trained Rambo, warns Teasle: *"You want a war you can't win?"*—echoing the message hammered at our government progressively from the left, center, and right during the war years. The invariable reply was the pious rhetoric Teasle spouts as he is sucked deeper into his lethal enterprise.

> TEASLE (*angrily to Trautman*): People start playin' around with the law and all hell breaks loose. . . . We're just a small time Sheriff's department, but we're expected to do our duty, just like the heroes in Special Forces. . . . You think Rambo was the only guy who had a tough time in Vietnam?

While it draws upon movies like *The Exterminator* or *Deathdream*, *First Blood* avoids tidy pseudo-resolutions. The film does employ exaggeration in the service of presenting a not unrealistic picture of the entity psychiatrists call post-traumatic stress disorder, a syndrome characterized by flashbacks and obsessive recollection of ungovernably painful experiences; anxiety attacks; withdrawal from ordinary social contacts; blunting of emotional responses, so forth.

Rambo's powerful argument with Trautman, as Teasle lies grievously wounded with the town in ruins, is diagnostic in more than one sense:

> TRAUTMAN: You did everything to make this private war happen. . . . This mission is over!!!

RAMBO: *NOTHING IS OVER!!!* . . . You don't just turn it off. . . . It wasn't my war . . . *you* asked me, I didn't ask *you!!!* . . . and I did what I had to do to win, but somebody wouldn't let us win! Then I come back to the world, and see all those maggots at the airport . . . spittin', callin' me baby-killer and all kinds of vile crap! Who are they to protest me? I've *been* there!

TRAUTMAN: It was a hard time for everyone, Rambo. It's all in the past now.

RAMBO: *FOR YOU!!!* Your civilian life is nothin'! . . . In the field we had a code of honor. . . . Out there I could fly a gunship, I could drive a tank, I was in charge of million dollar equipment! Back here, I can't even hold a job!!! . . . Where's everybody? All those guys now? Where's all my friends? . . . Sometimes I don't know where I am. . . . I don't talk to anybody, sometimes a day, sometimes a week. . . . *I CAN'T GET IT OUT OF MY MIND!!!*

First Blood portrays the veteran neither as omnipotent hero nor psychotic villain, but as a pitiful victim, lashing out at forces which he feels (and the movie would have us believe) are beyond his control. America created Rambo out of youth's idealism, then abandoned him. His last shred of identity derives from the craft and fellowship of a war no one wants to remember. In the end, he is led away to penal or therapeutic confinement, leaving us to wonder uneasily what validity his terrible sacrifices might possess.

First Blood avoids naming precise villains or reasons for defeat. It alludes to a shadowy "someone" who wouldn't let Rambo win. "His" identity is never established, but one senses "his" negligence verges on malevolence. "His" traces can be discerned in Teasle's compost of high-minded civic principles and low-handed revenge. The sheriff unwittingly steps into "his" shoes, and precipitates catastrophe.

Rambo: "Do We Get to Win This Time?"

Red Dawn and *First Blood* recuperate Vietnam on American soil. *Rambo: First Blood Part II* reengages the enemy several years later in the paddies where it all began, over the issue of captive American MIAs.

Little mention of MIAs was made in earlier veteran pictures. They became a signet of compromised national honor in several successful films produced shortly after *First Blood*. These include *Uncommon Valor* (1983), directed by Ted Kotcheff (who also directed *First Blood*), and Chuck Norris's *Missing in Action I* (1984) and *Missing in Action II* (1985). The Eastern enemy wears his characteristic mask of cruelty and deceit in these pictures. The enemy at home is no longer anonymous. He's a senator, or some other official of treacly liberal persuasion, jealous of his petty power, obviously no friend to the present administration.

The MIAs are cloned from the Bataan death march, starved and beaten slaves of the yellow man. Their existence is smoothly denied by one side, timidly pursued by the other. Typically, the American bureaucrat counsels prudence lest some delicate diplomatic balance be upset, while the wily Vietnamese hopelessly outmaneuver him. The prisoners are tangled in a bureaucratic web, duplicating the original restraints upon American valor. Statecraft is for fools or cowards. Only a rugged individualist can cut the Gordian knot, a man unafraid of breaking rules or heads.

Rambo: First Blood Part II pushes this scenario further toward the paranoid right. The hero is discovered on a rockpile, serving a prison term for his Oregon misadventure three years ago. Colonel Trautman offers him a chance for a presidential pardon if he participates in a Special Operations project to investigate the presence of MIA prisoners in Vietnam. "Do we get to win this time?" he asks.

At a high-tech Thai command post, Rambo receives a rankling order from Murdock, the slick CIA type in charge of the secret mission. He's only to photograph any prisoners he finds. He parachutes in and discovers MIAs are indeed interned at the camp where he himself was once imprisoned. He frees one, but is stranded at the pickup point when Murdock abruptly aborts the mission. An outraged Trautman realizes Rambo was never meant to succeed. Going through the motions of a search was intended to placate the public, while suppressing evidence of MIAs—if any were found—would eliminate humiliating negotiations and reparations.

Back at the camp, Rambo is sadistically interrogated by a Russian "advisor" and his goon sergeant. A beautiful contra helps him escape. She is almost immediately killed after they decide to go over the border. Ablaze with rage, Rambo single-handedly destroys the camp, releases the MIAs, and flies them back to the command post in a Russian helicopter after blasting his last enemy, the Soviet officer, out of the sky. He destroys Murdock's computers, but spares the trembling apparatchik. Trautman warns him not to become consumed with hatred for his country. Before walking into the mythic distance, Rambo asserts:

> RAMBO: Hate it? I'd *die* for it. . . . I want what they and every other guy who came over here and spilt his guts [wants] . . . for our country to love us the way we loved it!!!

Rambo unfolds its reparative theme through a series of perilous returns. The hero nearly is torn to pieces during the parachute drop; betrayed by river pirates hired to bring him to the camp, then by a representative of his own government; again confined by the Vietnamese; tortured by their Russian overlords. He escapes to lose a barely discovered love; he transcends defeat in two final revisitations; devastates the enemy, and intimidates the feckless Murdock into acknowledging responsibility for a lost generation of American warriors.

Rambo journeys back to the source of his trauma to gain his freedom and, the script implies, to heal his psychic wounds. But from the outset Stallone's performance makes it obvious that the hero is completely lucid, a far cry from the schizoid drifter of *First Blood*. As for Rambo's physique, Stallone has pumped himself into a living fetish. A traveling shot down his arm is held so close as to make his biceps resemble the Himalayas.[3]

Three years on the rockpile have not caused this remarkable recovery, but the New Decaturism of the day. The gauntlet of suffering the hero runs is not meant to affirm his resolve, but *ours*. His returns are stations of the cross in a high patriotic rite. Rambo takes upon his own person the torment of the MIAs and the nation's humiliation. Brought low, he rises in vengeance and flame to redeem America.

The comparisons with the Christian passion are obvious, especially in several torture scenes. Rambo takes one MIA off a cross. Later, he himself is lowered by the Vietnamese into a swamp with his outstretched arms chained to a yoke. Still later, his Russian interrogators spread-eagle him across an upright iron grill and jolt him with electricity. His nearly nude body writhing in muscular agony, grimacing as he fights back his screams, Rambo could easily be one of the flayed Redeemers favored by the Flemish school.

Foreign adversaries are depicted as satanic, in imagery familiar to World War II film buffs. The Vietnamese are lustful little butchers like the Japanese of old, complete with gold teeth and guttural snarls. The Russian interrogator owns the insinuating intelligence and icy arrogance of a 1940 Gestapo chief. Like the World War II movie, *Rambo* declares the foe inhuman, hence beyond Christian mercy.

The resurrected Rambo—he towers like a guardian archangel over the MIAs—does not merely kill, he *expunges!* In a sequence much applauded each time I saw it, Rambo aims explosive bolts at a fleeing Vietnamese soldier. The man stops, transfixed, no more able to avoid Rambo's avenging hand than the Almighty's. He is blasted to rags, not a trace of him remains, as if a single enemy should not befoul the earth after Rambo's day of judgment.

Rambo's Christlike character merges with that of another American hero: the virtuous frontiersman, threatened by the corrupting encroachment of civilization. Examples include Uncas of *Last of the Mohicans*, Natty Bumppo of *The Deerslayer*, and Tarzan of the apes. (Huck Finn is a youthful version, happy with Jim on his raft, removed from hateful feminine control.) Rambo is half-Indian. His Green Beret training liberated *his* Uncas: his alienation from mainstream society after the war reinforces his identity as Natural Man. A dreary civilian existence cannot offer him the affirmation of life in the wild.

The film's associated distrust of technology is positively Luddite. *Rambo* asserts that one is best tested on the bloody field through exercise of native brawn, brains, and a minimum of weaponry. Rambo dismisses electronic combat with a Wilshire Boulevard koan: "The mind is the best weapon." When his parachute is fouled, he cuts away his sophisticated hardware and drops into the jungle armed only with a knife, bow, and arrows. In the end, he destroys the mighty Russian supercopter through a clever ruse, then blasts Murdock's mainframes to bits.

The film waxes as paranoid over big government as big machines. Its vision of our country is intriguingly split. One America exists in a sanctified imaginary—a shining land of populist iconography and simplistic truths—fruited plains, purple mountains' majesty, halls of Montezuma, so forth. It's well worth dying for. The other America governs, and not well. Devious courtiers like Murdock are its creatures, gutless liberals, weak-principled do-gooders.

Rambo implies that if you don't get this corrupt leviathan off your back, it will bleed you dry. Or send you off to a badly managed war to be killed, maimed, forgotten. Ronald Reagan ran twice on the same divided vision of America, representing himself against himself, and won.

(One notes he has frequently quoted Rambo, and Dirty Harry as well.) Meanwhile, the practices of big, "bad" government he has critiqued continue proliferating.

Dangerous Recuperations

Saddled with a staggering national debt and a huge trade imbalance, floundering amidst conflicted economic signals, this administration no longer easily blames its predecessors. It repeatedly recommends escalating an already enormous military budget in aid of pursuing an intransigent, and at times provocative foreign policy. Its answer to many of the complex issues of the day—including the residual problems of Vietnam—is distressingly familiar: label a foreign enemy inhuman, despicable; make him a lightning rod for discharging populist anger and discontent whether in El Salvador or outer space. Beat the drums; blow the bugles; send out the recruiting sergeants again.

Art imitates life: *Red Dawn* rehearses invasion by a new Latin American foe, *Rambo* recalls the humiliations inflicted by an old Eastern one. Behind them both, the Russian adversary stands ever ready to visit plunder, rapine, and his godless policies upon us. Both films predict war with Russia, and none too subtly applaud its arrival. Both make war more thinkable by suggesting that nuclear holocaust can be avoided.

Red Dawn deploys a convoluted strategic rationale to deny apocalypse. The Russians need our grain, so they use their missiles sparingly. *Rambo* imagines the armament of Armaggedon simply doesn't exist; war becomes a matter of individual enterprise and honor, the good guy slugging it out with the bad guys, with the outcome as predictable as a western (in the end, Rambo even walks out of the frame like Eastwood or Shane). Stallone's *Rocky IV* (1986) pits the American champion against a Soviet opponent; the ads read: "World War III is about to begin." Next week with swords, indeed.

War also becomes more imaginable by disguising the grisly nature of wounding. Violence in the current war film rarely produces the gruesome outcome of today's "splatter" movies, or past pacifist pictures like *Beach Red*. *Rambo*'s violence is staged with a not unsatisfying balletic quality, reminiscent of the best spaghetti westerns, Peckinpah's cinema, and Walter Hill's work, notably in *The Warriors* (1979) and *Streets of Fire* (1984). This aesthetic of wounding, the previously cited "clean death" of the World War II G.I., are two of the many strategies used by the genre to mask war's terrible face.[4]

To their credit, many recent war films are making long overdue statements about the contemptible treatment veterans have received from an ungrateful, cumbersome system. *First Blood* is the best of a problematic lot in this regard. But the benefit of publicly exposing the veterans' wrongs is eclipsed by the danger of Hollywood's current prescription for our collective post-Vietnam distress. It is compounded out of the same heedless hawkishness that embroiled us in Vietnam in the first place.

Unwittingly or otherwise, both administration rhetoric and the bellwether productions of popular culture seem to be clearing the way for yet another generation of American youth to be enlisted in yet another dubious foreign adventure. Despite facile reassurances on the "manageability" of such an enterprise, the world itself would surely stand at pawn the next time around. Like our leaders, the New Decaturs of Hollywood are finally memorializing the Vietnam vet. But like the Bourbon kings, in the process of remembering, they have learned nothing.

Afterword

My army service ended in 1965. I came to oppose the Vietnam War within a few years of my discharge. Since writing the preceding essay, I have remained out of sympathy with one dubious American military adventure after another, as successive foes we sought to demonize fell, victims of their own incompetent expansionism. The execrable Sadaam—like many another petty dictator preceding him—was supported, then reviled by the same arbiters of our foreign policy. Whether continued sanctions with or without less massive military intervention would have likewise defeated him will never be known.

With the astonishing debacle of Desert Storm for Iraq, closely followed by the autodestruction of the Soviet imperium, New Decaturism resounds throughout the land with even greater fervor. Our leaders continue to be lulled by Hollywood visions of patriotic gore, rather than confront uncheering geopolitical/economic realities.[5] No cinematic monuments to our Iraq adventure have been filmed at this writing. In a sense, they need not be, since massive Pentagon censorship and the media's Tom Clancyish absorption in the gleaming gizmos of war seemed to make the Gulf conflict pass equably as one prolonged, sanitized *Top Gun*.

The audience has now left the theater, eerily uncomprehending or uncaring that Sadaam rules his blasted land and tortured people with renewed vigor. Meanwhile, our own desperate internal problems escalate, sorely scanted of cash lavished upon weapons of destruction, and fielding the half-million who used them.

"Dangerous Recuperations" was not intended to decry American bellicosity, as if other nations were exempt from the lure of bellicose enterprise. The racist signatures of *Rambo*, *Red Dawn*'s vision of an antagonist's despicable barbarism, are but the latest in a parade of such paranoid distortions since the dawn of history. Both in *Civilization and Its Discontents* and his exchange with Einstein,[6] Freud addressed the ubiquitous tendency of one individual or tribe to project upon some degraded Other the engrained lust for property, power, or the slaking of naked aggression sui generis.

Sam Keen has poignantly underscored the urgency in a nuclear age of acknowledging the processes by which the home team's cadre and casus belli are eternally sanctified, the opposition's eternally condemned.

In the beginning is the enemy . . . before we make a weapon or a war, we make an image of the enemy. First we think each other to death, then we invent a battle ax or a ballistic missile. . . .

Instead of being hypnotized by our enemies, we need to look at the eyes through which we see [them]. . . . All nations use basically the same visual metaphors, the same hostile cliches. . . . The enemy is always a demon, a barbarian . . . the aggressor, a liar, a madman, or some vile animal [who] can be exterminated without regret. . . .

There are real enemies, and we can't make conflict go away by pretending we're all friends . . . but the world has become too dangerous to portray those people as monsters, evil empires, ourselves as God's righteous warriors. Can we find a way to live with, and even struggle against people and nations whose interests are in conflict with ours, without dehumanizing them? Could we be heroes without making other villains?[7]

Psycho: The Apes at the Windows

The price of progress in civilization is paid in forfeiting happiness through the heightening of the sense of guilt. —Freud, *Civilization and Its Discontents*

My love of film is far more important to me than any considerations of morality.
—Alfred Hitchcock (to François Truffaut)

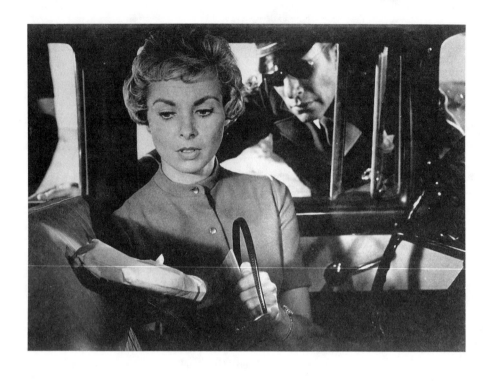

The implacable Hitchcockian superego:
Psycho's cop of the mind.

*E*nter Harold, punctual to the minute, in his usual uniform. The gray twill slacks, blue shirt, and brown oxfords have gone through as many reeditions as *Gone with the Wind*. Mother bought his herringbone jacket twelve years ago for his college graduation; he hated it then, hates it now, but has never taken it off. I observed yesterday that change upsets him, so today he is wearing his other necktie, after agonies of indecision before the mirror this morning: Was he putting it on as a concession to me, or to prove I was wrong? Either way, I've made a dent in his defenses, and the proof of my influence both frightens and angers him. He quick-marches to the couch, not looking at me—for that would further acknowledge my impact—lies down, every button securely buttoned against further assaults on his integrity. His hands are folded stiffly upon his breast, his legs locked in a painful parody of relaxation. He gives a fair imitation of a man on his way to an embalming. Even his voice is distant, sepulchral:

This morning, I awoke at 7:30 A.M., and, after dressing, ate breakfast. I was running a bit late, hence only had time for a single cup of coffee. Whilst riding the subway, several thoughts supervened. (1) It occurred to me I might ask out Edna again for next Saturday. However, I'm not entirely sure I want to see her so soon—I'll have to give the matter more thought. (2) A great deal of paperwork has accumulated; I hoped to clean it up before coming here. (3) I was worried, therefore, that I might be late, and you would think I was anxious because you said I don't like having my routines disrupted. . . . Well, I thought about *that*

a great deal. Although there is some merit in your formulation, I basically disagree.

Harold drones on, processing the precious stuff of experience into a
homogenous gruel, lacking zest or flavor. I keep awake by reminding
myself he's trying to bore me asleep. He embarks on a long disquisition
about his defective shortwave radio. I gently chide him that he's still trying to keep the status quo. He objects testily, explores every crevice and
quiddity of my wrongness, then, one minute to go, tells a dream he had
last night.

*He is at his desk, absorbed in his everlasting paperwork; he looks up, to see a band of apes
romping outside the windows. How could they get here? he thinks. I'm on the fiftieth
floor! They pound against the glass, their toothy simian grins unutterably obscene. In a
moment, the windows will shatter, they will swarm in.* He awakens in a cold sweat.

The psychoanalyst spends a good part of his days suffering along with
people like Harold. The treatment of the obsessive-compulsive personality is likely to be demanding, frustrating, and lengthy. In Freud's days,
obsessionals seemed more likely to present with crippling symptoms:
perverse thoughts—*Fuck God! Let Mother Die!*—descended from nowhere upon these most upright of citizens, which had to be redeemed by
obscure rituals, repetitive hand-washings, touching of doorknobs, arranging the pillows just so before retiring.

Classic analytic theory holds that these strange obsessions and com-
pulsions are only the tip of the iceberg, pathological spinoffs from an
underlying system of coping with stress by imposing rigid rules and restraints upon the self. Supposedly when the system becomes overloaded
beyond its limits, florid symptoms erupt into consciousness.

No one knows why, but many of today's obsessionals seem to present
the system entire without symptoms to the analytic therapist. If a serious
episode of compulsiveness has occurred, it will often have been many
years ago, during childhood or adolescence, and subsequently sealed
over. The adult patient is mildly depressed, vaguely unhappy, and lonely, yet frequently unaware of how desperately the obsessional "style" has
diminished the quality of life.

But it should not necessarily be assumed that to be obsessional is, per
se, always to be "ill"—at least, in the clinical sense. While tormenting
rituals may confine the obsessional, only a minority are so afflicted. The
obsessional *adaptation*—particularly sans symptoms or concern over
their limitations—is simply another way of being in the world; one ac-

corded high survival value in cultures such as ours, which still nominally reward the puritan values.

Typically, the obsessional individual is industrious, clean, orderly, thrifty, cautious, and doubting. Observe that Harold's prolix speech is shot through with references to his thoughts. Indeed, he thinks so inordinately about his thinking that there is but little room for him to feel. Feelings are risky commodities, unquantifiable, uncontrollable; and if there is one illusion the obsessional treasures, it is the possibility of absolute control over everyone and everything. The self is experienced as a computer, programmed to reduce the mysterious wholeness of existence into myriad petty duties and details that must be "cleared up" with relentless efficiency.

But feelings intrude, the ghost in the machine. And since the machine can never be brought to a state of perfection because of them, breakdown always seems imminent. Obsessionals dread the clamor of instinct, protecting themselves by a passion for the mundane. When I interpreted Harold's fear of change, I became a harbinger of change, and set the apes to dance around his defenses of intellectualization and isolation.

Intriguingly, it is these timorous souls who reveal most tellingly the cleavage between "civilized" morality and the netherworld of chaotic, primitive desire. Monsters from the id continually assail the obsessional: unacceptable wishes and desires constantly threaten homeostasis, the more so because the psychic repository of morality and conscience—the superego—is so unremittingly harsh. For the obsessional, an evil thought is as reprehensible as an evil deed. Being is pervaded by doubt whether to follow the lascivious prompting of the id, or bow to the implacable sanctions of the tyrannous superego.

How comes this misery to prevail? Some experts tout chemistry, or heredity, since obsessionalism frequently runs in families. Others believe a parent indoctrinated in the obsessional style during childhood inflicts it upon the next generation. Freud thought that obsessionals were "anal erotics" by nurture or nature, fixated in coping strategies that originate out of the amalgam of pain and pleasure during the second year of life, when the child delights in its own excrement, and learns the impact upon its parents of defecating and urinating at the right place and time (or the wrong place and time!).

The psychological issues of the anal stage extend beyond the potty. Erik Erikson writes:

The anal zone lends itself more than any other to the display of stubborn adherence to contradictory impulse because . . . it is the modal zone for two conflicting modes of approach, namely retention and elimination. . . . The sphincters are only part of the muscle system with its general duality of rigidity and relaxation. The development of the muscle system gives the child much greater power over the environment, in the ability to reach out and hold on, to throw and push away, to appropriate things and keep them at a distance.[1]

The two-year-old analist requires a mixture of firmness and respect more easily described than achieved by parents driven to distraction by the bewildering contradictions of the age. The child must be protected from intoxicating excesses of stubborn hostility, while cherishing its yearning toward autonomy. Toilet training can unfortunately become metaphoric of more global attempts to leash in the child's native exuberance, archetypal of other catastrophic shaming experiences that raise primordial doubts about dignity and worth. When such prevail, the self is likely to be perceived as a container of filth that must periodically and obediently be cleansed upon demand. Erikson warns that

if denied the gradual, well-guided experience of free choice, the child will turn against himself all his urge to discriminate and to manipulate. He will over-manipulate himself . . . develop a precocious conscience. . . . He will become obsessed with his own repetitiveness. . . . He then learns to repossess the environment and to gain power by stubborn and minute control, where he could not find large-scale mutual regulation. Such hollow victory is the infantile model for a compulsion neurosis.[2]

Parents act for society and themselves. The kindness or cruelty of their interventions is intimately related to the stringency of cultural prerogatives. Freud discovered early in his career that neurosis often attended the taming of the child's passions during its difficult passage toward maturity. In a work written during the last decade of his life— *Civilization and Its Discontents*—he theorized that society evolves with corollary repressive effects upon its membership, likening acculturation to the induction of an artificial obsessional state. If we are to live together without tearing each other apart, the strictest order must be set over unruly instinct:

Order is a kind of repetition compulsion, by which it is ordained once and for all, when and how a thing shall be done, so that on every similar occasion, doubt and hesitation shall be avoided.[3]

Civilization requires us to transcend our native messiness, our anality and carnality. As the baser drives give way to the sway of intellect, as we acquire the ability to sublimate, so are we cleansed of the angry ape, but also compelled by an increasingly oppressive morality to tremble with ever greater guilt over the id's incitements.

The escalating harshess of the culture's collective superego exacts a heavy toll in emotional suffering. War is yet another signet of that fearful price, an organized, legitimized release of projected aggression that threatens to destroy that which it was designed to protect. Freud was pessimistic about the possibility of liberating society from its obsessional tendencies. A single patient might learn to live neurotically, but the conventions of a neurotic world would never cease hemming him in— must even be respected.

We must remember that Freud was a model of bourgeois propriety in his personal life. Although he sowed the seeds of several revolutions, there was a strong conservative, yes, even obsessional streak in the man. Very likely, he never intended that his theories should be used in a strident call to arms against the manifold injustices society perpetrates in the name of its perpetuation. That call was sounded by wilder spirits like Wilhelm Reich, who Freud disavowed—as I rather think he would have disowned the subsequent Freudian left.

I have framed the personal and cultural manifestations of obsessionalism at some length, because the cinema of Alfred Hitchcock has been marked persistently by his obvious obsessional concerns. Above all by his insistence on the preservation of a prudent, ordered existence, lest the sanctions of culture be overthrown, the very substance of reality be rent asunder by monsters from the id; or lest the imperfect, sinning self be crushed by the pitiless avengers of the superego.

The roots of Hitchcock's obsessionalism can only be dimly surmised. His private life is supposedly as unremarkable as was Freud's. He has been quietly married for many years, keeps carefully apart from the glitter and scandal associated with screen luminaries. He admits to being exceptionally neat and fussy in his personal habits; to growing uncomfortable when his routines are disturbed:

I'm full of fears and I do my best to avoid complications. . . . I get a feeling of inner peace from a well organized desk. When I take a bath, I put everything back neatly in place. You wouldn't even know I'd been to the bathroom.[4]

His penchant for rigorous control in his work is well known. He constructs his films in the office with meticulous detail. His oeuvre essentially has been accomplished upon a mental sound stage, and it is in the setting of intense communion with the wellsprings of private fantasy that he finds greatest pleasure as a director. Shooting could almost be an afterthought. His editing is minimal. He supposedly scorns looking through the camera on set, since he has already composed his mise-en-scène with a formidable mind's eye.

In public—and he has always been the shrewdest publicist for his movies—Hitchcock teases us with impishly disarming references to the foulest evil. He beguiles with an avuncular presence; thus many still conceive of him as an entertaining bogeyman, who for pleasure and profit jangles our nerves with easily cast-off nightmares. In serious reportage,[5] he discusses technique with alacrity, but regards searchers after "deeper" meaning in his work with a mixture of disbelief and amusement. When pressed, he says he prefers to let his pictures speak for themselves.

He will give only the most perfunctory details of his autobiography— e.g., his fear of the Jesuits who schooled him; his repugnance for the police, which in an oft-repeated tale is ascribed to being sent by his father to a station house at age five, with a note directing the constables to lock him up for being "naughty." This is quite possibly a screen memory, one that distills volumes of life experience into a single traumatic recollection, perhaps emblematic of other episodes of disastrous shaming Erikson describes in the history of obsessionals.

However, it would be impertinent on the basis of such slim data to infer the nature or extent of Hitchcock's "neurosis"; nor does it much matter for my purposes if, in fact, he were neurotic at all. Whatever the status of his mental health, Hitchcock is first and foremost a supreme poet of ambiguity who has, under the aegis of light entertainment, made us witness the disturbing dilemmas of the obsessional viewpoint at first hand; made us cognizant of our own obsessionalism with a power denied to the clinician restricted by rational interest in the "rules" of diagnostics and therapeutics.

I have elected to address *Psycho*, for it represents the extremity of Hitchcock's black vision of human vulnerability and corruptibility. Themes elsewhere latent are blatant in this most shocking of his films, the nightmare from which there is no easy awakening for a commercial break.

Psycho's credits are presented to frantic, pulsing music[6] over an abstract pattern of horizontal and vertical lines that arbitrarily mesh, separate, and recombine; then ascend and coalesce into a modern cityscape. The camera hovers breathtakingly over skyscrapers, descends to pan across a shabbier neighborhood; then, in a series of dissolves, zeroes in on one building; one wall of windows; a single window with drawn shade. As in a TV newscast, titles converge at bottom frame:

PHOENIX, ARIZONA

FRIDAY, DECEMBER 11

TWO FORTY-THREE PM

The opening implies random selection: one could just as easily, as indifferently move to the left or right, to another block, another building, another time of day—and another story. Hitchcock's first perspective dwarfs his yet unseen characters and their unknown entanglements, rendering them supremely unimportant in a schema that cuts the city itself down to toy-size. Still, a choice has been offered. The director has borne us away from the glamorous center of the metropolis into seedier territory.

The camera hesitates, then slides furtively under the half-open window, into a drably furnished room where a semi-nude couple fitfully embrace, and pick over the bones of an unsatisfying midday tryst. She is Marion Crane (Janet Leigh), an attractive Phoenix secretary slightly past her prime, still single. Her lover, Sam Loomis (John Gavin), toils in a small-town hardware store to pay off his father's debts and his alimony. Marion hankers after marriage, Sam refuses on the grounds he won't have her live in poverty. It is an old, unresolved argument between them.

Loomis's divorce, his father's malfeasance (never explained) have disrupted a basic complacency. He's shouldered an enormous burden of meaningless responsibility, to slog on until stability is restored and his virtue proven to distant fates:

> SAM: I've been sweating for people who aren't there. . . . I sweat to pay off my father's debts, and he's in his grave. . . . I sweat to pay my ex-wife's alimony, and she's living on the other side of the world.

He relishes his martyrdom, since it earns him the good opinion of his neighbors and the right to wallow in self-pity. After the curious fashion of obsessionals, Sam thinks he's earned the right to a little pleasure, but too much, too soon would be unallowable. Perhaps some day, when his dues are sufficiently paid to the masochist club, he will "deserve" marriage. Until then, he keeps Marion at a distance and—having struck a bargain with his conscience—enjoys the sleazy side of their affair.

For her part, Marion has come to resent the disorder in her life and the taint of whoredom. She is hurt by Sam's secret delight in their illicitness, wants chaste respectability from now on. Sam will dine at the apartment she shares with her sister, as an approved suitor—"with my mother's picture on the mantle."

> SAM: And after the steak? Send sister to the movies, turn Mama's picture to the wall . . .

> MARION: They also pay who meet in hotel rooms. . . . I haven't been married once, yet.

> SAM: Yeah . . . but when you do, you'll *sweat*—live with me in a storeroom behind a hardware store. . . . I'll tell you what, when I send my ex-wife her alimony, you can lick the stamps.

He grudgingly agrees to upgrade their affair short of marriage, betraying an unpleasant mean streak in the comfort he takes at the thought of Marion's daydreams being ground down, as she "sweats" in the coils of respectability. He makes an unenviable hero—but then Marion is not a particularly appealing heroine, not at first, aside from her physical attractiveness. Small people hassling over small ends, seeking a modicum of approval in a dull, judgmental world.

Down through the years, Hitchcock has assaulted the sensibilities of just such conventional protagonists with deadly intrusions into their respectable lives. His people are usually of the bourgeoisie—lower through upper (occasionally, a character assumes the mantle of middle-class respectability to repair or conceal a disorderly lifestyle—like John Robie, the ex–cat burglar of *To Catch a Thief* [1955], or *Marnie's* [1964] prissy kleptomaniac). His male characters in particular tend to be weak or vacillating, although they may surprise themselves with newfound courage.

The most terrifying disruptions of the status quo occur in the most prosaic settings. In *North By Northwest* (1959), a Madison Avenue advertising executive is attacked by a crop-dusting plane in a midwestern wheat field. In an amusement park, the unimaginative tennis player of *Strangers On a Train* (1951) wrestles for his life with a psychotic killer, beneath a carousel madly spinning out of control. The more commonplace the hero and setting, the greater the viewer's anxiety, as the apparently diamond-hard surface of obsessional reality is fractured by the Apes at the Windows, the Monsters from the Id.

Hitchcock has increasingly ordered his mise-en-scène with the priorities of a surrealist painter—one thinks chiefly of René Magritte. Everyday objects and people are "objectified," presented with startling clarity, yet their configurations are also charged with dreamlike significance, subtly articulated with the unconscious fantasy and questionable motivation of the characters.

Psycho has little of the frenetic pacing of "suspense" films like *North By Northwest*. Its violence lasts only a few heartbeats. But despite the sharply etched quotidian of the surroundings, things are subtly out of joint from the beginning, the visuals more infused with an ineluctable strangeness, more laden with eerie presentiments than any other Hitchcock picture. The dialogue has an unnerving Pinteresque quality. Shut your eyes for a moment next time you see the film to discover what I mean. The most trivial statements are pregnant with meaning and menace. People do not speak, so much as their words collide; bounce off at a tangent, creating even in the act of love a pervasive tone of tense alienation.

Sex has always been a potent challenge to Hitchcock's obsessional order, the spur for unsettling experiences of archaic fear and aggression. Sex opens the Pandora's box of the unconscious, unleashing the mindless primitive. Lovers are never far from becoming murderers (e.g., *Dial M for Murder* [1954], *Suspicion* [1941]). The director frequently dwells upon "heavy petting," adolescent gropings on the verge of embarrassing interruption. The essence of Hitchcockian sensuality is prolonged tumescence—vide the interminable Bergman-Grant kiss of *Notorious* (1946). He has filmed only one definitive orgasm—in *Frenzy* (1971), where an engaging sexual psychopath rapes the frigid directress of a matrimonial agency upon her desk while the poor lady whispers her prayers. Afterward, with at least equal pleasure, he strangles her!

Psycho's sexuality is particularly colored by Hitchcock's peculiar blend of puritanism and lubricity. Sam and Marion's lovemaking defies small-town convention. Although they couple in Phoenix, the big city where morals traditionally become unglued, it is the harsh ethic of Fairvale,

Loomis's hometown, that shapes their anxiety over losing face. *Psycho* begins with an invasion of privacy. The audience—especially the man in the audience—is placed in the uncomfortable dual role of voyeur, panting after a better look at Leigh's luscious bosom, and moral watchdog, implicitly identified with Marion's dead mother, peering out disapprovingly from her picture frame.

Sam and Marion upbraid each other over arranging a legal sanction for their love while the promise of genuine intimacy, without a care for the neighbors, goes a-begging. Their furtive copulation is bracketed by her financial worries, and her fear of being accounted a spinster or a fallen woman. Still, their affair has been integrated into the status quo, granting them some release from routine, without destroying routine. Marion disturbs routine by trying to alter her circumstances, denying Sam her body. Her decision registers on destiny's seismograph, and an infernal retribution machine winds itself up, for the gods of Hitchcock's universe have decreed that her punishment is paramount to the preservation of order.

Back at her office, Marion endures the smug chatter of a recently married coworker, Carolyn, about her husband's proprietary attitude and her mother's nosiness. Lowry, her boss, enters with a drunken oilman, Cassady, who has just purchased a house for his soon-to-be-wed daughter. He leers goatishly at Marion:

CASSADY: Tomorrow's the day my sweet little girl—oh, not *you*—tomorrow she stands her sweet self up there and gets married away from me. . . . Eighteen years old, and she never had an unhappy day. . . . You know what I do about unhappiness? I buy it off. Are you unhappy?

He brandishes forty thousand dollars in cold, undeclared cash. Lowry hustles him out, gives Marion the money to put into safe deposit over the weekend. Carolyn observes forlornly that Cassady didn't flirt with her: "I guess he must have noted my wedding ring." On a sudden impulse, Marion goes into Lowry's office, sidesteps a crude proposition from Cassady, pleads a headache, and asks to be excused for the rest of the day after going to the bank.

Marion has returned from her troubled tryst to contend with petty vulgarians who goad her with reminders of her unwed state. Of course, Carolyn and Cassady are hardly content. Neither Cassady's money nor inebriation salves his pain, and there's a great deal of desperation underpinning Carolyn's prattle. But Marion is too immersed in her deprivation to be objective. Should these pampered dollies—Carolyn, Cassady's daughter—own respectability without a second thought as their natural due, while she must sweat on her back in a dingy hotel room for lack of funding?

No, let her be a winner once! Besides, Cassady will not miss the money, he came by it illegally, and Lowry probably will keep it undeclared too. Let her turn the tables, show the lecherous Cassady what it's like to be "taken." One discerns an odd complementarity between Marion and Cassady, a curious blurring between their disparate personae, a crossing of circumstances and motivation common in Hitchcock—like the proposed exchange of murders in *Strangers on a Train*. Cassady would have used his illicit gain to ease the pangs of loneliness, keeping a presence in his daughter's house. Marion is tempted to steal, thereby transforming Cassady's purpose into her own, forcing Sam into making the commitment that will protect her from a lonely spinsterhood. We have been seduced into applauding the theft, surrendering our scruples and assenting to Marion's criminality.

She does not go to the bank. We discover her alone, again half-nude, in her apartment. An envelope containing the money lies on the bed. As she dresses and packs, the camera insistently cuts back to the envelope, until in distorted close-up it fills the screen temptingly. The money evokes mingled resonances of desire and apprehension, security and sinfulness. Behind her, we see the bathroom door with a glimpse of the shower. She stares hard at herself in the mirror, snaps the suitcase shut, slips the envelope into her purse. The die is cast: in questing for an elusive respectability, Marion surrenders herself to the shameful accusations she feared!

From now on, she will be untied from the familiar, cut off and cast away from any deliverance. Her sister, in Tucson for the weekend, thinks she is spending a quiet weekend at home, as does Sam, for she has not told him she is coming with a pilfered deliverance. Her last touch with Phoenix reality is unnerving. At the wheel of her car, her mind invents Sam's startled reaction to her appearance. His voice betrays *her* unease—already she half-realizes that his hypertrophied conscience will not let him use the money; must make him view her in a new, unfavorable light. As she stops, Lowry and Cassady pass directly in front of her. She smiles nervously, waves; Lowry looks back with a puzzled frown, and she pulls away.

The next morning, she sleeps inside her car near the highway. A patrol car pulls up, an officer raps on the window. She wakens with a start, automatically tries to leave. He restrains her; she emanates an almost palpable aura of guilt.

POLICEMAN: There are plenty of motels in this area. . . . You should've . . . I mean, just to be safe . . .

MARION: I didn't intend to sleep all night. . . . Have I broken any laws?

POLICEMAN: No, Ma'am.

MARION: Then I'm free to go?

POLICEMAN: Is anything wrong?

MARION: Of course not. Am I acting as if there's anything wrong?

POLICEMAN: Frankly, yes.

Pure Pinter! The cop is genuinely worried about her welfare, but in one fantastic shot we see him through Marion's eyes: an enormous, goggled face towering over the car window, as she desperately tries to hide her purse from his omniscient gaze. He is the cop of the mind, the eternal vigilante every obsessional fears. He lets her go. She turns off the freeway, into a gaudy used-car lot, picks up a newspaper from a vending machine, scans it for mention of the theft. There is none, but the cop has returned, standing tall behind his vehicle, watching her intently. She sees him with a shock, and in an ironic role reversal, high pressures a fast-talking salesman into an exchange of cars before he can get his spiel off the ground. His bogus joviality undercut, the salesman, too, grows wary of her:

SALESMAN: You *are* in a hurry! Somebody chasin' ya? I take it you can prove that car is yours?

In the washroom, Marion extracts seven hundred dollars over a grimy sink. The camera is positioned above her so that she appears hemmed in, as by the walls of a prison cell. As she completes the purchase, the patrolman quietly eases his car into the lot. She panics, almost driving off without her luggage. From the angle of her departure, it's evident the cop has gotten a full view of her license plate. In one of Hitchcock's matchless compositions, an attendant, the salesman, and the cop, aligned in a portentous diagonal, stare after her.

During my army hitch, I treated several cases of a relatively rare syndrome called "travel psychosis." The patients were psychologically marginal men, who disintegrated during bus rides that took them from customary surroundings to a new post halfway across the country. Over long hours of monotony, their vision turned inward with disastrous results. Marion undergoes an analogous decompensation—hermetically sealed in her car, enmeshed in the flow of vapid scenery, a species of sensory deprivation erodes her contact with reality. Day fades, the lights of oncoming traffic strike her full face, creating the ambience of an interrogation chamber. She has converted those along her way into extensions of her punitive superego. Now her uneasy conscience rises up to torment her.

While Hitchcock has allied us with her, made us hope she can escape out of the gray frame of obsessional reality, he has also shown that she will never escape, for she *wants* to be caught. Had her near abandonment of her suitcase (an intriguing Freudian slip) been successful, she would have been left only with the clothes on her back, a prototypical fugitive. The money at this point possesses no significance beyond establishing her guilt. As she drives on, she plunges deeper into the darkness of a fugitive mentality, restlessly rehearsing the events leading up to her almost certain arrest.

We hear the patrolman agree with the salesman that she acted like "a wrong one . . . I better have a look at those papers, Charlie"; Lowry's sudden recollection, when she fails to show up at work, of seeing her in her car; Cassady's demand for revenge—"I ain't about to kiss off forty thousand dollars, I'll replace it with her fine soft flesh!" These are her forecasts, but also her *fantasies*. Cassady's threat is conjured up as much out of her masochism as her intuition. She *needs* to be punished sadistically.

Hitchcock shows a Shakespearean flair for setting the natural world reverberating with the prevailing emotional climate. Lear's rage at his daughters evokes the howling tempest; in *Marnie*, lightning flashes punctuate the heroine's descent into traumatizing memory, and in *Psycho*, Marion's orgy of self-condemnation hurls down a savage rainstorm, clouding her vision, emphasizing her lost spiritual state. Morally derailed, she drives around for hours through the deluge until she spies a sign glowing through the blurred windshield—BATES MOTEL . . . VACANCY. The frenetic music fades on a long held note, leaving the soothing patter of the rain and the slap-slap of the wiper blades.

She dashes out of her car into the motel. The office is empty. From the porch she sees, perched on the hill above, the very model of the dark old house of gothic tale and horror film. The figure of a spare old woman is silhouetted against one of two lit windows. One almost smiles at the banality of it all—surely Hitchcock has more imagination! But the Bates's house is ominous beyond self-satire, a bizarre incongruity counterbalanced against the nondescript motel below, and the other lackluster environments Marion has passed through during her abortive flight.

At the sound of her horn a gangly young man, Norman Bates (Tony Perkins), bounds out of the house. Marion has heard only the imaginary voices of her accusers since the debacle at the used car lot, so Norman's homely welcome comes as a blessing. The motel is completely vacant, its only guests strays from the beaten path:

NORMAN: They moved away the highway—but there's no sense dwelling on our losses, we just keep lighting the lights and following the formalities.

The obsessional's credo! While Marion registers under a false identity, he reaches for a key to the third cabin, then with a furtive sideways glance picks the key to the unit adjoining the office instead. He takes her to the cabin, while showing her around points to the bathroom, but can't bring himself to name it. Pathetically attracted to her, he is every inch the upright, uptight all-American mama's boy, yet withal so ingratiating that one is inclined at first to overlook his eccentricity. He asks her to supper, and leaves. Marion unpacks, wraps the money in her newspaper. As she places it on the bed, she hears the indistinct voices of Norman and an old lady quarreling:

MRS. BATES: And *then* what, after supper—music, whispers? Go on, go tell her, she'll not be feeding her ugly appetites with my food or my son!!

NORMAN: Shut up! SHUT UP!!!

He returns, crestfallen, with a tray of sandwiches and milk. He's too nervous to eat in her cabin, so they go into the parlor behind the office. Their meal is overseen by a enormous stuffed owl mounted high on one wall. Norman, it seems, practices avian taxidermy to relieve the tedium of his stultifying existence—"A hobby's supposed to pass the time, not fill it." His father died when he was a child; he had his mother all to himself until several years ago, when she fell in love with a man who convinced her to sink her life's savings into the motel. When it failed, he died under mysterious circumstances. Mrs. Bates's sanity snapped, turning the mother into an invalid child and the son her nurse.

NORMAN: You know what I think? . . . We're all in our private traps, clamped in them, and none of us can ever get out. We scratch and claw, but only at the air, only at each other.

MARION: Sometimes we deliberately step into those traps.

NORMAN: I was born in mine. I don't mind it anymore.

Like many seriously troubled people, Norman possesses an unhealing insight; but his duty appears unassailable and he accepts it absolutely. Marion is moved, with us, to sympathize with this odd fellow. She takes his side against his deranged mother—a fatal error in judgment. When she suggests that mother be committed, Norman grows furious:

NORMAN: An institution . . . a—madhouse? . . . Have you ever seen the inside of one of those places? . . . The laughing and the tears . . . the cruel eyes watching you?

MARION: I only felt . . . it seems she's hurt you. . . . I meant well.

NORMAN: People always mean well. (*bitterly*) They cluck their thick tongues and shake their heads and suggest, oh so delicately . . . (*suddenly affable again*) Of course, I've suggested it myself . . . but I hate to even think about it. She needs me . . . it's not as if she was a maniac . . . she just goes a little mad sometimes. We all go a little mad sometimes . . . haven't you?

MARION (*firmly*): Sometimes just one time can be enough. Thank you.

Hitchcock has engineered another crossing: the equivalency between Marion and Norman is underscored as she registers. The two face each other across the counter; by adroit camera work and lighting their profiles seem mirror images, as their plights mirror each other. They are both caught in draining, parasitic relationships: Norman ministers to his sick, minimizing mother; Marion to her weak, degrading lover. As they talk in the parlor, Norman's agreeable mask slips away, and we sense his madness. Mutatis mutandis, in comprehending Norman's awful resignation Marion is able to pull herself together, and renounce her fugitive identity. She tells Norman she will return to Phoenix next morning:

> MARION: I stepped into a private trap back there. I'd like to go back and try to pull myself out of it, before it's too late for me, too . . .

She leaves. Norman stands in darkness, surrounded by his repellent trophies, the owl perched menacingly over him as if about to strike. His expression hardens. He removes a picture from the wall—a pneumatic nude assaulted by two satyric men. He peers through a rough peephole at Marion undressing near her open bathroom door. Just as she removes her slip, the camera cuts away to Norman's unblinking eye, filling the screen in sideview, then back to Marion donning her robe. He and we have been deprived of her nakedness—another unconsummated sexual act, and this time unmistakably perverse. Norman glares accusingly up at the decaying old house, then bounds up the hill.

Marion checks her bankbook to determine what will be left after she pays for the getaway car. She tears up the jottings, flushes them down the toilet, eases off her robe, displaying her shapely back. A close-up of her bare legs as she steps into the tub. She draws the curtain, turns on the shower—close-up of the showerhead—she offers herself up luxuriously to the streaming water, closing her eyes and stretching out her long, delicate neck.

We have been subliminally primed for this moment from the beginning of the film, teased by repeated shots of her, half-nude, covering and uncovering herself. The motel bathroom has been anticipated by the previous marginal awareness of the bathroom in Marion's apartment, and the filthy lavatory of the used car lot. The painting of the ebullient rape covering Norman's peephole gave a tiny intimation of the horror about to occur. Through the translucent curtain, we see the bathroom door open; a tall, indistinct shape slips in. Then, to the agonized ululation of the strings, the curtain is torn aside, revealing a shadowy old woman—we see only her eyes, her hair drawn into a tight bun and, indelibly engraved upon one's riveted consciousness, an enormous upraised knife.

Hitchcock's skill at montage reaches an extraordinary summit in the shower murder sequence. As James Naremore observes, we are actually shown very little intrinsic violence.[7] Yet, such is the rhythm established by the elegant shuffling of sixty separate camera set-ups that one reels with the impression of an unparalleled savagery, echoing down the corridors of the mind like the shrieking violins. Hitchcock intercuts between Marion's screaming lips, the knife rising and falling; an ejaculatory spurt of blood soils the gleaming white bathtub; the knife makes a tiny bloodless belly puncture; an overhead view shows Marion trying to twist and turn away from her attacker, as she shields her breasts.

The old woman rushes out as quickly as she entered. Close-up of Marion's upper torso and face—miraculously spared—slowly sliding down the wall as her eyes fix, glaze over. Her blindly outstretched hand clutches the curtain, ripping it away from the frame hook by hook as she pitches forward onto the floor. The music descends in a series of deep, minor-key groans, then ceases, leaving only the patter of the shower, reminiscent of the unaccompanied rainfall when she entered the imagined haven of the Bates Motel. Her blood mingles with the bathwater, gurgling down the drain in a small clockwise whirlpool and, in a masterstroke of aesthetic balance, the camera spirals back counterclockwise from a freezeframe of Marion's staring eye, to show drops of water gleaming on her cheek—are they real tears, or gratuitous?—and her dead face pressed awkwardly against the floor. As the water continues to stream down, the camera drifts leisurely across the bathrobe into the bedroom, pausing significantly at the newspaper still on the bed, then passes over to the window, and Norman cries from the hill: "*Mother, Oh God! Mother!! Blood!!!*"

Obsessionals suffer under a general interdiction of sexual pleasure, but they are particularly haunted by guilt over childhood voyeuristic and exhibitionistic fantasies. The wish to observe the sexual activity of others, initially one's parents, and the need to display oneself as a sexual object, are normal components of the child's instinctual heritage; smoothly integrated, if all goes well, into later sexual activity (one takes delight in drinking in the sight of the beloved, and in being similarly admired). But if these wishes to see and be seen are ringed about with the scathing humiliation so prevalent in the early history of obsessionals, it is likely they will later become highly conflicted gratifications, stamped with a peculiar confluence of fear, shame, and secret longing—and may easily verge over into frank perversion.

Hitchcock's films are filled with voyeurs, with heroes or villains watching others unobserved, for sinister or worthy purposes. Recall the famous tennis match scene in *Strangers on a Train*: the heads in the audience swivel, obedient to the flight of the ball, while the villain stares unmovingly through the crowd at his victim playing below. *Rear Window* (1954) is an extended essay on the vicissitudes of voyeurism. Its hero is a professional "watcher," a news photographer apartment-bound by a broken leg, alleviating his boredom by spying on his neighbors across the courtyard. His visual eavesdropping nearly precipitates his death at the hands of a murderer he has discovered. More than meets the conscious eye is stirred by Hitchcock's clandestine surveillances, because he has so artfully tapped the unconscious erotic basis of our desire to watch, unknown, out of the darkness.

As a rule, Hitchcock presents sexual disorder and perverse wishes through a glass darkly, concealed in the cloak of criminality. The frigid heroine of *Marnie* acts out rape fantasies in reverse, by plundering her employers after winning their confidence. Bruno Antony's homoerotic yen for Guy Haines in *Strangers on a Train* is embedded/hidden in the emphasis placed upon the exchange of murders for profit, instead of lovers' vows. But in *Psycho*, Hitchcock has dropped all pretense of concealment. Norman Bates is an unregenerate Peeping Tom, and we are manipulated with exceptional cunning into participating in his dirty business. In fact, we have been placed precisely in the position of the obsessional's ego—wooed by the forbidden delights of the id, then trampled by the remorseless punishment of the superego.

Psycho began with a voyeuristic invasion of privacy to which we assented without question. We have been interminably tempted by Janet Leigh's spectacular body, until the director pointedly makes Norman's eye our own, his frustration our own, and compels us to watch Norman watching Marion, the better that we may appreciate the depth of our complicity. Then he repays us in full. We are forced to attend the ultimate invasion of privacy, gagging upon our voyeurism as Marion expires in a frenzy of bloody eroticism, leaving us spent and obscurely guilty— like an adolescent who has just masturbated into the toilet bowl.

We identify with Norman-the-watcher, but also empathize with Marion, unwitting exhibitor and focus of desire. We wince when the knife pierces her vulnerable flesh. Hitchcock's attitude toward his women has always been frankly ambivalent. They are snares or helpmeets, keepers of the hearth or treacherous Jezebels. Often, like Sam Spade and other film noir male protagonists, the hero must puzzle out a heroine's good or evil intentions to save himself. It is only at the end of *North By Northwest* that

Roger Thornhill realizes Eve Kendall wants to marry rather than murder him.

Although by reputation personally uxorious, Hitchcock emerges in his pictures as an enthusiastic lady-killer. He has been exterminating women since his earliest silent work (*The Lodger* [1926]. *Frenzy* (1971) contains an enormous amount of not so latent misogyny: a Scotland Yard inspector tracks down a modern-day Jack the Ripper, while his loving wife serves up repugnant dishes at home from her course in haute cuisine. In the midst of apparent domestic bliss, she could almost be poisoning him!

Hitchcock's perceptions of Marion veer back and forth between sympathy and dispassionate distaste. To Cassady and Mrs. Bates, her putative executioner, she's a malevolent seductress. Sam resents her for withholding her favors, Norman grows furious when she turns her body away from his avid eye. The director may betray a buried resentment toward woman as perennial tantalizer in *Psycho*, but he also feelingly shows Marion as an abused sex object (her resemblance to Marilyn Monroe, on this score, is remarkable). Sam has leeched the life from her, Cassady longs to butcher her, Norman's sensitivity gives way to sordid lust at the peephole, the meanest manipulation of her yet, before she steps into the shower to consolidate her victimhood forever.

But Hitchcock's sympathy is never absolute: it is tempered by an objective awareness of her self-destructiveness. He implies that something broken in her sought out the role of chronic loser before the theft, allying her unprofitably with Loomis. I have noted how during her flight she masochistically provokes unpleasant treatment from total strangers, a well-meaning cop who could have saved her, and the used-car salesman whose worst offer she took without a thought.

But, granted all this, one must still be struck with the bitter unfairness of her death. She alone, however wrongfully, has striven to break the fetters of obsessionalism that bind Sam and Norman to their thankless duties. She alone has tried to flee from the thankless rituals of obsessional reality. "They also pay who meet in hotel rooms," she said in Phoenix; now the circle has come full round in the Bates Motel room. At the liberating moment of insight into her "private trap," she pays an exorbitant price for disturbing the status quo. I always like to think she would have given back the money, quit her dreary job, and booted Sam out of her life, but we shall never know. The frozen tear on her dead cheek renders poignant testimony to all her lost possibilities.

Even after repeated exposures, the shower scene still leaves one numb with disbelief. It is incomprehensible that Janet Leigh should simply cease to be. Never before had a star of such magnitude, a female sex goddess, been so utterly expunged in midstream. Thus Hitchcock drives home the incontrovertibility, the awesome finality of death. Our yen for sanctioned sex and sadism has been dreadfully surfeited by Marion's crucifixion. With Leigh gone, the comfortable conventions of the Hollywood suspense vehicle have been totally violated. *Psycho*, half-completed, dangles in midair, apparently deprived of its narrative center.

Hitchcock alleviates our disequilibration with a typical obsessional device—the big cleanup. Norman rushes into the bathroom, fights back a wave of nausea, then grabs a mop and pail and sets about putting everything methodically to rights like the automaton housewife in a TV detergent commercial, scouring down the bloody tiles, bundling the corpse in the shower curtain. His relentless ritual cleansing is punctuated by fragments of Marion's nudity, heaping necrophilia upon voyeurism as yet another perversity of which we will stand guilty should we be pricked by a queasy desire to view the remains a little closer.

Norman stuffs the body in the trunk of her car with her pitiful belongings, then pitches in the folded newspaper. Marion's crime, so momentous within her frame of reference, has been reduced to an addendum of concealment as she herself has been negated. Norman drives to a swamphole conveniently bordering the Bates property, and pushes the car into the morass. The previous shots of filthy sinks, gurgling drains, and flushing toilets coalesce into one magnificent, appalling anal image. Down, down into the muck goes beautiful Marion, her white car, and the forty thousand dollars—dust unto dust, dirt unto dirt.

But the car sinks only halfway, then stops. Norman gnaws his thumb: we are instinctively with him, hoping it won't get stuck. After a few anxious seconds, it vanishes irrevocably. He flashes a mirthless little grin, a quick study in obsessional satisfaction—all done, all gone—my, that felt good! He joins a long, impressive roster of Hitchcock's sympathetic villains, attractive monsters from the id we are encouraged to root for against our civilized judgment.

These creatures woo sedate citizens with their charming plausibility; their evil frequently comes within a hairbreadth of eluding detection. Hitchcock clearly empathizes with them and part of him, I suspect, dearly wants them to get off. In this regard, recall that the producers of *Suspicion* (1941) insisted he rewrite the original ending in which Cary Grant kills his mousy wife. The new denouement, with Grant properly repentant and his marriage rehabilitated, is singularly unconvincing.

Dissolve to Sam Loomis's hardware store in Fairvale. Sam is visited by Marion's sister, Lila (Vera Miles), who blames him for Marion's disappearance. They are confronted by Milton Arbogast (Martin Balsam), a private investigator hired by Marion's employer. Arbogast comes on as strong as Marion's patrolman, but we will find that, like the cop, he truly wants to help. Thus the "watcher" is either a decent sort, or an agent of the persecuting superego, depending upon one's guilt level and need for punishment.

Arbogast infers that Sam may have plotted the robbery with Marion, possibly with Lila's collusion. He canvases the motels in the vicinity. At the Bates's, Norman denies knowing Marion, but his boyish insouciance fragments under the detective's skillful probing. Caught in uncomfortable contradictions, he stammers and twitches—now his perimeter suffers unfriendly intrusion. Arbogast elicits that Marion did indeed stay overnight at the motel, dined with Norman, and infers she "met" Norman's mother. When Arbogast suggests Norman might still be hiding Marion in return for sex, he becomes angry, refuses to let the mother be interviewed, and orders Arbogast out.

Arbogast telephones Lila that Sam is innocent, says he is going back to the motel to check out Norman's story. He enters the dark old house, slowly climbs the steep staircase. As he gains the top, the camera swoops upward to give a bird's-eye view of a door opening off to one side. The strings emit a shrill shriek, as the old lady dashes around the corner and strikes Arbogast full in the face. He stumbles backward, his hands and feet flailing for balance, down the stairs. Mrs. Bates flings herself upon him, the gigantic knife upraised as the scene darkens . . .

When Arbogast fails to show up, Sam procrastinates until Lila demands that he go to the motel, where he discovers only the silhouette of the old woman in the window (Norman has handily swamped the shamus). Sam and Lila contact Chambers, the Fairvale sheriff, a crusty rural type who tries to dispose of the affair with plain horse sense. He suggests Arbogast got a hot lead from Norman, immobilized them with his call, then took off alone after the money. Norman is phoned, and supports the sheriff's theory. But one item doesn't yield so conveniently: Sam and Arbogast both claim they saw Norman's mother, yet the sheriff reveals that Mrs. Bates died ten years ago by her own hand, after poisoning her unfaithful lover!

SHERIFF: If the woman up there is Mrs. Bates, who's that woman buried in Greenlawn Cemetary?

The odor of sanctity emanating from Norman's martyrdom suddenly is charged with a whiff of brimstone.

Back at the Bates's house, Norman enters his mother's room. From behind the closed door, we hear her cackling: "No, I will *not* hide in the fruit cellar, ah ha, you think I'm *fruity*? I'm staying right here in my room, and no one will drive me out of it, least of all my big, bold son!!!" The obscene vigor of the raucous old voice, the maniacal attacks, do not sort with the frail, still figure Norman carries down the stairs, into the cellar.

The sequence is marvelous, vintage Hitchcock, amusing and terrifying. The camera pivots at that same staggering height from which we watched Arbogast fall. The sheriff said that Norma Bates lay in her grave, but we have just heard her arguing with her son. Norman bears her like a paralytic, yet we have had horrific evidence of her mobility. The mind reels on the verge of scarifying revelations. We are left suspended over a metaphysical void.

Hitchcock frequently employs vertigo as a visual metaphor for the state of emotional imbalance he carefully constructs in his characters and audience. Naremore comments that, more than mere devices to arouse suspense, Hitchcock's epiphanies at the abyss (e.g., the Mount Rushmore and Statue of Liberty finales in *North By Northwest* and *Saboteur* [1942], respectively) are "poetic figures, perfect expressions for the chaos which disrupts the lives of his protagonists."[8] (*Vertigo* [1958] is an extended contemplation of this theme, hinging upon the hero's actual fear of heights.) Patients may become vertiginous when some dark psychic corner is illuminated and the intuition of the familiar is fractured by the resurfacing of buried wish or memory. I have treated several cases where dizziness arose de novo while a deeply repressed fear of death was being analyzed. Arbogast, one recalls, died struggling for balance, his commonplace explanations for Marion's disappearance shattered by Norma Bates's demoniacal apparition.

Dissolve from Norman's descent into the fruit cellar to a view of the Fairvale church spire against a crisp Sunday sky. Hitchcock artfully balances the "below" of psychotic disorder against the dubious reassurances of order and morality asserted "above" through rituals of faith in a small-town Deity. On the church steps, the sheriff tells Sam and Lila he visited Norman earlier that morning, found him completely alone. Perhaps Sam is the victim of "illusions"! For once, Loomis rises above his engrained compulsiveness and is unconvinced by appeals to reason. He and Lila drive to the motel, register as husband and wife. While Sam draws out Norman in the office, Lila steals away to explore the house.

Sam and Norman are photographed in profile as they talk across the desk, echoing the earlier "doubling" of Marion and Norman. Beyond an uncanny physical resemblance (Sam seems a more robust, "filled out" version of Norman), both are basically timid men unaccustomed to abrasive confrontations. But a competitive, almost sexual tension hangs over their pleasantries, as if Sam intended to rape Norman rather than expose his criminality. Lila makes a parallel assault upon Norman's privacy. In a series of eerie tracking shots, the house seems to rise and float toward her, instead of her climbing toward it.

The atmosphere within is heavy with solitude. The cluttered Victoriana, aside from its inherent strangeness, belongs almost palpably to others—*None of your business*—PRIVATE, KEEP OUT—the old house seems to flash. Yet, as in a nightmare, Lila is compelled onward, her anxious progress crosscut with Sam's penetration of Norman's defenses below. Mrs. Bates's room is immaculately preserved, its appointments precise reflections of the mother's obsessive, anhedonic nature: a sterile washbasin, an armoire with a prim row of high-necked dresses, a sculpture of lace-cuffed hands clasped in prayer. The large double bed contains deep indentations that nag at the edge of awareness.

Meanwhile, Sam presses Norman to confess that he would grab at the chance to escape the poverty of the motel. (Both the professional and amateur sleuth, having harnessed their bourgeois imaginations to the money, cannot conceive a motive other than profit to explain Marion's absence.) "This place happens to be my only world!" Norman cries, "I grew up in that house. . . . My mother and I were more than happy!!" Despite his iniquity, we are moved by his pathetic illusions about a past that saw his spirit broken on the rack of his mother's inflexible will. His room is filled with the artifacts of childhood—toys, schoolbooks, a stuffed teddy bear—a small, squalid place enclosing vast emptiness.

Suddenly realizing that Lila is gone, Norman knocks out Sam and hurls himself up the hill. Lila ducks into the basement, tiptoes into the fruit cellar, where a silent old woman sits, her back turned. Lila touches her shoulder tentatively—"Mrs. Bates . . . Mrs. Bates?" The chair swivels . . . *and here is Norman's mummified Mum, her wizened flesh stretched over the ancient skull, her leathery lips pulled back into a charnelhouse grin!*

The violins take up Lila's scream: and a wigged Norman stands at the door in matronly drag, a sheep in wolf's clothing, the knife brandished and ready to pounce as Sam comes up behind him, seizing him by the throat. Norman's body convulses into an intolerable arc, his face spasms into a hideous grimace—the wig flies off, his dress rips, and he collapses in a ruined heap. The pendulum swing of a bare bulb creates the horrid illusion of movement in Mrs. Bates's empty sockets, and it seems that she has been resurrected in her son's dissolution—the final, dreadful "crossing" of the film.

Dissolve to the county courthouse. An officious psychiatrist (Simon Oakland) reports the results of his interview with the entity that calls itself Norman's mother. From "her" story, he constructs for Sheriff Chambers, Sam, Lila, and a few bystanders the "scientific" explanation for the horrors at the Bates Motel:

Mrs. Bates was a "clinging, demanding woman." For years, she and her disturbed son had lived "as if there were no one else in the world." Then she took a lover, and Norman killed them both. Afterward, overcome with remorse, he dug up and preserved her corpse to erase consciousness of his crime, play-acting her presence as a defense against "danger and desire." The masquerade escalated to the point where "Mother" became as real as himself, then more real. "He was never all Norman, but he was often only Mother. And because he was so pathologically jealous of her, he assumed she was as jealous of him." Pretty young women aroused "Mother" to insane vengeance, while "Norman" would wink out of existence to awaken later, horrified at "Mother's" crimes. Marion was at least "her" third victim; Norman was the first, and now the last, for he has simply ceased to be . . .

The film's psychiatrist speaks inexactly to the basis for Norman's madness—the twisted solidarity with his mother. Basic trust, a durable sense that the self is worthy of care, evolves out of a dialectic of pleasure between mother and child, a complex matrix of shared satisfaction (the nursing situation is paradigmatic). Later, as she once ministered to the infant's helplessness, a reasonably healthy mother will demonstrate her affection by encouraging the growing child's efforts to maintain mastery over its environment.

Unfortunately, because of unresolved neurotic difficulties a troubled mother may encourage the child's overweaning dependency.[9] For instance, in caring for her baby she may be caring for the still-ungratified infant within herself; she may paradoxically feel abandoned if she must relinquish that care. Unwittingly, she invades the child's developing autonomy; implying that without her comforting presence the child will be unable to function, or will fall prey to catastrophe in a hostile world.[10]

The child of such a mother is frequently "adultified" as well as "infantilized," forced to fulfill needs that should be met from another quarter. ("A son is a poor substitute for a husband," says Norman to Marion.) One discovers a continuum of psychic disorder roughly corresponding to the extent of the mother's (or a surrogate's) unnecessary intrusions into the child's life-space. At sickest extreme is the malignant symbiosis fostered by an eccentric, egocentric woman like Norma Bates.

In this stultifying partnership, Norman came to find existence equally tormenting with or without his mother; he hated her for dominating him, loathed himself for his crippling neediness. And it is not unlikely that Mrs. Bates also came to resent Norman's intrusions into her life, sought to remedy this burden by taking a lover during Norman's adolescence. Norman had, in a sense, won the Oedipal victory, gaining exclusive possession of Mother when his father died. There is no gainsaying his rage when Mother turned away from him to another; adolescents have been known to kill under these circumstances.

However, let us not be too quick to buy the psychiatrist's convenient explanation. Every critique of *Psycho* has simply assumed Norman murdered Mom and her lover simply because "Mother" told the doctor so. Paranoids like Mrs. Bates do not admit to being or doing wrong. So one must ponder an alternate possibility: *Norman is guiltless of his mother's death. Mrs. Bates killed her unfaithful, swindling lover, then took her own life. The "Mother" who thereafter became institutionalized in Norman's skull accuses him to exculpate herself!* This is entirely consistent with what can be gleaned of her manipulative, malevolent character.

But even if Norman were guilty, he did not exhume Mother out of remorse, as the psychiatrist urges, but primarily out of *loneliness*. He sought to recreate the demeaning protections of the symbiosis and maintain the nursery illusion of eternal sustenance, if only Mrs. Bates could be preserved—*How many nights has he lain on that indented bed, clutching her corpse?*

Over the years, "Mother" grew more crazily oppressive and possessive, as she would have if she had she remained alive, and uninvolved with anyone but her son. The young women who stumbled upon the motel and aroused Norman were ruthlessly eliminated by "Mother" to keep the precious union intact. Norman executed Marion and the other girls in an altered state of consciousness. From his perspective, each murder was a symbolic rape-revenge against his seductive, rejecting mother, as well as a brutal disengagement from her influence for which she, not he, would take the blame. Lila and Sam carried out the threat for which Arbogast died, by exposing Mrs. Bates's decaying mortality. Norman, rather than face the reality of his utter aloneness, then took flight backward into the womb of time, returning from whence he came, leaving "Mother" to rule in triumph over the husk of his body.

Norman's macabre hobby was pitched at redeeming his mother's shriveled ruin. His stuffed birds are also mute representations of the negated ego, the damaged self certain latent psychotics experience as a dead hollowness enclosed within an obsessional envelope.[11] Mummy looks like Norman's dummy, but in fact he has always been *hers*, despite token resistance. With the terminal submersion of his personality, his dummyhood becomes absolute, unassailable.

One is irritated—by design, I think—at the presumptuousness with which the pompous psychiatrist disposes of Norman, as if he were a bizarre insect to be pinned and cataloged. Hitchcock's strong attraction toward Freudian psychoanalysis has always been curiously diffident, even slapdash, in its undisguised manifestations. He is least satisfying a Freudian when trying hardest to be one; does his best when Freudian themes are woven unobtrusively into the films.

Contrast the bogus dream sequences of *Spellbound* (1945), the heavy armchair psychologizing of *Marnie* and *Psycho*, with *Psycho*'s authentic ambience of the dream, as in Lila's excursion through the Bates's house; with *Psycho*'s wealth of visual free association, appreciated only on repeated viewings; with its subtle insistence on the influence of childhood conflict upon adult destiny; its evocation of sexual aberration with a minimum of garish cues. Hitchcock would probably agree that one must be terribly wary of the blandishments of depth psychology, lest one deny the mystery of what can never be known about other people. At one level, "scientific" speculations merely constitute another obsessional peg from which to hang one's faith in rational order while the id seethes and the superego hovers, contemptuous of puny reason.

We are fetched away from the psychiatrist's facile explanations by "Norman's" request for a blanket—"He feels a little chill," says a guard with unconscious irony. We see Norman's shell, sitting still as death in a bare cell, and the sight defies all rationalizing. "Mother's" voice speaks off-camera.

It's sad when a mother has to speak the words that will condemn her own son. . . . They'll put him away now, as I should have years ago. He was always *bad* . . . and in the end, he attempted to tell them I killed those girls and that man . . . as if I could do anything but sit and stare, like one of his stuffed birds. . . . They're probably watching me . . . well, let them, let them see what kind of a person I am (*the mad eyes dart down to a fly, crawling on its wrist*). . . . I'm not even going to swat that fly. . . . They'll see, and they'll know—and they'll say . . . why—*she wouldn't even hurt a fly!*

It peers cannily straight at us, its lips firm into a tiny, knowing smile. For a fraction of an instant, we register Mrs. Bates's rictus behind her son's skin; then, an actual skull; then dissolve to Marion's car, winched out of the fecal swamp.

With this grim deliverance we have touched psychic ground zero, reaching an ending beyond "THE END" of a mere thriller, encountered as subversive, as nihilistic a vision of human cruelty and insignificance as any called up by Lear in his raving, or in the barren recognitions of Samuel Beckett. Endgame, indeed!

Exploitation is the core experience of relatedness in *Psycho*, and in the darkest corners of Hitchcock's universe. The film unfolds as an articulating chain of abuse: we are, the director tells us, destined to be each other's victims, victimizers, or both. Sam Loomis is victimized by his dead, failed father. He abuses Marion's love; Marion cheats her employer, and turns the tables on Cassady, who sought his pound of flesh even before the robbery. Norman seduces Marion into trusting him, then murders her, but he is a zombie, the marrow of his ego sucked dry by the same mother he has possibly slaughtered, definitely gutted and stuffed.[12] Caring and closeness have everywhere degenerated into prying and preying. The past preys upon the present; the parent preys upon its helpless offspring (mothers most of all); and God, who wears Hitchcock's inscrutable features, shits us into the world to shit us out again.

André Bazin and Eric Rohmer postulate that Hitchcock's God is Catholic, specifically Jansenist.[13] For Raymond Durgnat, He is cruel, capricious, Calvinist.[14] To the analyst, He embodies the very essence of the obsessional's cruel, sanctimonious conscience. However He is named, on whatever premise, He emerges as the incarnation of His Maker: a sadistic, omnipotent Santa Claus who always knows if you've been good or bad, renders few gifts, and mocks the mixed motive. He created the abominations of Norman and Mother, for which He holds both equally to blame. He sends Marion Crane into the swamp, resurrecting her carcass to her irredeemable defamation. Since no one will ever know her change of heart in Norman's parlor, she will be remembered as that sexy girl who stole all that money and got herself killed. Poetic justice! Served her right, with those tight sweaters!

In *King Lear*, the blinded Gloucester cries: "As flies to wanton boys are we to the Gods—they kill us for their sport."[15] In Sam's store, after Marion's murder, one of Hitchcock's wacky old ladies searches for a painless insecticide. She is the Lord of the Flies, and we are ruled by analogous Providence. The best one hopes for in this life of pain is numb extinguishment by the imponderable forces coolly regarding us from afar, as we claw and struggle within our private traps.

Norman Bates has lived at the antipodes of estrangement from that vital status quo, that precarious respectability that normals like Marion and Sam pursue as proof against the rule of Chaos. Freud, despite his obsessionalism, was at least able to offer some surcease from the torment of the blaming superego, asserting that knowledge of the past and of one's disavowed drives might yet create a more tolerant view of the embattled self, allowing a less rigid adaptation to an authoritarian culture. Hitchcock, for all his genius, can give no better prescription for the alienation he portrays so tellingly in *Psycho* and throughout much of his mature work than the obsessional's credo: there is little that can be done to stave off madness or retribution, the apes at the windows or the cop of the mind, except to keep one's eye squarely on the task at hand, mind one's business, attend to one's duty, and never hope for much pleasure or freedom—except, of course, at the movies!

Several otherwise elegant studies of *Psycho* have been marred by assumptions that Hitchcock intended something more therapeutic than an affirmation of obsessionalism. Leo Braudy believes that the director is challenging the complacency with which we thirst vicariously after evil in the theater's darkness.[16] *Psycho* makes "the irresponsible audience" acknowledge "the rooted violence and perverse sexuality that may be in our motives." For James Naremore, *Psycho* is a monstrous, yet healing joke— "some viewers have been offended—but if we could not laugh, we would go mad."[17] Robin Wood, whose work I greatly admire, has argued most cogently on Hitchcock as therapist manqué. He, too, finds balm in *Psycho*'s sardonic humor—"it enables the film to contemplate the ultimate horrors without hysteria, with a poised, almost serene detachment."[18]

Unfortunately, audience response does not betoken healing or mastery of the "ultimate horror," our entrenched fear of death. Who—especially a woman—has been able to step into a motel shower with equanimity since *Psycho* was set loose upon an unsuspecting public? At best, we laughed a little, screamed more, and then were only too glad to thrust the film out of consciousness. At worst, a few marginal souls (I have interviewed two at Bellevue) suffered brief psychotic episodes during *Psycho*. No, the serene detachment Wood applauds is not ours, but very particularly Hitchcock's.

If the director is challenging us with our darker desires, I submit it is with the moral force of a tu quoque argument. After all, *Psycho* had its inception in *his* imaginary; in this overweaning interest in "rooted violence and perverse sexuality." By making us responsive to, and responsible for his preoccupations, he has exonerated himself and spread the blame, reaping enormous profit in the process. The imputation of "irresponsibility," if made at all, should be resituated where it belongs—with the director himself, especially since *Psycho*'s box office triumph has spawned a plethora of execrable imitations that have often debased cinema. Hitchcock has often issued pious pronunciamentos about the callousness and brutality of our age, yet he must stand implicated in much ubiquitous brutality of movies today. And if *Psycho* is a joke, the joke has surely been played on us, at our expense literally and figuratively, since we have paid admission to be degraded, dragged through the mire of Hitchcock's contempt—like *Psycho*'s characters.

Afterword

Since 1975 Hitchcock criticism has become something of a cottage industry for film scholars of various persuasions. *Psycho* has been probed sui generis, or as part of larger critical projects. The director's life has also been probed past his genteel evasions, to suggest that he was not always as personally repressed (or benevolent) as he endeavored to represent. I will touch on a few highlights in criticism of the work rather than deconstruction of the man.

William Rothman's magisterial *Hitchcock: The Murderous Gaze* emphasizes the director's rigorous formal control in aid of asserting his disquieting vision of spectatorial disavowal. Much of *Psycho* contains Hitchcock's "profoundest reflection on the nature of the camera and the conditions of his own authorship."[19]

Rothman's intricate close reading traverses some of the psychological territory charted in my essay. He limns the claustrophobic entrapment of the film's universe, cannily equating the shower curtain with the film screen—the magic curtain we had assumed would keep us separate and safe from the filmic world. As he violates our illusion, just so does Hitchcock cut down Marion in her naked narcissism, at the very moment of her pitiful certainty that she has secured a haven where she can be washed free of her crime, can author her own salvation. Rothman concludes: "What lures us into the world of a film may be a dream of triumphing over death, holding death forever at bay. But *Psycho* decisively demonstrates what Hitchcock's work has always declared: the world of a film is not a private island where we may escape the conditions of our existence."[20]

Tania Modleski comments further on Hitchcock's ambivalence toward Marion. She finds his oeuvre replete with images of ambiguous sexuality (such as the Norman/Marion doubling), which threaten to destabilize the gender identity of viewers and protagonists alike. The direst threat is to male spectators, for whom "fascination and identification with the feminine continually undermine their efforts to achieve masculine strength and autonomy . . . a primary cause of the violence towards women that abounds in Hitchcock's films."[21]

Modleski asserts that Mrs. Bates speaks a fundamental truth in exculpating herself. Her son's guilt foregrounds the culpability of men who seek to assuage their fear of obliteration by the mother or her substitutes through identifying with the supposed aggressor, becoming destroyers themselves. Norman's murder of Marion, his furious cleansing of the motel bathroom, the corpse's subsequent "swamping" comprise a "ritual of defilement," expunging all traces of the polluting feminine. "Thus do men's fears become women's fate."[22]

Modleski believes Hitchcock intuits the murderous misogyny in his work even as he has it acted out. The female spectator may derive pleasure not—as some of the director's detractors have complained—through masochistic identification with the victimized heroine, but through enhanced awareness of masculine oppression, of the subversive powers men anxiously try to quell. "Though our monstrous father may have made us fear our own image of ourselves, he has also (no doubt against his will) given us reason to hope that we will be able to survive patriarchy's attacks."[23]

In an impressive recent critique, R. Barton Palmer finds *Psycho* exemplary of Hitchcock's "metafictional" thrust in the later American work, i.e., the construction of a fictional illusion along traditional lines, and the laying bare of that illusion, generating considerable formal tension thereby.[24] *Psycho*'s narrative trajectory passes through a succession of classic genres—melodrama, detective, thriller, horror. Each genre successively collapses, its conventions defamiliarized, outrageously or subtly undermined.

With his dark Freudianisms and ironic rejection of free will, Norman is Hitchcock's primary subversive force. At base, the film asserts a radical noirish pessimism against the centrist optimism of mainstream Hollywood. Hitchcock refuses a comfortable storytelling tradition based on convenient resolutions and suppressions, to document the futility of desire in a world ruled by blind, unhappy chance. In sum, "his films are entertainments which reveal the darker realities upon which such vicarious pleasures are based."[25]

Stephen Rebello gives a comprehensive account of *Psycho*'s inception, production, and aftermath.[26] One learns that Hitchcock had been worried in the late fifties that Henri-George Clouzot might have snatched his laurels as presiding genius of cinematic shock with *Les Diaboliques* (1955). The director had been carefully tracking the box-office successes of low-budget horror films for some time. His sense of the public appetite for such fare, together with his competitiveness toward Clouzot, were the chief spurs for undertaking *Psycho* against considerable opposition.

Rebello definitively explodes the fiction that Hitchcock did not actually direct the shower sequence. He mentions *Psycho*'s influence on subsequent horror movies, a subject addressed at length in the next essay on *Alien* and "cruel" cinema.

6

Reimagining the Gargoyle: Psychoanalytic
Notes on *Alien* and the Contemporary
"Cruel" Horror Film

I admire its purity . . . a survivor, unclouded by conscience, remorse, or delusions of morality.
— Ash, Science Officer, the *Nostromo*

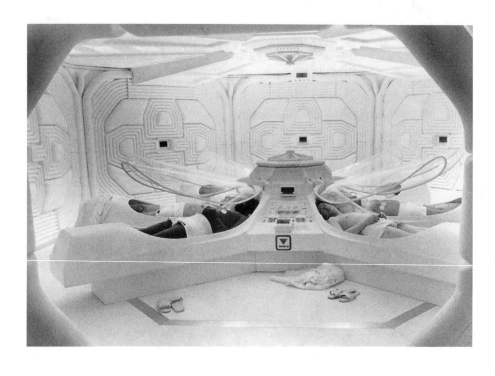

Alien: Nostromo's crew awakens from
hypersleep and the "Mother" computer's
meager sustenance. With the
unmasking of the Company's plot to
capture the monster, "Mother's"
questionable nurturing will turn
definitively noxious.

*I*f *Hair* proclaimed the Age of Aquarius, *Close Encounters of the Third Kind* (1977) surely celebrated its last gasp. According to Steven Spielberg's vision, our troubles would be resolved by Aquarian consciousness-raising sessions conducted by relentlessly benevolent extraterrestrials. But then a stretto of disasters put paid to the aspirations of Woodstock Nation. Three Mile Island, the plunging dollar, the spectacle of the American imperium held hostage by shabby ideologues—these and sundry other narcissistic injuries refurbished our pessimism, setting us to brood upon apocalypse.

With the situation so grim below, how could we remain sanguine about the good intentions of celestial messengers? Through that obscure feedback process by which the cinematic dream factory translates inchoate collective angst into extravagant scenarios, we have been served up an outer-space ghoulie to match the proper paranoia of the day—*Alien* (1979)!

Despite its contemporary iconography, *Alien* hearkens back to the malignant conception of unearthly life found in fifties science fiction, during another watershed of national self-doubt and paranoia. In the setting of spreading global communism, fading postwar prosperity, and the renewed threat of nuclear holocaust, Hollywood disgorged an army of implacable invaders, feasting upon flesh and blood, like the brainy carrotman of *The Thing* (1951), or cannabilizing consciousness, like the emotionally neutered Pod People of *Invasion of the Body Snatchers* (1956).

Alien contains numerous citations to these fifties classics, allusions to *Forbidden Planet* (1956) and similar arcana that excite cultists, but hardly make for big box office. Nor does *Alien*'s populist political stance and debatable feminism explain its staggering popularity. *"In space, no one can hear you scream,"* the promo poster tantalizes. It shows a cracked egg, backlit harshly. Dared to discover the source of this soundless scream, we go to the theater, gag on bloody recognitions, then—according to demographics—return again for more. The "repeater" phenomenon of past "weird" films has become even more significant with recent horror hits like *The Exorcist* (1973) and *Alien*. How to explain it?

I have elsewhere suggested that part of the weird genre's vast appeal resides in its flamboyant catharsis of our *timor mortis*.[1] This bizarre cure becomes worse than the disease it addresses when horror surpassing ordinary psychological tolerance cancels spectatorial pleasure, nullifies catharsis. Many viewers then undergo a kind of post-traumatic stress; the film acts upon them as a nightmare from which it is difficult to fully "awaken" after leaving the theater.

The creators of vintage fantasy mostly refused to violate our childlike faith that the weird movie might scare us but never really harm us— saving the rare catastrophic reaction of the exceptionally vulnerable viewer. This fragile trust was irrevocably abrogated by Alfred Hitchcock's 1960 benchmark masterpiece, *Psycho*. The English Hammer Studios productions flooded the screen with stylized gore in the fifties, but *Psycho* truly legitimized the show of violence to large general audiences. With extraordinary craft, Hitchcock welded to the excesses of the Grand Guignol a panoply of disturbing, perverse psychological motifs—rape, voyeurism, necrophilia—which had previously been explored more distantly and tactfully. Never had viewers been so cunningly seduced by a mere "thriller" into attending scenes of eroticized butchery.

Paradoxically, this species of trauma encourages repeated exposure, not out of masochism, but the very human wish for *mastery*, to prove to the vulnerable self that one can face mortal danger and survive. Many viewers rushed to *Psycho* on a dare as they would later rush to *Alien*, and got far more than they bargained for. They told their friends; everyone came back in droves. Concentration camp survivors, in a desperate attempt to master the unmasterable, often dream themselves back into torment. Analogously, *Psycho*, more than any previous horror film, compelled us against our better judgment to seek out hell at the Bijou.

"Cruel" Horror Cinema

Psycho's financial and artistic success spurred the escalation of violence throughout cinema, especially within the weird genre. It became the prototype for a subgenre I will categorize as "cruel" or "hardcore" horror, comprising pictures that skirt the edge of the impermissible visually and psychologically, or plunge over the edge.

Shot on low budgets, employing unknown actors and waning Hollywood luminaries, many cruel films piled up fortunes on the drive-in/exploitation circuit. The best—or most notorious —of these frightful cheapies are *Texas Chainsaw Massacre* (1974), *Night of the Living Dead* (1968), *The Hills Have Eyes* (1977), *Last House on the Left* (1972), and, more recently, *Halloween* (1978), *Friday the 13th* (1980), *A Nightmare on Elm Street* (1985), and sequels. Huge profits from exploitation screening eventually restored cruel cinema to the legitimacy *Psycho* had acquired. Expensive, high–production value shockers like *The Exorcist*, *The Omen* (1976), and *Carrie* (1976) generated megabucks through massive distribution to family audiences. Although the number of cruel films produced has somewhat declined, the subgenre still does well at the box office, and exceptionally well in videotape.

It is a monument to *Psycho*'s enduring power that its elegant or execrable spinoffs continue to reflect its cynical appraisal of the human condition and its coolly harmful attitude toward the audience. In cruel cinema, any possibility for a healing catharsis is deliberately sacrificed in favor of overwhelming the viewer's capacity to endure psychic pain. The attack may be crafted with exquisite visual manipulations, and little if any actual onscreen violence—viz., John Carpenter's work in *The Fog* (1980). It may be unremittingly raw, as in the nonstop carnage of George Romero's films. Or it may modulate between a raw and cool approach, as in the cinema of De Palma.

The Weltanschauung that informs *Psycho* and its cruel successors is paranoid/Hobbesian. Hitchcock predicates exploitation as the central experience of relatedness. He elaborates an articulating chain of victims and victimizers which culminates in a monstrous exploitation situated at the epicenter of family life—the tainted symbiosis between Norman Bates and his malevolent mom.[2] Since *Psycho*, the cruel movie has busily engendered similar monstrosities, born out of disturbed family relations (*Carrie*), or inserted into the family by malignant outside forces (*The Omen*, *Rosemary's Baby* [1968], *The Exorcist*). Alternately, the family entire is presented as a deviant monster (*Texas Chainsaw Massacre, The Hills Have Eyes*). For a lengthier discussion of this trend and its ramification, the reader is referred to Robin Wood's admirable essay, "The Return of the Repressed."[3]

Cruel cinema has also powerfully discoursed on the exploitative viciousness Hitchcock saw lurking within family life. Sometimes a family member will transform suddenly into a monster, turning savagely upon spouse, parent, siblings (*Night of the Living Dead, The Children* [1980]). Or, monstrous from birth, the child-beast feeds upon strangers (*It's Alive!* [1974]). The monstrous family preys upon its own, or maintains its perverse solidarity by attacking outsiders (*The Hills Have Eyes*). Murder and rapine flourish, but the signatory crime of cruel cinema is *cannibalism*.

The taint of cannibalism is subliminal in *Psycho*. Hitchcock dwells predominantly on the devouring of psychic identity—a theme privileged in the weird genre. Norman and his mummified Mum dine upon each other's egos. Mrs. Bates's withered husk is emblematic of that foul feast, the ghastly image of her shrunken skull, her leathery lips pulled back into a charnelhouse grin, evoked a ravening orality. Vastly potent, it provoked less fastidious talents after Hitchcock to "embody" the devouring of the self's substance, in the loathsome consumptions of the cannibalistic family monster.

The celebration of cannibalism reaches its zenith with the most traumatizing movies ever made—George Romero's *Dead* trilogy, *Texas Chainsaw Massacre*, and *The Hills Have Eyes*. In the Romero cycle, the newly dead rise again through some inexplicable agency to become ghouls. Amidst the wholesale slaughter, the cannibalistic corruption of family relationships is particularly harrowing. Mortally wounded loved ones succumb, then resurrect to tear their bereaved into pieces. *Texas Chainsaw Massacre* and *The Hills Have Eyes*, respectively, present psychotic and mutant families which sustain themselves by eating intruders. Their bloodthirsty orgies leave nothing to the imagination. Norma Bates's mummified skull is repeatedly reincarnated: in the half-eaten skull that first reveals ghoulish attack in *Night of the Living Dead*, in the skull-cum-lamp of *Texas Chainsaw Massacre*, in the severed head of the tourist father which the mutant patriarch of *The Hills Have Eyes* impales upon a stake.

Besides deriding the family "togetherness" valorized by the American heartland, these films also satirize the competitiveness central to the

American dream. In *Dawn of the Dead* (1979), Romero's zombies are drawn to a huge shopping mall. They totter about the aisles in a grotesque parody of conspicuous consumerism until living prey attracts them. In *Texas Chainsaw Massacre* and *The Hills Have Eyes*, the cannibalistic behavior of the deviant families is wittily counterpoised against the competitive striving of the "normals" who have wandered onto their turf. Capitalism is pictured as a less egregious form of the deviant's cannibalism, a normative rapacity sanctioned by culture and family. Wood mordantly observes that the family of *Texas Chainsaw Massacre* only carries to its logical conclusion "the basic (though unstated) tenet of capitalism that people have the right to live off other people. . . . Cannibalism represents the ultimate in possessiveness, hence the logical end of human relations under capitalism."[4]

I will now undertake a reading of *Alien* as legitimate inheritor of *Psycho* and its cruel lineage regarding its stylistic conventions, its frontal attack upon viewer sensibility, and its reinvention of the above motifs in outer space—particularly its Hobbesian perception of degraded relationships within family and state. My interpretations are based on what the film shows and says, plus information furnished by Ridley Scott, *Alien's* director and guiding intelligence.[5]

Alien's Mise-en-scène

The film opens with the letters "A—L—I—E—N" slowly etching themselves in a futuristic/runic script. Behind them the camera tracks across the galactic void. Cut to a long shot of a space vehicle, hovering over subtitles:

Commercial Towing Vehicle: *"The Nostromo"*

Crew: *Seven*

Cargo: *Refinery processing twenty million tons of ore*

Course: *Returning to earth*

After these slim facts about the *Nostromo* and its mission, the viewer is set squarely down *in media res*. One then pieces out an exceptionally vivid impression of *Alien's* time, unencumbered by those self-conscious explanations about "how we came to be here" that so often has marred the science-fiction film.

The *Nostromo*'s formidable technology constitutes a dull given for its people. The ship is a high-tech rustbucket, a old warhorse of the interstellar "Company's" merchant fleet, returning not from Ulyssean adventures, but prosaic commercial enterprise. Its crew is also unextraordinary. Like their well-worn surroundings, they are utterly and rather wonderfully *there*, a collection of competent loners one would find aboard a similar vessel in ancient Phoenicia or the East India trade.

Most viewers come to *Alien* old cinema spacehands, too—not as inclined to gasp at outer-space vistas after a glut of *Star Wars* (1977) special effects. *Alien*'s creators have subsumed the audience's tacit acceptance of the previously marvelous, in order to manipulate the gleaming mechanics of "straight" science fiction toward darker ends.

The *Nostromo* complex consists of several refineries—half-spheroids topped by towers and spires—linked to a central tug module. In the first long shot the entire structure looks like a warren of abandoned gothic cathedrals, suspended in midair. One's impression is distinctly *not* of the future, but of some indeterminate fantasy realm—Oz, or more pointedly, the terrible dark houses of vintage horror cinema: Dr. Frankenstein's mountain laboratory, Dracula's aerie, even the Bates's Victorian mansion.

The next shot is a tight close-up of the *Nostromo*'s massive ventral plane rumbling across frame. This detailed immensity has been a commonplace of genre icononography since *2001* (1968), rendering tomorrow's apparatus awesome and tangible. But here, instead of being lit starkly (another commonplace), the ship's surface is sunken in shadow, vaguely threatening. The *Nostromo*'s "terrible house" equivalencies, combined with the darkness of the ship's surface in the subsequent passing shot, at once kindle a feeling of disquieting ambiguity that pervades the flat "suchness" of space-age technology throughout the film. More than any previous work (including *Metropolis* [1926]), *Alien* evokes simultaneous resonances within the horror and science-fiction canons in representing a future milieu.

This feat is accomplished by extraordinary design which imbues futuristic hardware with haunting "horrific" connotations quite apart from function: viz., the hieratic helmets—they resemble *Aztec skulls!*—resting upon the dead computer terminals in the deserted control room at the film's beginning. Ridley Scott's vision of *Nostromo*'s hardware also shifts facilely between the locutions of science fiction and the horror/suspense film. For example, the decks are first presented as a maze of unexceptional storerooms, conduits, grills, and greasy machinery. As tension mounts, Scott transforms them into a tenebrous labyrinth, filled with false leads and murderous cul-de-sacs, through which the crew members stalk or are stalked by the elusive monster.

I cite only one of the numerous paraphrases of classic horror cinema during these sequences: Brett, seeking Jones the cat, approaches *Nostromo*'s cavernous undercarriage storeroom. Through subjective camera work, the gates seem to advance *toward him*, charged with an ineluctable menace—just as the front doors of the Bates house in *Psycho* seem to move eerily toward Vera Miles, as she goes to penetrate the mystery behind them.

The unsettling quality of the "ordinary" future environment foregrounds the unabashed weirdness of the wrecked derelict. Much of the uncanniness in the derelict's exploration derives not from the outlandishness of the vessel, but from the nagging similarity of its structures to human organs, particularly the organs of reproduction (reflecting *Alien*'s preoccupation with monstrous gestations).

The entire craft resembles a stupendous uterine-fallopian system. The crew members enter the ship through one of three unmistakably vaginal hatches. The main deck is shaped like an enormous spine/rib cage. Kane, lowered into the bowels of the derelict, discovers the Alien hatch laid out in the pelvis of a mighty vertebral column. The fossilized "space jockey's" giant skeleton rests upon a control chair, from which juts a huge penile shaft. The chair itself resembles an operating table; here, eons ago, some unfortunate pilot from another race died of the same catastrophic Caesarean which later terminates Kane.

Science fiction frequently offers an "acceptable" rationale for frightening psychotic or archaic mental phenomena. Clinical corollaries of the derelict's megalithic anatomy are found in the changes in body image experienced during a hallucinatory drug trip or an acute schizophrenic episode. One recalls Victor Tausk's intriguing hypothesis that the paranoid schizophrenic projects the skewed sense of his own body into the crazy design of the "influencing machine."[6]

These distortions are thought to be extravagant elaborations of early percepts of self and "Other." The uncanny feelings aroused in the viewer by the derelict's great innards may likewise be rooted in infantile oceanic impressions of one's body and of the immense, ineffably mysterious physicality of nurturing adults. In this regard, the investigation of the derelict has been interpreted as a symbolic return to the maternal womb and beyond, an oneiric quest for truth about the origins of being.[7]

The Anatomy of a Monster

No matter how evocative the milieu, the monster film ultimately stands or falls on the believability of its inhuman protagonist. Many promising films have foundered when the monster stood ludicrously revealed—a "man in a rubber suit." Neither talent nor cash was spared by *Alien*'s production team in manufacturing a credible being. Superbly executed and artfully deployed, the Alien is one of the most frightening monsters ever brought to the screen. The qualities owned separately by the best of the breed have been gathered together under one hide: the creature is *mysteriously ungraspable, viciously implacable, improbably beautiful,* and *lewd.*

Ungraspability

Weird literary masterpieces like the stories of M. R. James triumph through discretion, an elegant paucity of illustration. In the horror film the naked face of Thanatos is also best sparingly revealed, lest the indescribable be described or the unnamable named. Like the dim memory of repressed trauma, what frightens us most is likely to be half-glimpsed, seized and rehearsed in each viewer's intuition of the terrible. In this regard, Ridley Scott made an astute decision, over the objections of others in his production team, to show his exquisitely designed monster briefly and ambiguously.

The explosion of a seething tongue of flesh out of the Alien egg lasts the blur of an instant. The only version of the creature that registers in detail is the "face hugger"; besides the egg form, it's the most quiescent of the Alien's stages, befitting its relatively passive function as Kane's nurturer. The "chest burster" form is still for a few seconds before it careens out of the mess.

The adult Alien is seen in quick flashes during its attacks on Brett, Dallas, Lambert, and Parker, briefly when Ripley meets it on her way to the shuttlecraft, and for no more than several minutes in the final sequence. In the sum of all its mutations, the Alien is on camera less than any other classic cinema monster, with the possible exception of *The Thing*'s Carrotman (who also makes lightninglike entrances and exits, and whose longest appearance occurs in a final confrontation with his human adversaries).

The adult Alien is photographed so obliquely that a coherent gestalt can never be constructed. When it drops upon Brett it seems like a huge phallic tube. During Lambert's slaughter, one only sees a sinuous tail curling around her leg. Fully 90 percent of the Alien footage consists of close-ups of its head and jaws, from which one bears away a hobgoblin vision of metalloid skullbrow, cruelly curling lips, needle-teeth dripping luminescent saliva—*Alien*'s reprise of Norma Bates's skull. The entire creature appears for the first and last time in the shuttlecraft, but the viewer's sight is obscured by flashing strobes within the ship, and by the dazzling engine exhaust outside. Scott thus compels the viewer to piece together an impression of the monster based on tantalizing fragments, fleshed out by the potent nuances of subjective fantasy, surely the scariest beast of all.

The Alien's enigmatic appearance is further compounded by its *mutability*. King Kong's genes dictate no other form but hairy apehood, nor is Frankenstein's monster about to burst his stitches and assume other shapes. But like the Old Man of the Sea, awful transformations are native to the Alien's life cycle, central to its survival. The awareness of its quick-change potential keeps the viewer in a state of even greater unease, anticipating what chimerical composition the creature will choose in its next reincarnation.

In keeping with this ambiguity of shape, Ridley Scott deliberately provides the sketchiest information about the Alien's developmental phases. It is a Linnean nightmare, defying every natural law of evolution, by turns bivalve, crustacean, reptilian, and humanoid. It seems capable of lying dormant within its egg indefinitely. It sheds its skin like a snake, its carapace like an arthropod. It deposits its young within other species like a wasp.

Intermediate or alternate stages are hinted at, but never clarified. Scott deleted a sequence in which Ripley discovers Brett and Dallas in cocoons. Dallas is still alive, in agony and recognizably human. Brett is dead; the shrunken husk of his body contains the larval Alien, and has further progressed in dreadful metamorphosis toward the egg form. From this scene, one could easily discover that the eggs in the derelict's hatch were deposited within the bodies of its crew millenia ago to await another unwary host. But Scott obviously thought closure satisfaction would be better sacrificed in order to keep the Alien an awesome enigma.

One further intuits that the Alien's mutability is not solely dictated by a fixed if remarkably various life cycle, but by formidable mechanisms that allow it to change literally second by second, in conformation with the changing stresses of its milieu. It thus responds according to Lamarckian *and* Darwinian principles. When it attacks Ripley, it looks much smaller and more humanoid than before. Several observers, Ridley Scott included, have rather horribly suggested that its next manifestation would be fully human—at least on the outside!

Implacability

Movie monsters frequently provoke fear and pity because they embody the persecuted outsider, excluded from quotidian joys and sorrows. In Karloff's poignant portrayal, Frankenstein's creation became a misunderstood, battered child who identified with its oppressors. It only gave back in kind the ill treatment afforded by its laboratory "parents" and society at large. Even Dracula drew a measure of compassion in Lugosi's performance because of the eternal torment of his immortality.

The Alien stems from a different line of monsters, creations that provoke terror untempered by sympathy because of the inhumanity of their form, their divorce from human concerns, or the catastrophic nature of their onslaughts. Examples of "unsympathetic" monsters with inhuman shapes include the giant insects, lizards, and crustaceans of the postatomic era (*Them* [1954], *The Giant Gila Monster* [1959], *Attack of the Crab Monsters* [1957], assorted globs of undifferentiated protoplasmic goo like *The Blob* [1958] or *Caltiki, Immortal Monster* [1959], vile extraterrestrial phantasmagoria like the demonic Martian grasshoppers of *Five Million Years to Earth* [1967]).

The unsympathetic creature's lack of empathy may originate in its lack of wit, wedded to an enormous appetite. On the other hand, its brainpower may be so vastly superior (viz., the invaders of *War of the Worlds* [1953]), that humankind exists for it as mere fodder, or so much underbrush to be cleared away. Its attack is devastating, merciless. The victim is expunged, erased, body disintegrated, dismembered, or consumed; or else the marrow of psychic identity is sucked dry, leaving an envelope of dumb flesh for colonization.

The Alien being is patently inhuman in its earlier versions, and the adult form is never sufficiently humanoid to promote easy identification. Its IQ is problematic; it cannot be easily dismissed as a digestive machine propelled by a peabrain—*Jaws* in space. It demonstrates exceptional cunning while hunting the crew in its instant grasp of the *Nostromo's* layout, and its decision to secrete itself board the shuttlecraft. It is not inconceivable that it can read the crew's thoughts (the possibility they might communicate with it is never entertained).

The ruthlessness of the Alien's attack is typically unrelenting: its victims are sundered or totally annihilated. Kane is eviscerated by the nativity of the beast; Brett is hauled off by the adult Alien, leaving only a scream behind. Dallas vanishes in the airshaft as if into thin air, a dot on Lambert's tracking screen—there one moment, gone the next.

Cornered by the Alien, Parker is garrotted—by what is not made clear. Next, there is a quick shot of an uncertain gourd of flesh (head? belly?) pierced by a toothy ramrod. Then the Alien's tail snakes around Lambert's leg, and the camera cuts briefly to a close-up of her terrified face. When Ripley arrives, all the viewer is allowed to see is Parker, hunched against a bulkhead, intact but obviously dead, as Lambert's naked and bloody foot dangles out of focus in foreframe. By careful editing, Ridley Scott leaves the exact manner of the victims' passage nearly blank, once again compelling the viewer to conjure from fantasy the direst account of their deaths.

Beauty

Much of the Alien's fascination resides in its unexpected loveliness. The "face hugger" and "chest burster" stages are frankly repellent. But the adult Alien owns a sumptuous elegance. The robotic simulacrum of the heroine in *Metropolis*, and the Gillman of *Creature from the Black Lagoon* (1954) nearly approach this nacreous beauty. The creature's architecture is skeletal, fleshed out with a kind of flayed musculature reminiscent of Vesalius's anatomical engravings. The bony elements are supplemented by strange, streamlined mechanical structures, cartilaginous rods and pistons. The creature's skin is glistening black; a long, lustrous grey porpoise head is fitted behind a skull's facies; the outside jaws are studded with rows of stainless-steel teeth. Here is the charnelhouse aesthetic of the medieval Dance of Death; the hellish apparitions of Bosch; the figurations of Tibetan demonology.

Sensuality

A few inhabitants of Monster Alley are not without lubricious intentions—viz., Kong's moony courtship of Anne Darrow, or the Frankenstein monster's confused erotic designs upon its creator's fiancée. However, sensuality is not usually within the purview of the unsympathetic movie monster. With rare exceptions—the mutant amphibians of *Humanoids from the Deep* (1980)—the unsympathetic creature's depredations are too obliterating, its appearance or disposition insufficiently humanoid to project a believable sexuality.

The Alien manifests no erotic intention until its lust erupts during the final showdown with Ripley. Until then, the crew members have shown little sexual interest either, compared with the clumsy yearnings weird cinema frequently depicts between heterosexual shipmates cloistered in deep space, mad doctors and their intended brides, intrepid military types and their scientist girlfriends. When Ripley steps out of her fatigues, she becomes intensely desirable and achingly vulnerable. The sight of her nearly nude body is highly arousing in the context of the film's previous sexual neutrality, as well as the relaxation that follows the *Nostromo*'s destruction and the creature's supposed death. Precisely at this moment, the Alien unfolds out of its hiding place.

Unlike the blinding speed of its earlier assaults, it moves slowly, languorously. It stretches out its phallic head as if preening. Ripley, her horrified gaze fixed hypnotically upon it, retreats stealthily into the equipment locker. It extends a ramrod tongue, tipped with hinged teeth dripping with luminescent slime (actually, K-Y jelly!), and hisses voluptuously. The very air is charged with the palpable threat of rape—and worse. There is no square-jawed hero to rescue this damsel in distress. Unlike Fay Wray and a legion of impotent screaming Mimis, Ripley saves herself. Her combat with her exhibitionistic assailant bears the patents of sexual engagement.

She slips into a space suit, crooning a *love ditty* to curb her panic: "You . . . are . . . my . . . lucky . . . star . . ." Repeating "lucky . . . lucky . . . lucky . . . ," she creeps out of the locker and straps herself into the pilot's chair. Her breathing, amplified within her helmet, is heard in accelerating gasps and moans (a libidinous variation on the famous sequence in *2001* [1968] in which Dave Bowman's breathing is heard echoing in his own ears as he disconnects the murderous HAL).

The Alien rushes upon her, maddened by poisonous gases she has triggered. Her face is sweaty, her expression dazed, very nearly ecstatic. With an orgasmic wail, she slams her hand down upon the control panel and blows away the hatch. The monster hurtles out, then grips the entryway. She discharges an ejaculatory bolt from the grapnel gun that strikes the creature full in its chest, flinging it into space. Simultaneously suffering with her, and voyeur to her victimization, the viewer (especially the male viewer) experiences a powerful commingling of raw sexual excitement and mortal terror, an effect often sought but rarely achieved so well in suspense cinema.

Innards and Other Outrages

Like Hitchcock and De Palma, Ridley Scott incites terror in *Alien* through a clever blend of suggestion, indirection, and confrontation. The film contains almost as little actual onscreen mayhem as *Psycho*. Horror is elicited rather by sophisticated manipulations of the medium.

Alien's considerable cruel reputation is based on two extraordinary gobbets of overt violence flung in the viewer's face: the birth of the Alien through Kane's shattered chest, and Science Officer Ash's dismantling by Parker. The "chest burster" sequence merits particular attention since it is probably the main reason many people have been dared into seeing the movie, or have returned to see it again.

Scott sets up the scene by lulling the viewer into a state of false calm. The anxiety which has been adroitly built up abates with the creature's supposed death and Kane's reawakening. The viewer identifies with the crew's relief; is disarmed by their highjinks during the celebratory meal; then is plunged into even deeper, disorganizing terror by Kane's awful fate. This "ratchet" effect—sharply lowering tension with a leaven of humor, then sharply escalating it so that it impacts more profoundly—is a staple of the genre, and never employed to better effect.

When Kane sickens, Parker and Ash wrestle him onto the mess table. His chest heaves, swells, a stain of blood spreads over his tunic, then the head of the infant Alien thrusts viciously out, spattering the appalled onlookers with gouts of gore and visceral shreds (Scott had his actors unexpectedly showered with entrails bought from a nearby butcher shop to achieve their howls of shocked surprise!). The Alien looks like a dehisced organ or loop of gut, until it fully emerges as a murderous embryo. One is marginally aware of Kane's hands in the frame's periphery, clawed in agony. Parker lunges forward, a knife in his hand. Ash stops him. The creature emits a sizzling hiss and rockets away, a long, reptilian tail whipping out behind it.

The most traumatizing aspect of the sequence is Kane's unexpected *disembowelment*. The overwhelming loathing and fear related to evisceration has rarely been addressed in the analytic literature. While the smooth exterior is readily conceptualized, a completely realistic or pleasing picture of the "insides" is not likely to be found in the average citizen's body image. A nauseous vision is usually summoned up of a smelly claustrum, stuffed with slippery ropes and lumps of flesh. One knows the vitals are vital to life, that food is processed, energy generated, the seeds of life itself planted within one's proper entrails, but it still seems necessary to the psychic economy to keep the guts safely contained, relegated to darkness.

Disembowelment abrogates this touchy sequestration irrevocably. The self's fragile envelope is definitively breached: once the abdomen is ripped open, how can Humpty Dumpty ever be put right again? After his tiny invader leaves him a gutted husk on the mess table, Kane's deadness is absolutely unassailable, a crushing narcissistic wound like Janet Leigh's death in *Psycho*, to viewers who had imagined themselves omnipotently secure outside the screen.

The discovery that Ash is a robot doesn't make the spilling of *his* entrails less unpalatable. His evisceration, coupled with his bizarre resurrection, is even more traumatic. Ridley Scott gives the viewer a closer look at Ash's guts—unwholesome gizmos that spout greenish hydraulic goo. After Parker decapitates him with a fire extinguisher, Ash's head is rewired at a distance from his unpacked torso. His voice a dispassionate gurgle, a tiny smile plays across his lips as he expresses genteel sympathy for his shipmates' fate: "I can't lie to you about your chances, but you have my sympathy." The utter morbidity of the moment beggars description.

Kane serves as prime focus of *Alien*'s complex birth imagery. His intrusion into the hatch, his penetration of the blue force field, the touch of his hand that discharges the Alien out of its egg, all may be read as symbolic fertilizations. Kane is thereby uncannily implicated as subject *and* object in a horrific account of the primal scene. As if in talion retribution, the scene recoils upon *him*; his punishment for viewing and participating in the forbidden act of conception is a spectacular (!) death precipitated by the Alien's birth.[8] I submit that each viewer's catastrophic response to Kane's disembowelment may well be determined by reactivation of personal archaic fantasies about the primal scene and the birth process, in addition to the dynamics elucidated above.

Finally, the "chest burster" sequence epitomizes the leitmotif of *Alien*: within a dark claustrum filled with real, simulated, or symbolic vitals, a supremely potent menace lurks, waiting to tear apart and devour its un-suspecting victims. For Kane, the menace literally lives within his guts. For the remaining crew, their ship becomes one great cloaca through which the beast prowls, Grendel-like, to pick them off at its pleasure. Their plight acquires an added claustrophobic piquancy by the immensity of galactic space surrounding them into which they can neither "shit out" the Alien, or expel themselves. The menace concealed within Ash's bionic entrails is his secret function as the Company's creature. And the Company is the direst menace of all, a treacherous Leviathan that gnaws away at the vitals of *Alien*'s society.

Of Corporate Depredations and the Family Monster

The *Nostromo*'s crew may be analyzed as a symbolic family. In this context, Dallas, the Father/Captain, appears initially passive, increasingly withdrawn, until he is completely eliminated midfilm. The real source of power within this family system is "Mother," the computer. "She" and the Company she prefigures are futuristic versions of the classic "bad" witch-mother of myth and fairy tale.

The crew is symbiotically dependent upon "Mother," but her nurturing is at best ineffective, exemplified in the meager sustenance provided by her life-support systems in hypersleep. When the crew awakens, her ministrations turn definitively noxious. With full knowledge beforehand, she reroutes them to certain doom on the asteroid. After Ripley exposes her complicity, the female warrant officer emerges as the nearest thing to a "good" mother on board. But Ripley can only rescue herself and Jones, the ship's cat, narrowly escaping "Mother"'s last revenge, the *Nostromo*'s detonation.

One is told almost nothing about *Alien*'s culture, but powerful inferences about it can be made by studying the crew. For the most part they are skilled technicians from a conforming middle or upper-middle class. They observe the outward tenets of contemporary American democracy. No one is a focus of obvious discrimination because of sex, class, or color (Parker is black). Everyone seems well fed, well educated, and reasonably well off.

Differences exist in station, but an air of easy, unauthoritarian informality is maintained, possibly consistent with the *Nostromo*'s status as a merchant rather than a military vessel. Each individual's competence is tacitly respected. Ripley, one notes, perceives Ash's failure to provide more information about the Alien more as a function of his untrust-worthiness rather than ineffectiveness. The importance of teamwork is implicitly emphasized.

Yet on closer scrutiny the *Nostromo*'s democracy smacks of the anthill. The crew address each other by last names only, work efficiently like anonymous cogs. Women stand on exactly equal footing with men to the point of androgyny; they use no makeup, wear the same serviceable clothing as their male counterparts—floppy surgical whites or fatigue uniforms. Although not unattractive, both sexes evince little if any sexual interest.

Except for a few convivial moments, the crew's interactions are impersonal, tense, and slightly abrasive. Hardly a trace of empathy exists, with the notable exception of the "chum" bond between Parker and his taciturn fellow mechanic Brett (their origins seem working class). Some affection is also elicited by Jones the cat, indicating the capacity for engagement has not withered entirely, if only with the nonhuman environment.

As the Alien's threat escalates, relations aboard grow more alienated. Dallas betrays a nasty paranoid streak. When Ripley tries to discuss her suspicions about Ash, he snaps: "I don't trust *anybody!*" The crew seem bound to each other only by shared fear and vulnerability. They betray little real mourning for their dead except for Parker's grief when Brett is killed. Even Ripley, who evolves into the most humanized character, never overtly shows more than momentary anguish over her lost comrades.

Kane's maimed funeral rites offer a paradigm of the pervasive dehumanization afflicting the crew. Dallas reads no formal service over him, an intriguing departure from the convention of fifties classics like *Forbidden Planet*, in which departed shipmates were assured of a Christian burial in deep space. Instead, the captain coldly inquires: "Does anyone want to say anything?" and when no answer comes, flushes the corpse out of the airlock as dispassionately as emptying a toilet.

It is strongly implied that the source of the *Nostromo*'s impoverished relationships lies in an overweening lust for gain, a life-denying greediness that has extended from the highest levels of *Alien*'s world to become rooted within the individual psyche. The theme of insatiable orality is subliminally sounded in the beginning of the film: the camera tracks through the empty mess to a close-up of two perpetually feeding plastic gooney birds, bobbing up and down over a cup of water.

After the crew awakens, their first conversation involves Parker's noisy demands for a larger share of the profits. He claims those who do the dirty work below decks are exploited by the technocrats above (shades of *Metropolis*). When Dallas orders the landing, Parker protests that since *Nostromo* is a commercial ship he will only undertake a rescue operation for extra pay. He complies after Ash drily points out that a clause in his contract makes the investigation mandatory "under penalty of total forfeitures of shares. *No MONEY!!!*"

Parker strikes a keynote of sour appropriativeness that echoes throughout the film. His type is recognizable today, the "I'm all right, Jack" union stalwart, jealous of petty prerogative, spoiling for a strike, his true ideology to the right of Bismarck. But one should not be misled by the coarseness of his rhetoric; those who walk the upper decks share his greediness. Their motives are merely more suavely disguised. Dallas, for instance, does not seem any more touched by mercy in conducting the rescue operation. The captain is simply a better servant of his employers.

Ingrained personal selfishness may be taken as a pallid reflection of the maniacal greed of the corporate masters ruling *Alien*'s society. They would appear to govern a corrupted galactic democracy that maintains the pretense of libertarian ideals while shamelessly plundering outsiders, and covertly abusing its own citizens. The resources of the *Nostromo* are deployed to exploit a distant planet's natural resources. In past centuries, the lucre from similar missions legitimized subjugation and slaughter of colonial populations. Even the death of those enlisted by the exploiters in pursuit of their golden dreams could be justified by appropriately compensating survivors. The *Nostromo*'s real mission, and the heartless manner in which it has been contrived, illustrate the depth of inhuman exploitativeness which has developed out of the earlier terrestrial excesses of capitalism.

It may be extrapolated that the Company actually deciphered the derelict's transmission some time *before* the *Nostromo*'s departure. After gleaning that a highly dangerous presence had been encountered by whatever agency responsible for planting the warning beacon, the Company suspected this entity might be useful for its "weapons section." Perhaps it battles with other giant conglomerates like our own Krupps or DuPonts for galactic hegemony, as it hawks ordinance across the universe.

Since it constantly seeks a competitive edge, the Company opts to keep its profile low while retrieving the Alien. Sacrificing safety for stealth, it elects *not* to send a large, well-equipped expedition. Instead, an ordinary merchant vessel is chosen whose course has already been scheduled to take it near the planetoid on which the acoustic beacon is located. Hopefully, the beacon site can then be reconnoitered, and the Alien recovered under the guise of a rescue operation, without unduly alerting the suspicions of the crew *or* potential competitors. After all, investigation of unknown transmissions *is* required under prevailing maritime law. A rescue operation *is* what the crew members will probably think they are undertaking to earn their pay, and will perhaps keep thinking if survivors are actually found together with whatever danger lurks on the planetoid.

Besides preserving security, the use of a merchant vessel also saves the major cost of outfitting an expedition. The profit-obsessed Company can therefore possibly kill two birds with one stone, acquiring both the *Nostromo*'s cargo and a new weapon. The complete success of the gamble is, of course, contingent on a docile, or at least manageable Alien—never a reliable possibility in the genre since Kong broke out of his chrome-steel chains at the Rialto.

But the mission's complete success is by no means mandatory. The Company has neither provided the crew with disintegrator weapons to vaporize the creature, nor the means of creating a force field to contain it—devices well within the capabilities of a faster-than-light technology. One theorizes that the highly limited low-tech defenses alloted to the crew—the best they can jury-rig are primitive prods and flame-throwers—attests to the Company's miserliness, as well as its bias in favor of eliminating the human crew to preserve the Alien (and the cargo).

To cover every contingency, the Company substitutes for the *Nostromo*'s regular science officer an android totally obedient to its will, programming Ash and "Mother" to implement its intentions on the mission. One surmises the Company prefers to bring back the Alien without incident without disclosing the evil uses to which it will be put, if Ash can fog the issue by insisting the creature needs to be studied for its intrinsic research value or possible humanitarian benefits. But Ash is also empowered if necessary to sacrifice crew, survivors, the cargo, himself, to return the Alien to the "weapons section." His tactics are passive-aggressive and obfuscatory until Ripley discovers the conspiracy. Then he explodes into an impersonal fury quite matching the Alien's.

Conceive, then, that the "family" of the *Nostromo* is victimized by three monstrosities, within and without. The clearest danger to its integrity is the Alien, but it is monstrous *only* from its victims' viewpoint. Objectively, there is nothing evil in its nature, for its ceaseless feeding and breeding merely fulfills the imperative of its genetic code—to survive in shifting, inimical environments.

Ash is the second monster, inserted from outside to dwell deceitfully within the family's bosom, preserving group integrity if such will further his aims, but equally capable of destroying the group to protect the Alien. But Ash is no more culpable or intrinsically evil than the creature, for he is not his own man. His morality is preprogrammed, a cog-and-wheels Darwinism engineered by others to make him a tool fit for their dirty tricks. For him, the Alien's purity constitutes a robotic ego-ideal, and he is more than halfway toward achieving it . . .

The authentic moral monstrosity of the piece is the Company, and its fellow corporate predators. The Company's materialism has infected the heart, corroded relationships almost beyond redress, struck hurtfully at the center of individual, group, and family identity. Like the family of *Texas Chainsaw Massacre*, the Company's feeding upon others to survive and prevail is completely ego-syntonic. It perceives nothing in the least reprehensible about its machinations.

Cruel Cinema as Sullied Polemic

Many critics have theorized that art reflects the psychic tensions generated by a culture's historic, economic, and technological circumstances. Inimical conditions are believed to provoke dark, disintegrative resonances in the psyches of a culture's members. More "affirmative" percepts may evolve whenever favorable environments promote higher levels of cultural integration. Employing formal devices consistent with medium and prevailing stylistics, the artist is said to "capture" the culture's "negative" or "positive" collective psychological valence, a process which occurs largely outside conscious intent.[9]

The motion picture has been widely heralded as an exquisitely sensitive litmus for collective psychic tensions. Weird cinema offers a particularly sensitive index of disintegrative cultural thrusts, elaborated into an idiosyncratic vocabulary of apocalyptic imagery. Both trashy and artful productions of the weird canon therefore deserve serious attention in a politically committed critical practice. Robin Wood observes that the very *lack* of seriousness with which horror movies are conceived and received encourages *loosening* of censorship for maker and viewer. Superficially innocuous, or downright disreputable weird films may consequently be far more "radical and fundamentally undermining than works of social criticism, which must always concern themselves with the possibility of reforming aspects of a social system whose basic rightness must not be challenged."[10]

In opposition to the liberalism of "establishment" reformists like Capra or Kramer, cruel cinema has been waxing exuberantly nihilistic about sacrosanct American values for some time. *Alien* is the culmination of this trend: it recapitulates in one concentrated scenario the cruel film's fragmented or disguised preoccupations with the deterioration of the quality of life—notably of family life—and the degradation of the social contract under the aegis of capitalism.

The omnipotent monster who preys on puny humans is a common figure in art from earlier phases of cultural disintegration. As the despair of the Dark Ages gave way to the hope of the Gothic Middle Ages, the indominable Grendel dwindled into the gargoyle, a peripherally removed figure of fun, waiting in the wings to flourish again in darker times.[11] *Alien* moves the gargoyle back to center stage. Late twentieth-century corporate capitalism, with its unslakable thirst to propagate its vast institutions, is nominated as the sinister force which has reincarnated the omnipotent beast.

The condemnation of a callous, consumerist ethos, obliquely set forth in *Texas Chainsaw Massacre* and the Romero *Dead* opus, now emerges undisguised. The Company, playing out its intergalactic scenario of contemporary boardroom smash-and-grab, is emphatically labeled villainous; the Alien recognized as avatar of its unholy scavenging.

The script implies that the Alien is also a warning to the Company cast in its own image. For had the creature been brought to Earth, a dreadful retribution would surely have followed as it fed upon the flesh of its rescuers and bred its own kind with Malthusian vigor. Ripley's courage narrowly averts the extinction of her culture. It is left moot whether she will unmask the Company's perfidy after her return, which might precipitate a galactic Watergate or even send interplanetary revolutionaries to the barricades.

Several critics have suggested that *Alien* is agitprop in genre masquerade. Lyn Davis and Tom Genelli believe the film functions "as a kind of wakeup call to present-day society . . . to shock us out of our psychic 'hypersleep.'" Our "technological society" breeds environmental and economic ills as numerous as the Alien's mutations because "our left brain 'mothers,' the computers and technocrats who run them, are unable to *generate* what is needed to solve these problems."[12] The authors further categorize the Alien as the dernier cri of the presumably ungenerative "masculine principle, total aggression without emotion or regard to life." The answer to the phallic expansionism it symbolizes is the affirmation of "the conservation instinct which we need to reacknowledge, to reincorporate within our collective human body."[13]

This "feminine principle" is epitomized by *Alien*'s heroine. Ripley, as avatar of Kali, the Mother Goddess, perceives the danger of letting Kane and the other explorers back aboard. She is ready to sacrifice a few lives so that millions may live. She searches out the Company's scheming; exposes Ash's empty "fathering" of the Alien. She jeopardizes her own escape to rescue Jones the cat, demonstrating her empathy with the nonhuman manifestations of the life force.

I found the Davis-Genelli arguments doubtful in 1980. They seem even less helpful in reassessing *Alien* and the problematics of cruel cinema in 1986. Several decades of work in psychoanalysis and feminist studies enjoin wariness about erecting gendered "principles" as eternal spiritual/biological verities. Beyond their essentialism, Davis and Genelli have fundamentally erred—perhaps falling prey to wishful thinking—in ascribing to *Alien*'s creators a degree of mindfulness that simply doesn't sort with its deliberately traumatizing aspects. *Alien* remains a masterpiece of the genre. But it also replicates the uncompromising hurtfulness, the amoral "cool" of *Psycho* and its cruel inheritors, while teasing the audience with a politically "engaged" facade.

Robin Wood remarks that contemporary horror cinema brings "to a focus a spirit of negativity, an undifferentiated lust for destruction, that seems to be not far below the surface of the modern collective consciousness."[14] Not content with mocking the values of its characters as it tears their flesh, cruel cinema assails its audience with that same spirit of negativity, destructiveness, and exploitation Davis and Genelli would have us believe *Alien* decries. And what vast profit is garnered in the process—shades of the Company!

The past few decades have witnessed the spread of violence throughout American culture, perpetrated within the family, on our streets, sanctioned at the highest levels of government, whether in the napalming of children or in subsidizing foreign torturers. The show of overt violence in media has become a commonplace never conceived of in the worst excesses of yellow journalism. Television news passes equably from the commercial break to the unsparing depiction of the atrocities of war and urban crime. We have gradually become inured, desensitized to violence. Its victims grow increasingly "thinglike," exciting only the briefest twitch of pity or horror before the bloody scene dissolves to the hawking of toothpaste and designer jeans.

It seems to me that cruel cinema merely takes up where the TV screen leaves off, with a greater cachet to treat characters and audience as dumb objects to be exploited toward enormous gain. In the course of transforming the collective angst bred out of a corrupt and corrupting capitalism, the creators of cruel movies, wittingly or otherwise, have allowed their medium to become tainted by the sordid practices of their bête noire. The creators of *Alien* have perhaps beheld the greedy beast lurking in its lair more accurately; but then, to paraphrase Blake, they have become what they beheld.

In sum, films like *Alien* cannot legitimately be recommended as polemics against capitalism. They should instead be properly recognized as collective artistic derivatives of its depredations, peculiar signifiers of a primordial selfishness, a boundless narcissism that pervades the age and diminishes the spirit. They are deeply testamentary to those terrible fractures of ego-desire which Father Thomas Merton discerned as the most certain result of a "life centered on 'things,' on the grasping and manipulation of objects."[15]

With rare exceptions, cruel cinema's means of production and ideology are dictated by corporate parameters. At best, then, its texts constitute sullied jeremiads. They dimly apprehend the primordial selfishness infecting late twentieth-century capitalism, but can only recommend convenient escapist, individualistic solutions.[16] At worst, they are signatory of its callous manipulations of our fellow creatures and our environment, which have brought us to the brink of universal ambiguity, destructiveness, and despair.

7

Fiction into Film—Problems of
Adaptation: Improper *Bostonians*

The cinematic *Bostonians* tinkers with
Henry James's subtle intimations of
Olive Chancellor's unacknowledged
lesbianism into the conventions of
soft-core porn.

*H*enry James's *The Bostonians* is *Schreckroman* masquerading as social satire, as chilling a tale of identity rape as *Invasion of the Body Snatchers* (1956). Behind the civilized veneer of the Jamesian mise-en-scène, devious depredations are regularly visited upon the innocent. Whether in the name of love or unrepentant lust after domination, desire for a vulnerable object often verges upon its abusive possession. The rankest such exploitations are visited by the servants in *Turn of the Screw* upon their young charges. *The Bostonians* antedates that novella by some twenty years, and eerily anticipates its predatory theme.

James's näif in *The Bostonians* is Verena Tarrant, an entrancing young woman in her late teens or barely beyond. She is the only child of an itinerant charlatan, the repulsive Selah Tarrant, latterly a mesmerist in attendance to Boston's postbellum bohemian set. Her no less objectionable mother is a narcissistic simpleton, whose social pretentions far exceed her doubtful station.

Although not well educated, Verena owns a surprising gift for oratory. The North has won, and women's suffrage has succeeded abolition as the burning issue of the day. Verena debuts in fringe salons, speaking out on the "great cause." It's quickly evident that a greater public awaits her. While profit does not interest her, others have high hopes of coasting to wealth and fame on her gifts. Her father passes himself off as her rhetorical generator, "starting her up" with mesmeric flimflam. Her mother and a penny-dreadful journalist lag not far behind in great expectation at her expense. James's ironic account of Verena's tawdry antecedents, of high-minded reformers, base exploiters, vague eccentrics and blarney merchants, sets the stage for the fateful triangulation that will consume her.

We first see Verena at a gathering of the faithful through the eyes of two unlikely companions: Olive Chancellor, a patrician Back Bay ideologue, and Basil Ransom, her darkly handsome distant cousin from Mississippi. Olive has pursued one cause or another throughout her life before lighting upon feminism. Currently she counsels compromised housemaids, who persist in fleeing her dreary ministrations and returning to "Charlie." So deeply repressed as to be absolutely unaware of her lesbianism, Olive can only conceive that heterosexual attraction is a testament to the male ego's essential rapacity and the blind ignorance of its object.

Ransom is a veteran of the late war; the scion of a fallen plantation family, come to New York to redeem his fortunes. He struggles on the brink of failure as an attorney, while scribbling high-minded broadsides on the nation's sunken ideals. He yearns for greatness in a grim, quiet way. His detractors rag him for lagging several centuries behind the liberal times. According to his own chilling estimate, he is that much ahead.

In the novel's remarkable opening scenes, James subtly limns the hash of motives that compels Olive to bring a strange, dangerous bird like her cousin across her doorstep. Olive's cherished fantasies spring from a yeasty compost of altruism, misanthropy, masochism. She fairly burns for martyrdom; St. Joan is her ego-ideal. From a distance, Ransom seems a fitting enough object for her charity, like her housemaids. But in person he appeals obcurely to a vast potential for gratuitous suffering. A joking, deeply unrepentant conservative, he opposes every issue that has sent her to the barricades.

There's also an indefinable whiff of danger about the man: his startling sexuality challenges her very being—he's the personification of every "Charlie" who mocked her labors. Nearly instantly, she fears and loaths him almost as much as he dislikes her. Yet, in a triumph of perversity, the two cannot be quite quit of each other. Out of a wish to reform him (more likely, the counterphobic drive to grapple with the very danger she intuits), Olive tenders Ransom an invitation to her feminist salon. He accepts with alarming alacrity. Her panic attack in the carriage bearing them to the meeting and Verena's lecture is prescient of coming disaster.

Both Olive and Ransom immediately fall captive to Verena Tarrant's charms. Olive is so smitten she asks Verena to live with her, paying off her parents discretely. During the next few years, Olive educates the pliable oratrix in feminist history, lending a substance to her discourse it previously lacked. Drab, painfully shy and completely humorless, Olive intends that Verena shall be her clarion/avatar. Verena' physical presence clearly intoxicates her, but her desire is totally sublimated through intellectual exercise. Each woman remains poignantly unaware she has entered into an unconsummated Boston marriage.

Meanwhile, Ransom's New York business affairs limp along and he goes unpublished. Verena is not much consciously on his mind, but she has never really left it either. During a business trip to Boston, he impulsively contrives to visit her, engendering one of the most perceptively drawn wooings in literature—as satisfying in its own way as Tolstoy's account of the Levin-Kitty infatuation in *Anna Karenina*.

Olive entreats Verena to resist Ransom with every means at her command, waxing increasingly desperate as her "ward" slips away. In the early days of Ransom's courtship, Verena deludes herself into believing she, too, only seeks to convert him. But it's she who turns and turns again. Small perfidies to spare Olive's feelings give way to major deceptions, broken promises, then hysterical pleas for rescue. All to no avail: the relentlessly ardent southerner pursues Verena to the seaside hamlet where Olive's entourage is summering, and tramples down her defenses. At length he wins her heart and demands a fearful price for his devotion. He has finally been published; plans to enter politics, and will not abide a wife who espouses abhorrent views, most particularly in public. Verena must cease her lectures and be content to keep his house.

On the heels of this terrible demand, the death of the admired abolitionist Miss Birdseye seems to compromise Ransom's victory. Olive bears Verena off to prepare the launching of her first major speaking tour at Boston Music Hall. But at the eleventh hour, Verena cannot bring herself to go on. Ransom spirits her away, in tears, to "a union, so far from brilliant . . . [that] these were not the last she was destined to shed." Olive is left to endure the martyrdom she has desired so mightily. "I am going to be hissed and hooted and insulted!" she flings over her shoulder at her departing cousin. James mordantly notes that a respectful hush attends Olive's entrance on the stage: "It was not apparent they were likely to hurl the benches at her . . . even when exasperated, a Boston audience is not ungenerous."[1]

James leaves no doubt about the infelicitous future of a marriage that embodies the triumph of hormones over good sense. Levin and Kitty are made for each other, matched nicely in personality and passion. But it appears inevitable that Ransom and Verena will unmake each other, once the hectic flush of courtship fades. Her exuberant spirit cannot thrive under Ransom's rule. She will probably slide into depression if she persists in submitting to his rule. Should she rebel, Ransom will daily confront in his drawing room the adversary he thirsts to do battle with in the public arena, with far less delight.

I infer Verena's continuing docility and despair as the probable course of this disastrous union. For all her verve, there is an anxious softness central to her character, a fatal desire to yield. No wonder: she is a mesmerist's daughter! James inscribes Selah Tarrant and his wife at the margin of his tale. Olive buys Verena's parents off, Ransom tenders them little notice of his suit. The author virtually ignores them after his scathing initial biography.

Freud demonstrated that the dreamwork defensively projects key conflictual elements into the dream's periphery. Their marginalized symbolic elaborations are then likely to be perceived by the dreamer as trivial when, in fact, they are often crucial to translating the dream's meaning. The narrative work of *The Bostonians* casts the elder Tarrants into an analogous fictive periphery. Nevertheless, they—or, more precisely, Verena's percepts and introjects of them—hold the key to understanding her tortuous involvement with two late-adolescent love objects, and her ultimate election of Ransom.

James paints Selah Tarrant as a minor charismatic sociopath who entranced his addled wife with promises of a brilliant career in some unspecified limelight. Instead, he has barely eked out a living at the edge of the reform movement, passing from one bunkum enterprise to another. Mesmerism allows him to exercise his native grandiosity while dominating others and reaping small profit. His wife has grown dissatisfied at the cheating of her hopes, but there is no evidence she has ever ceased looking up to her low down spouse.

Verena has been a devoted child to both her parents, despite her vaudeville upbringing. In late adolescence she still remains remarkably uncritical of them. Although she has embarked upon a career in the wider world, she is still heavily dependent upon the Tarrants (and they upon her); so far admiring of Selah (and unsure of herself) that she permits him the ignobility of mesmerically "starting her up" like a ventriloquist's dummy.

From her parents and their fringe associates, Verena has taken instruction in fashionable leftist philosophies of the day. The participants in the women's movement she meets at her first lectures lay the groundwork for transition, until Olive Chancellor's infatuation provides the decisive leverage for her to leave home. Ostensibly, she is now freer to speak for herself, unencumbered by her father's absurd, stifling presence.

However, Verena is far from being her own person. The Tarrants saw her as their meal ticket. Olive, while not as crassly exploitative, still neglects Verena's "otherness" to actualize her own unconscious vision of Verena as the charismatic spokesperson she can never be. She's poignantly unaware that her "arrangement" with Verena must be provisional, given the latter's exuberant heterosexuality. Olive basks in a sublimated fantasy of eternal big-sisterhood. In characteristic adolescent fashion, Verena draws strength from her friend's intelligence and fortitude, while chafing at the mounting repression of Olive's tutelage.

Under healthier circumstances, Verena would inevitably leave Olive, strike out on her own, possibly even become involved with a man of likeminded politics. She is actually offered such an opportunity by Henry Burrage, a wealthy New Yorker dabbling at Harvard. Although affable enough, Burrage possesses not a jot of Ransom's formidable sexual appeal. Nor does marriage to Burrage offer the neurotic possibilities for ego submersion afforded by Ransom (an element of domination is supplied by Burrage's mother, a socialite matriarch who would rule her son by matching him with a partner she deems an equal lightweight!).

Through her commitment to Ransom, Verena tragically pitches away the promise of her youth. She retraces her steps to the entrapment of her origins, attempting to resolve early conflict by marrying it. She grew up witnessing a ruthless scoundrel lording it over a foolish woman who could only realize a diminished identity through his dubious achievement. Quite possibly she identified with her mother's subsidiary role even as she competed with her.

Now she undertakes marriage to her father's double, a man of inordinate ambition and second-rate ideas, whose deferential attitude toward women is the obverse of his monumental chauvinism. Although not en-

tirely insensitive, Ransom proposes—entirely for her good as he con-
strues it—to subject Verena to the enslavement her oratory censures.
Thus she passes from being Selah's dummy, through a somewhat healthier detour as Olive's vocal alter ego, to take up her old role again as Ransom's domestic dummy. Hardly the stuff of comedy.

The Ismail Merchant/James Ivory screen version of *The Bostonians* (1984)
has been hailed for its fidelity to James's fiction. I have commented on the
novel at some length precisely because the film quietly ignores or departs
from its source in several significant respects. I hope to show that the
result, while a jewel for viewing, is deeply subversive of James's designs.

The complex first-person narrative scheme of *The Bostonians* poses
well-nigh insurmountable resistance to adaptation, not unlike the inherent problem of translating John Fowles's convoluted first personage in
The French Lieutenant's Woman. I mark at least *two* first personae in *The
Bostonians*: one is summarily detached, mimicking the narration of classic Hollywood cinema, which erases the signs of its presence to foster the
spectatorial illusion of unmanipulated reality.

James's "second" narrator descends from the Olympian stance of the
"first" to flutter helplessly over the action; one associates to Franklin
Pangborn, Edward Everett Horton, and those other genteel capons in
thirties and forties cinema, who fussed off to the side while the protagonists pursued the plot's main business. Here, for instance, is James
describing Verena and Ransom in the midst of an overheated exchange
during their Central Park excursion:

> If the moment I speak of had lasted a few seconds longer, I know not what mon-
> strous proceeding . . . it would have been my difficult duty to describe; it was
> fortunately arrested by the arrival of a nursery-maid pushing a perambulator and
> accompanied by an infant who toddled in her wake.[2]

Such fusty meddling creates unsettling contradictions: James cleverly
disavows/affirms authorial presence and "responsibility." He inscribes
himself at the edge of his narrative, constructing a congenial, fuddy-
duddy identity which appears to dissociate him from his characters as if
they followed their tangled destinies on their own.

This is, oddly enough, the space inhabited by Selah Tarrant. *But Tarrant is James's dummy, and James the ghost in the machine, "onlie begetter" of the
tale, of the manipulations and depredations practiced upon Verena Tarrant with
her unconscious collusion.* The apt cinematic analogy, therefore, is *not to*

Horton and Pangborn, but the Hitchcock of *Psycho*. At the beginning of that bleak masterpiece, he shows his avuncular presence boarding a bus. Having quit the scene in the flesh, he reassumes a godlike directorial stance. He constructs, as from above, a complex chain of exploitation and abuse, culminating in Janet Leigh's brutal murder, in which both her character and the uneasy spectator are made to seem complicit.[3]

Ruth Prawer Jhabvala's adaptation does not attempt to capture the ambiguities of James's narrative position; perhaps, as I have suggested, this lies beyond adaptation. If the savage repression of Verena's identity were more accurately limned as the horror in the drawing room James implies, the genteel elegance of the mise-en-scène might be sub-liminally perceived as gloss, concealment—visual counterpart to the rococo flourishes of James's "civilized" narrator. As it is, the surroundings remain just that, prettily "authentic."

The film's central failures reside in a simplistic rendering of Verena and Ransom's characters, articulated with a conventional romantic reading of a much darker text. Directorial viewpoint, adaptation, and casting are all responsible for these derelictions. Ivory and Jhabvala lighten up Ransom's unpleasant, bullying aspect and turn him into a Harlequin-novel staple: the dashing Confederate swain, Rhett Butler-cum-ideology, who sweeps away the heroine's objections and whisks her off to magnolia heaven.

Christopher Reeve is not bad playing this type: he has the looks, the gaze, and most of the accent. Reeve often brings an ingenuous intensity to his romantic roles which I found unexpectedly moving in *Superman* (1978) and *Superman II* (1980). However, his screen persona is so reso-lutely amiable as to defeat any representation of villainy, even the faintest hint of meanness. He was disastrous as the psychopathic minion of *Deathtrap* (1982). In *The Bostonians* it is not that he is bad, but that he's so adept at the film's misprision of Ransom.

Madeline Potter's Verena constitutes a double inadequacy, both as the romantic heroine the script intends (a function of Potter's serious limita-tions, at least in this role), and the talented, conflicted late-adolescent that James wrote about (a failure owing to Jhabvala's maladroit adapta-tion). She is physically unsuited for the part—it would be more correct to say she is unsuited for Reeve. She projects not a spark of sexuality, and her expression, as the old theatrical gibe goes, runs the gamut from *A* to *B*. She mainly simpers, and one quickly tires of her. It is hard to believe that Ransom wouldn't be turned off, too.

Vanessa Redgrave's Olive Chancellor nearly redeems the entire project. One simply could not imagine another actress taking the part after this exquisite realization. Redgrave has the right physical characteristics, uncannily captures Olive's gaunt rectitude, her perennially rattled nerves, the absurd excesses of her commitments, the almost touching naivete of her sublimations. Such zealots become painfully vulnerable when the heart is finally awakened, dangerously morbid when love departs. Redgrave's desperation, as she intuits Verena's drift during Ransom's summer siege, is absolutely heartbreaking.

However, serious questions must be raised about the blatancy with which Olive's profoundly latent homosexuality is trumpeted at a modern audience. Olive and Verena are constantly surprised in decorous clinches. The New York boardinghouse scene that has them languishing about in chemises is nearly situated within the conventions of soft porn. James needs very few words, none of them explicit, to tell us everything we need to know about Olive's sexual preferences. Measuring the general wrongheadedness of the adaptation against Redgrave's sensibility, one extrapolates that the responsibility for vulgarly underscoring Olive's lesbianism should be properly assigned to the former.

The finale of the cinematic version of *The Bostonians* compounds the numerous errors that began with the amputation of the vital establishing scenes between Ransom and Olive before the salon. After she commits herself to Ransom, Verena's tears are hardly glimpsed; the crucial inference of her future unhappiness, which James draws in the last line of his novel, cannot easily be construed from Ivory's direction. The Boston Music Hall audience is outraged, and does indeed appear ready to hurl benches, until Olive ascends the podium and gives a ringing speech affirming the feminist cause. Plunged into sorrow, she nevertheless is resolved to carry on the good work alone. The film considerably softens James's emphasis of Olive's masochism and thirst for martyrdom, in aid of applauding her heroism. This is by no means an insignificant lapse.

In the novel, Ransom experiences a rare moment of compassion after he realizes he has won Verena; he is gladdened that the crowd does not humiliate Olive. The film actually takes a much more patronizing attitude toward her by portraying Olive's bravery before the audience's extreme displeasure. It first implies that Verena's choice of heterosexual romance with the dashing southerner is "healthier" than the barren sublimations of her Boston marriage: this denies that Verena's motives for wedding Ransom are more neurotic than the forces that impelled her

toward Olive. Olive then quickly recoups Verena's loss through identifying with her, emerging triumphant with her own political "voice."

The film text thus unravels around two contradictory ideological
positions. The first, appropriate to its construction of a liberal view-
er/subject, is fashionably feminist; the second is unregenerately sexist—
betraying the patriarchal taint of pseudo-reformist cinema like *Personal
Best* (1982). According to this bias, lesbianism may be marginally acceptable as a holding operation or transitional state until Mr. Right
comes along. An "authentically" gay woman like Olive who dares to intrude into heterosexual territory may garner a few crumbs from the
table. But inevitably she winds up a lonely ideologue, or with her
damaged sisterhood in some semi-sordid lifestyle consonant with her
second-rate sexuality.

Although his conservatism softened later in his life, James had no
qualms about his opinions on the women's movement when he wrote his
novel. His views were probably as derisive as Ransom's, embodied in his
satiric depiction of the radical salon where Olive and Ransom meet Verena. However, the author's concerns in *The Bostonians* were *not* primarily
polemic. The politics of his characters interests him less than their psychology. Ideological conflict provides a backdrop against which the savage struggle between Ransom and Olive for possession of Verena Tarrant's spirit is played out.

James's vision of Olive is lucid and sure. He is not uncomfortable with
her misanthropy, does not worry about offending a liberal audience, and
suffers no compunction to redeem or reward her after Verena flees with
Ransom into the night. Consequently, his final picture of her is infinitely more honest, psychologically richer, and more ambiguous than the
film's.

In the novel, Olive reacts to the devastating narcissistic injury of Verena's loss not with brave rhetoric, but by retreating into masochistic
grandiosity. Savaged by Verena's defection, she savors the expectation of
further punishment from the abandoned spectators she identifies with.
She projects upon them a rage which, ironically, they do not vent upon
her. This is where James leaves her and where I believe she should be left.
Her triumphant speech in the film does as much disservice to James's
purposes as did Nahum Tate's "improved" ending of *King Lear* to Shakespeare's.

After one of the more yahoo cinema summers on record, hallmarked
by the sadistic inanities of *Indiana Jones and the Temple of Doom* (1986), I

wanted to like a film with the substantial intentions of *The Bostonians* better. But intentions are no substitute for substance. The Ivory/Merchant production is visually stunning—especially the scenes shot on Martha's Vineyard. It is not without other pleasures. But besides being ideologically suspect, it offers at base only the romantic frissons of the latest regency or gothic potboiler, instead of James's strange, rather sinister history.

Addendum: James's appraisal of *The Bostonians'* minor characters is particularly shrewd. In this respect, the film matches its source, both in adaptation and interpretation. Wesley Addey has been a largely unsung mainstay of Broadway and Hollywood for decades and a particular favorite of mine. Since Selah Tarrant figures so large in the above exegesis, I was happy to see the vile mesmerist deftly unmasked by Addey; he does a marvelous quick study in humbug cupidity. Other acute performances include: Nancy Marchand as the formidable Mrs. Burrage; Linda Hunt as Dr. Prance, the skeptical "doctress" attending the feminist community; Jessica Tandy as the aging abolitionist, Miss Birdseye; and Wallace Shawn as Matthew Pardon, an impertinent journalist.

Afterword

Despite its signal importance to the industry, adaptation has been scanted by film scholars until recently. Most discussion has focused on the treatment of literary texts. A critical majority formerly believed that cinematic intrusions into fiction—the classic novel in particular—were bound to be naive and clumsy by the very nature of the practice that spawned them. Even a few earlier film critics joined the literati in claiming that the psychological depth of a canonic novel could never be achieved on film.

There has certainly been no lack of maladroit Hollywood adaptations. But filmic interpretation of the printed page has often proven quite faithful in spirit and pure representation, even providing unexpected highlights/insights about the original in peculiarly cinematic terms.

By now, it is generally conceded that differences in receiving and interpreting words, as opposed to the moving image, do not warrant the facile conclusion that reading a book is less passive; engages the better part of intellect; is somehow a nobler process than the no less complex act of reading screened images. Most film and literary scholars have abandoned the elitism of yesterday in favor of more reasoned approaches to adaptation, employing the instruments of semiology, psychoanalysis, and other sophisticated strategies.

Rather than berate adaptors for their failures, critics should more properly recognize that they themselves "have been indolent about creating a vocabulary to articulate the characteristic qualities of cinema," according to Peary and Shatzkin.[4] Unpolemic comparisons between novel and film novelization are drawn in their collection of essays, and in a number of other excellent studies.[5]

This body of work illustrates cinematic analogies to literary devices, and facilitates understanding of the unique processes through which cinema enunciates narrative. My inquiry into *The Bostonians* was implicitly directed toward such ends. I continue to find its sense of James's purposes deeply flawed, both formally, psychologically, and ideologically. Ivory/Merchant's *A Room with a View* (1986) serves E. M. Forster far better.

8

On the McMovie: Less Is Less at the Simplex

FIRST SALESMAN: I sold those sardines I bought from you to the A&P for three dollars a tin.
SECOND SALESMAN: That's great! You only paid me a dollar a tin!!
FIRST SALESMAN: Yeah—but now customers are complaining they taste awful!
SECOND SALESMAN (*blanching*): Taste awful? Those sardines weren't for *eating*—they were for buying and selling!!! —Old joke

In the Huxleyan prophecy, Big Brother does not watch us, by his choice. We watch him, by ours.
—Neil Postman, *Amusing Ourselves to Death*

Sylvester Stallone, as the eponymous
hero of an exemplary McMovie, *Cobra*
(1986): "The emptiness of these
characters—another core aspect of the
narcissistic personality—is formidable.
With their constricted speech and
limited interpersonal repertoire, they
appear crafted from air."

*H*ollywood has been accused of pandering to lumpen taste, only to have its efforts lauded at a later point. Movies once deemed egregious trash are now venerated as genre classics, and are sifted for potent significations. A critic is thus wary about rendering yet another terminal diagnosis of an industry that has recuperated so often from dire critical appraisal, let alone box office disaster. Nevertheless, it does seem to many observers in and outside Hollywood that American motion pictures have been steadily declining in quality for some time.

Kael's benchmark 1981 New Yorker piece, "Why Are Movies So Bad," as well as recent articles by Denby, Shales, and others, speaks not to a temporary crisis, but to a fundamental, possibly durable deterioration in the Hollywood film.[1] It has also been suggested that, beyond critical discontent, general audiences are growing disaffected with the trivia regularly served up at the local sixplex. Without citing his sources, Denby states that: "Many adult moviegoers—and perhaps some of the kids, too—. . . feel abandoned and betrayed. They continue going, of course, because they have to go to *something,* but they aren't necessarily happy. American movies, the liveliest in the world a decade ago, have become an object of contempt."[2]

The subject of this chapter is an arch-signifier of Hollywood's compromised quality—a film hallmarked by a monumental vacuity, a per-

This essay was written in 1986 and first printed at the annual meeting of the American Psychiatric Association in 1987.

vasive impoverishment of means, ends, and ideology which cuts across genre. I characterize it as a "McMovie," analog to the nutritional replicants hawked by America's fast-food monoliths. Like the selling of the Big Mac, merchandising the McMovie is privileged over its content. The shortfall between huckster's promise and the product's bankrupt reality is correspondingly blatant.

The McMovie does not properly fit into that idiosyncratic category of the "good" bad film—the intriguing failure shown to general audiences, or memorably awful picture exhibited on the schlock/exploitation circuit. Some McMovies are not without momentary pleasures. Others are unrelievedly awful. But all ring with a distinctive hollowness, a dull inability to move the viewer—if only to hilarity—that sets them apart from pictures like *Mommie Dearest* (1981) or *They Saved Hitler's Brain* (1963).

The above critics have described several features of the McMovie passim, in the context of commenting on the causes of Hollywood's perilous condition. I will first discuss McMovie phenomenology at length, then expand upon the reasons already advanced for its emergence. A central psychoanalytic focus of my analysis is the unbridled narcissism of many McMovie protagonists. I will explore the disturbing implications of this finding with respect to the psyches of McMovie viewers, makers, and producers, as well as the collective cultural ethos.

McMovie Categories

By their very nature McMovies are grossly imitative. They are chiefly encountered in purest culture as either (a) obvious sequels, or (b) unattributed rehashes or downright rip-offs of more substantial, or at least more interesting earlier "action" and "weird" genre films. Prevailing McMovie categories are briefly described as follows.[3]

1. War, cop, and urban vigilante movies: *Rambo: First Blood Part II* (1985), *Top Gun* (1986), *Iron Eagle* (1986), *Invasion U.S.A.* (1985), *Commando* (1986), *Sudden Impact* (1983), *Year of the Dragon* (1985), *Cobra* (1986), *Death Wish II, 3,* and *4* (1982, 1985, 1987), and *The Exterminator I* and *II* (1980, 1984).

These films overtly reprise or echo financially (and often artistically) successful pictures of the last two decades (*First Blood* [1982], *Dirty Harry* [1971], *Death Wish* [1974], *Serpico* [1973], *The French Connection* [1971]). They often move the original's ideology to the rabid right, reflecting the current simplistic conservative thrust in American politics.

"New Decaturist" films like *Rambo* also recapitulate the narrative strategies and jingoism of World War II agitprop.[4]

2. Adventure, spy, western, and "fight" movies: *Indiana Jones and the Temple of Doom* (1984), the later James Bond films (notably *Octopussy* [1983] and *View to a Kill* [1985]), *Heaven's Gate* (1980), *Pale Rider* (1985), *Rocky III* (1982), and, particularly, *Rocky IV* (1985). Many of these films exhibit more covert rightist tendencies than their military counterparts.

3. "Splatter" and science-fiction classics: *A Nightmare on Elm Street 2* and *3* (1985, 1987), *The Hills Have Eyes, Part II* (1984), *Texas Chainsaw Massacre 2* (1986), the entire *Friday the 13th* series, *Halloween II* and *III* (1981, 1983), *Return of the Jedi* (1983), and *Aliens* (1986).

4. Films privileging the test of adolescent or young adult athletic skill—a "you-can-do-it, go-for-it, kid!" subgenre: *Flashdance* (1983), *Breakin' 2: Electric Boogaloo* (1984), *American Anthem* (1986), *Quicksilver* (1986), *The Karate Kid, Part II* (1986) and *Part III* (1989).

These pictures are also rehashes of recent worthier films—*Saturday Night Fever* (1977), *Breaking Away* (1979), *The Karate Kid* (1984), so forth. Earlier precedents for the current rash of adolescent show-biz McMovies are found in vintage thirties and forties musicals wherein neighborhood teenagers, sanctioned by one cause or another, decided to "*have a show!*"

5. Various "star" vehicles of mixed or anomalous genre such as *Rhinestone* (1984) and *Fever Pitch* (1985).

6. Teen and preteen educational/sexual "rites-of-passage" pictures: *Porky's I, Porky's II: The Next Day, Porky's Revenge* (1981, 1983, 1985), *My Science Project* (1985), and *Weird Science* (1985).

7. Spielberg or Spielberg-cloned films privileging the folkways of childhood, notably the travails and triumphs of misunderstood or "misfit" children, such as *The Goonies* (1985), among others.

Anatomy of the McMovie

The following attributes typify the classic McMovie (films categorized in this chapter as "semi-McMovies" contain many McMovie characteristics, but own greater coherence and some redeeming value, if only as entertainment (e.g., *Beverly Hills Cop* [1984], *The Breakfast Club* [1985], *Romancing the Stone* [1984]). A fair case can be made that most mainstream Hollywood pictures today are at least semi-McMovies.

Unlike earlier "bad-bad" pictures made on the cheap, the McMovie may look and sound slickly credible, since it is often crafted with the solid technical expertise bought by twenty or more millions of dollars. However, its narrative, character portrayal, and dialogue suffer from a ubiquitous barrenness. It lacks the symbolic evocations or psychological resonances of a picture by a minimalist master like Bresson, or even of a taut film noir.

The McMovie's plotting is spare, with a paucity of subplotting (e.g., depressed Valley Girl transplanted to Manhattan meets black ex–jumprope champ-cum-waitress, sweats buckets, gets crowned Doubledutch Queen of New York). The narrative, especially of sequel McMovies, has a curious perfunctory quality. It seems to exist merely to set the scene for outbreaks of military or urban violence, break dancing, slice-and-dicing, and special effects.

Loose plot ends and insufficiently developed characters are left dangling, as if the scriptwriter had forgotten—or simply ceased caring—about them.

Nick Nolte's girlfriend in *48 Hours* ([1982], a semi-McMovie), is played by Anette O'Toole. The character is strongly established at the outset as an astringently intelligent foil for Nolte's crudity. Then she inexplicably diminishes into a nagging voice on a barroom phone, a brief target of the hero's sexist put-downs and hang-ups. By the end of the film, she exists virtually under the sign of erasure.

The screenplay contains inconsistencies or downright absurdities. Plot premises seem to dissolve out of sheer sloppiness, lack of rigor—as if the thirst for action, laughs, or complex special effects has shorted out the writer's logic circuits.

In *Cobra* Nietzchean psychotics vow to purge society of its "weaklings." They proceed to kill young and old, black and white, male and female, strong or weak alike. Nowhere is it implied that the group's indiscriminate choice of victims is an ironic reflection upon the barbarism underpinning its leader's windy philosophizing.

In *Invasion U.S.A.,* a Russian spymaster masterminds the infiltration of America by a terrorist army, arguably the most *visible* secret force ever filmed. The spy's nemesis is Chuck Norris, a scruffy G-man. Norris holes up at Atlanta police headquarters and challenges the enraged Russian to a terminal shoot-out. The terrorists—played by possibly the entire Yugoslav and Spanish military— are drawn into a killing zone and wiped out by Norris, with some help from the National Guard.

McMovies are replete with coarse *allusions* to other movies. In attributed sequels, these serve to jog the viewer's presumed defective memory about the previous film. Allusions may also be deployed to confer upon the McMovie a cachet of excellence, or at least success, by association.[5]

Aliens (1986) was written and directed by James Cameron, who also co-wrote *Rambo* and directed *The Terminator* (1984). Among many citations of *Rambo* in *Aliens:* an elite task force of galactic "Colonial Marines" is outfitted like American soldiers from the Vietnam conflict. The "grunts" form up before entering their interstellar troop carrier with much macho posturing, ramming home of phallic rifle-bolts, lashing on of armor—reminiscent of Rambo's preparations before entering the plane returning him to Nam. Scenes of the aliens' juggernaut attack, and their "queen's" shocking resurrection after her supposed incineration, allude to corresponding scenes from *Alien* (1979) and *The Terminator.*

The McMovie's pacing is faster, with more shots per scene and more scenes overall than the average Hollywood narrative of previous years. Acceleration of pace and increase in shot density combines with other aspects/defects to give the McMovie a distinctively fragmented texture.

McMovie music is louder, and plays at this higher decibel level for longer intervals than in classic Hollywood cinema, as does the sound of gunfire, explosions, automobile and airplane engines in chase sequences, so forth.

Character development in the McMovie is pared to the barest essentials required for suturing the viewer into genre conventions, a tendency most evident in the McMovie sequel. Items of dress, weaponry, stylized expressions or gestures epitomize character in cartoon strokes. Potent visual metaphors that were originally coupled with strong scripts inspire no enduring interest in spin-off McMovies. When stale, illogical narrative fails to flesh out character or motivation, Indiana Jones's whip and Eastwood's squint degenerate into empty iconography.

The McMovie's utterance is minimal and often peculiarly stilted. Vocabulary is moderately to radically constricted. The sheer number of words may actually be increased in the discourse of adolescent or preadolescent McMovies like *The Goonies,* but the overall verbal variety of this pubescent babble is sharply reduced.

Within the McMovie action genres, discourse is frequently stunted, guttural and of the gutter. Fewer words and shorter sentences constitute a peculiar cinematic Newspeak. Heroes are prone to clipped assertions of courage or contempt. Dirty Harry's punk putdown ("Go ahead, *make my day"*), Rambo's Wilshire Boulevard koan ("To win war, you have to become war") may thus be read as verbal parallels to visual signatures of costume or armament.

Such strutting epigrams—discovered most frequently in the cop, urban vigilante, military, and adventure subgenres—testify to the *self-inflation of many McMovie adult male protagonists*. Taken with other presenting problems, it warrants the diagnosis of *narcissistic personality disorder.*[6]

The origins of this entity continue to puzzle analytic theoreticians.[7] Nature and nurture have been variously invoked in ascribing pathological narcissism to:

1. Obscure constitutional influences that might intensify oral aggression, heighten vulnerability to anxiety—especially related to aggressive impulses—and/or enhance native narcissistic supplies.

2. Failure of the mother or mother-surrogate to respond empathically to testaments of the child's selfhood. (An unbiased psychoanalysis would presume that a parent or surrogate of either sex in an intimate caretaking role could exert similar toxic effects.) Because of excessive withdrawal, intrusion, or a mixture of the two, the parent is unavailable for reliable introjection and integration into the child's healthy narcissistic matrix.

3. The mother's (or her surrogate's) vision of the child as touchstone, fulfillment of her own bristling narcissism, allied with some real or imagined quality of "specialness" in the child looks, talent, so forth. Once the child has been rated an immensely valuable "thing"/commodity, he/she comes to identify with the self-aggrandizing aggressor, perceives him/herself as hollowly magnificent, and views others as dumb objects to be charmed, manipulated, exploited.

4. Being reared in family circumstances redolent with entitlement, in which family members inappropriately stroke each other's narcissism to a high gloss, and generally fail to initiate the child into necessary recognition of the rights and needs of others.

It is not unreasonable to assume that each narcissist presents a unique compost of these factors, articulated with noxious influences from contemporary culture (see below).

The very existence, let alone the causes of his narcissism are of negligible concern to the action McMovie hero. Like his real-life clinical counterpart, he perceives little if any problem within. Any reasons for interpersonal distress are likely to be located squarely in the outside world.

Kernberg analyzes the enormous capacity of pathological narcissists for projection, projective identification, and withering devaluation, when he notes that in narcissistic personality disorder "the normal tension between actual self on the one hand, and ideal self and ideal object on the other, is eliminated by the building up of an inflated self concept within which the actual self and the ideal self and ideal object are confused. At the same time, the remnants of the unacceptable self images are repressed and projected onto external objects, which are devaluated."[8] Significant warping of superego development is an ominous outcome of the pathological fusion between ideal self, ideal object, and actual self-images. Integration of the superego is compromised

because the process of idealization is highly unrealistic, preventing the condensation of such idealized images with actual parental demands and with the aggressively determined superego forerunners. Also, actual self-images, a part of the ego structure, are now pathologically condensed with the forerunners of the superego, and . . . interfere with the normal differentiation of the superego and ego. Although some superego components are internalized, such as prohibitive parental demands, they preserve a distorted, primitive aggressive quality because they are not integrated with the living aspects of the superego which are normally drawn from the ideal self and object images . . . [that] are missing in these patients."[9]

In an intriguing parallel to the pathological narcissist's intrapsychic "script," many McMovie action genre scenarios justify the hero's absorption in his own purposes, and rationalize an appalling aggressivity, rife with paranoia, into "righteous" retaliation. Narcissistic entitlement and rage become *données,* absolutely syntonic to character and text. The hero's outbursts of untrammeled violence are repeatedly aimed at vile punks, ghouls, or "gooks" who richly deserve to "get theirs."

The narcissistic character disturbance is hallmarked by a grandiose sense of self-importance and uniqueness, an inordinate preoccupation with fantasies of overweening power, attractiveness, or intellectual brilliance. Apposite to the perennial distrust of pure intellect in American popular fictions, the action McMovie is more likely to privilege its hero's courage and brawn over brains (although a degree of cleverness in pursuit of the enemy is sanctioned). Two distinct types emerge.

The "Dirty Harry" heroic figure arrogantly flaunts his possession of the skills and guts to do society's dirty work. His scornful devaluation is directed beyond the criminal element at less venturesome colleagues, or hypocritical do-gooders who condemn him until desperate circumstances force his services upon them. Alternately, the hero is self-sacrific-ing, modest about his vast potency, a rock of manly dignity—like Rocky or the anonymous "Preacher" of *Pale Rider*. In this case, the humility compelled by the script is frequently belied by the steely egotism of the actor shining through his character.

These men manifest the narcissistic personality's cool indifference, resolute lack of empathy, exploitativeness, and disregard for the personal integrity of all save themselves. But a deadly "mission" undertaken for the common good usually mandates their behavior—hunting down ur-ban "scum" or terrorists, or searching out MIAs in postwar Vietnam. The mission is undertaken alone, or with the help of a similarly inclined buddy who often winds up killed or wounded (Dirty Harry's partners), or rendered hors de combat in some other fashion (Colonel Trautman in-*Rambo*). Away from the mission, many heroes live alone, in sketchy sur-roundings with no lover and few friends.

These narrative locutions may be interpreted psychoanalytically as elaborations on, and covert rationales for, the overwhelming fear of de-pendency that is often a core dynamic in pathological narcissism. For the narcissistic personality, dependency threatens exposure to the depreda-tions of the "Other"—reincarnation of a depressed, withholding, or coldly spiteful parent, also perhaps an embodiment of the patient's sim-ilar dark inclinations, now disavowed and projected.

The McMovie hero can be allowed to depend on a buddy only because the buddy is the hero's narcissistic *mirror,* a filmic version of the nar-cissistic patient's "pseudo-friendship," in which another party is per-ceived merely as a reflection of the patient's grandiosity. Thus, the Cobretti/Stallone sidekick in *Cobra* enthusiastically endorses his men-tor's marginal lifestyle, his derisive view of superiors and media liberals, and his murderous willingness to break laws in order to enforce them.

The arrogant hero revels in the role of despised outsider. Various tex-tual strategies contrive to force the humble hero into the role of per-secuted scapegoat, like Rambo or Paul Kersey of the *Death Wish* series. Arrogant or humble, the hero acts with godlike assurance, a law unto himself, a menace to foe and friend alike. His aggressive risk-taking es-calates even further after suffering defeat or humiliation (another classic signet of hypertrophied narcissism). When the hero's enterprise is sub-verted by a vicious enemy, the hero's reactive viciousness is implicitly abscribed to a necessary identification with despicable foes:

In *Year of the Dragon,* Stan White, a top New York detective, is assigned to rid Chinatown of tong rule. His passion for justice thinly conceals a megalomanic thirst for triumph over his adversary, a rabidly ambitious young gang boss. His brash provocation precipitates the murders of his wife and several peers, then the brutal rape of his TV journalist girlfriend. He is ubiquitously condemned until a final bloody victory completely redeems his reputation and romance.

Consonant with the narcissistic personality's exhibitionism and craving for the limelight, the camera lingers lovingly over the action McMovie hero, often over his uncovered body—as in *Rambo*'s traveling shot down Stallone's biceps, or in *Top Gun*'s ample display of its aviators' pectorals and buttocks.

The audience's gaze is directed at the hero as it once was fixed upon the dangerous ladies of forties cinema. Hayworth in *Gilda* (1946) and Stanwyck in *Double Indemnity* (1944) were transfixed by the camera's "look"—temptation for male viewers, flawed ideal-cum-object-lesson for women.[10] Their seductive menace was terminally neutralized through marriage, imprisonment, or death. But the McMovie's narcissistic "hunk" is stroked by the camera solely toward his elevation; admired by men, worshiped by women for his literal and figurative "balls."

The macho McMovie hero does not speak to, but at or through others. His discourse is more appropriate to belligerent threat or profane putdown than ordinary conversation. His grinding lack of empathy renders intimate dialogue more unnerving and disjunctive. In *Top Gun,* Tom Cruise says all the right words to Kelly McGillis, but transmits not a jot of tenderness, nor elicits any corresponding spark. The narcissism of the actor, *not* merely of the brash aviator he plays, feels so entrenched that the hero's repentance after the death of his best friend rings singularly unconvincing. Because of the blare of his ego, Stallone's chaste love scenes with his beautiful Vietnamese contra in *Rambo* register equally invalid.

The emptiness of these characters—another core aspect of the narcissistic personality—is formidable. With their constricted speech and limited interpersonal repertoire, they appear crafted from air. Their home environments—if they have homes—are literally barren, or barrenly ridden by convention as in the *Rocky* sequels. Those relationships they are allowed are impoverished and stilted. They are work- or "mission"-consumed; manifestly bored away from the dangers of the job, if they are ever shown in this capacity. They exist mainly for frenzied pursuit or cruel combat. The script has them caring not a whit for the general praise or blame attendant upon their progress, but it is in the swirl of this attention that they truly come alive.

Past Hollywood action genre heroes possessed some of these tendencies—e.g., the protagonists of Howard Hawks's films—but owned far more substance. If Popeye Doyle of *The French Connection* (1971) lived like a slob, related poorly, and only thought of putting an elegant drug czar behind bars, the *character* was at least created in depth.

Narcissistic tendencies in youth-oriented McMovies are not as toxic as in adult action genres, and are generally more in accord with the developmental vicissitudes of adolescence. [11] Adolescent self-absorption can be accompanied by considerable grandiosity and insensitivity toward others. Substantial self-inflation may occur whenever teenagers are gripped by a typical "dream of glory" related to some romantic, athletic, creative, or spiritual pursuit. With time and maturation, most youngsters revert to a more modest view of the self and its powers.

In the "you-can-do-it" McMovie, adolescent dreams of glory are far more grandiosely presented and realized than in the average teen musical of former years. Beyond the usual local achievement—raising money for a charity, saving the community center—a young protagonist (less frequently, a group of teenagers) is launched on the road to general fame, or may actually have become a celebrity by the end of the film—e.g., *Turk 182* (1985).

The practice of athletic or dancing skill is curiously portrayed in the "go-for-it" McMovie subgenre. Sweat is much in evidence: it artistically dapples the adolescent's brow and body during exhausting workouts. But a highly mobile camera, exhilarating music, and quick cutting foster the impression of effortless effort, curiously vitiating any sense of actual pain and gain.

Rather little useful on-camera instruction occurs in films like *Flashdance*. A teacher—frequently out of the mainstream—may propound aphorisms, or speak bluntly to the hero or heroine's lack of determination. But there isn't much real substance imparted about dance, sport, martial art, whatever. Occasionally, consistent with the American approval of rugged individualism, formidable expertise is acquired on one's own. Criticism of recognized experts may at first constitute a major obstacle to success, but is usually negated by a stellar performance.

Flashdance climaxes with an audition for a classical ballet company. The panel of judges is skeptical about the heroine's shortage of formal background or training. But they are knocked out of their socks by a routine which smacks more of the disco bar than the *barre*. It establishes her gymnastic prowess, but affords only trifling evidence of balletic talent. She wins the post hands down.

The viewer may thus infer that fame as an adept of kendo, karate, ballet, or break dancing lies easily within the grasp of any youthful aspirant. Talent *is* required—but since its precise nature is rarely specified, presumably anyone can own it. A few lessons will suffice, supplied by an unorthodox teacher or a dusty old book, a modicum of fashionable sweat, and a fabulous relationship with oneself.

Many McMovies about adolescents are informed by *a radically simplistic view of pubertal and postpubertal development*. A naive perception of youth's intricate psychological vicissitudes typifies the college musicals of the thirties and forties, the Beach Blanket and Teenage Rebel pictures of the fifties and sixties, and the late seventies classic *Animal House* (1978). In the McMovie, it is inflected by contemporary Hollywood's permissiveness toward the show of sex and violence.

Psychoanalytic developmental theory customarily divides adolescence into three stages: early (about eleven and a half to fifteen), mid (approximately fifteen to eighteen), and late (eighteen until twenty-one). In a contemporary pluralistic culture, adolescent developmental issues may actually not attain satisfactory closure until the mid- or late twenties.

The earlier phases of puberty are marked by an eruption of instinct-driven urges that matches the spurt in physical growth. By the time most youngsters reach their late teens or early twenties, they have integrated problematic sexual/aggressive feelings into a stable self-image. A reasonable degree of mental (and sometimes geographical) separation from the family of origin will have occurred. The individual now begins to hammer out a viable adult identity in work, love, and play.

In many teen McMovies adolescents appear as impulse-ridden hedonists or rebellious depressives, monomaniacally preoccupied with sex and/or aggression. A predilection for fun, fighting, or fornication is encountered not only in lightweight fabrications like the *Porky's* films, but also intrudes into pictures with serious pretentions:

The older high school students of *The Breakfast Club* (another semi-McMovie) wrestle with typical late-adolescent identity problems, to varying degrees of success or psychopathology. While their conflicts are formulated with some skill, the narrative insists on clumsily forcing them into rote turns of giddy or explosive behavior, characteristic of fourteen- rather than seventeen-year-olds. At the conclusion, youngsters who previously had scorned each other because of differences in social background or ideology are romantically paired off—as if it weren't feasible that boys and girls who had struggled so painfully toward rapprochment couldn't merely remain trusted friends.

McMovies about neglected, misfit, or misunderstood children re-capitulate an analogously shallow developmental vision of childhood, as well as a cloying naivete about childhood "innocence." Plucky waifs were immensely popular in the silent era—e.g., the storm-tossed pre- or early-adolescent heroines of Mary Pickford, or Jackie Coogan's *The Kid* (1921). The little näif who prevails after being exiled or temporarily es-tranged from bourgeois society appears again in *Peck's Bad Boy* (1921), the *Little Rascal* and *Our Gang* shorts, various Shirley Temple vehicles, and the "Leave It To Beaver" and "Dennis The Menace" TV series. *E.T.* (1982) is the principal begetter of the adorable misfit kid McMovie. In my frankly jaundiced opinion, it's at least a semi-McMovie.

Adolescent and child McMovies hold adults in even lower regard than their predecessors, aside from archetypes like the wise teacher, and the courageous divorced or widowed parent. Grown-ups are pleasant ciphers inscribed at the edge of youthful action, fools and impotent fumblers, or openly malevolent authoritarians. Spielberg-produced or -influenced ju-venilia may portray parents as reasonably loving and competent, but be-tray an unpleasant paranoid streak toward adults outside the family, es-pecially those connected with government.

One looks in vain for the very old amidst the well-favored young in most McMovies, perhaps another signature of the narcissistic inability to confront the facts (and limitations) of life. If elderly people appear at all in any length, it's usually as victims of crime, or figures of fun.

Etiology of the McMovie

Film Industry Economics

The rise of the McMovie is most clearly linked to developments in the *commodification* of cinema, an inherent thrust in Hollywood business no less than business practice elsewhere, if tempered by the industry's pecu-liarities. However, the sheer amount and sophistication of film market-ing has escalated formidably over the past two decades, attendant upon shifts in perspective about filmmaking deeply imbricated in corporate influences over production. I will describe these phenomena at length, then touch briefly upon more controversial contributing factors to the McMovie's genesis.

The changes in movie industry economic operations relevant to this discussion have been outlined by Kael, Monaco, McClintick, Litwak, Bach, and others. [12] The classic Hollywood studio, with its durable cadre of administrators, skilled, and semi-skilled workers, virtually disappeared by the sixties. With it went the old moguls' rigorous on-site control. Government trust-busters played a major role in breaking up the "majors," but eventually studio control would pass to even more powerful corporations and conglomerates. Today's studios are likely to be part of other vast corporate holdings, related or quite unrelated to cinema.

Many executives hired by conglomerate megaliths to run studios do not own the nut-and-bolt expertise of their predecessors. Their apprenticeship is likely to have been served in television, law, or Wall Street. Even though they may perceive themselves as devoted cineasts, their bottom-line concern is the profit-and-loss statement.

Today more than ever, studio chiefs must be responsive to distant companies whose leaders may know even less about film, and who are more likely to view the merchandising of movies from the same shareholding perspective as the hawking of soft drinks or cigarettes (or sardines). With the average cost of a picture hovering around fifteen to twenty million dollars, decision making up and down the corporate ladder tends to be risk-aversive. Nevertheless, players of the new Hollywood game continue to be lured by the promise of fantastic lucre, as well as the power and glamour associated with the film business.

Movie people agree there is plenty of profit in making decent films well, and more than a few very well. But an ordinary hit won't suffice anymore. Since the phenomenal success of *Jaws* (1975) and *Raiders of the Lost Ark,* enormous pressure has prevailed to score big with another "blockbuster" movie. A Christmas or summer blockbuster generates monstrous grosses through massive general showings, repeat viewing, sensational foreign sales, videocassette rights, toy and clothing promotions, *everything* on one roll.

Until very recently, the industry has taken it as received truth that the chances of a film becoming a blockbuster depend on its popularity with younger viewers, notably teenagers and preteens. Litwak states "the studios often act as if [adolescents] were their only customers." [13] There may be some validity to this belief. A 1984 Motion Picture Association of America study indicates that 36 percent of the average American movie audience is twelve to twenty years old (another 18 percent is age twenty-one to twenty-four; thus 54 percent of the audience is age twelve to twenty-four, inclusive). [14] Although adolescents and preadolescents may constitute an absolute minority in any given audience, the MPAA study also suggests *they go more often to the movies, and return more often to a film already enjoyed.* [15]

Today's studios do not make movies; they rather participate in an intricate dance of deals around the hopes of others to make movies for them. In omnipresent pursuit of the elusive blockbuster, studios seek or are sought by powerful agents, stars, producers, in mutable packages and combinations. A one-line no-brainer "high concept" ("*ALIEN—JAWS in space!!*"), vaguely attached to a famous star and director in the hope of luring the young, may energize a deal more potently than a viable screenplay appealing to a more selective older audience.

Most deals never come to fruition: they only serve to stoke future deals and the egos behind them. If a picture finally emerges from a labyrinth of Machiavellian negotiation, it is often made by a film company assembled for that purpose alone. The studio then undertakes the job it now does best—marketing.

Millions of dollars are regularly budgeted for promotion—enough to finance many a less promising (or more controversial) but potentially high-quality picture. A single massive national advertising campaign usually hypes a new film's saturation release across the country. Audience response to a new movie during the first few weekends after its opening is deemed a valid gauge of hit status, and hopefully blockbuster potential. So is the attendance of young viewers.

If big box office revenue isn't generated quickly, and the sense obtains (justified or otherwise) that the market—particularly the younger market—hasn't reacted quickly and favorably, a film may be pulled out of circulation just as quickly, even with good reviews. It may then resurface abroad, or in videocasette, or—rarely—be rereleased to theaters later with a new promotion slant, or a different title. Or it may disappear altogether.

In the setting of this relentless mercantilism, the raison d'etre for the McMovie's vapidity would seem to spring from its inevitably derivative nature. Risk-shy corporate sachems believe their best chance for achieving a new blockbuster lies in reinventing an old one. Hence the obsessive cloning of whatever combination of star and genre has most recently generated megaprofits. Occasionally, McMovie makers reach further back, lifting a text from the last blockbuster but one, or some halcyon Hollywood effort.[16]

Dogged imitation and allusion rather than experimentation, even within narrow genre confines, usually dictates the newest Vigilante Vengeanceflick or Flash-in-the-pan-dance—in short, the latest McMovie. By now, McMovies have passed through several generations. Uninspiring prototypes have spun off sequels, which have birthed still drearier successors—a Barthean chain of replication unfolding into ever-declining signification.

A McMovie screenplay is a hack effort—more often than not the ghost hand of a fine recent or old film, or the cruder version of an already flawed narrative. The ineptitude of the script proceeds from its derivative intentions, and the perception (conscious or otherwise) of its viewers as so unintelligent, unmotivated, or distractable that they will overlook narrative defects—or even regard them as virtues. McMovie writers may also be unaware of the mediocrity of their work because of their own limitations (see below).

The broadest possible plot strokes, glyphs of character, and clumsy distillations of dialogue are deployed to rehash the original screenplay, fleshed out with whatever chases, gunplay, dancing, splatter attacks, or special effects are necessary to the coarse duplication at hand. In an attributed sequel, it is not unlikely that greater subtlety in the script may actually be discouraged, lest the drawing power of the source be compromised.

The McMovie screenplay may be dashed off between other projects by a skilled writer out to earn a fast—and very large—buck. It may be cut to fit a producer's or agent's mercantile vision by a novice writer, eager for the quick strike that will propel him into the vastly more esteemed and profitable craft of directing.

The script may be deliberately submitted incomplete, for others to alter to their taste. Or it may start out a complete, competent product, only to be hacked away at by a star, director, producer, other writers—*anyone* connected with a project—as it is dragged through deal after deal. After numerous appalling revisions, it may emerge as a McMovie's tacky armature.

The wooden quality of McMovie acting is a function of the screenplay's leaden lines, as well as unskilled or perfunctory direction. But actors are far from being the McMovie director's helpless victims. Stars have considerable input in shaping the McMovie script, and are increasingly involved in its production.

While the rewards are high, the price paid for sacrificing talent to such meager ends can be devastating. After bringing considerable capability to diversified roles, stars like Clint Eastwood and Charles Bronson have gradually become ensnared, their skills narrowed, by their identification with a McMovie hero.[17] It's no less unsettling to see the range of newer talented actors and actresses leashed in by a McMovie appearance—e.g., Pat Morita in *The Karate Kid, Part II* or Sigourney Weaver in *Aliens*.

Narcissism

Giant egos have always flourished in Hollywood, at the summit of industry success, on the way up or down. A strong conviction about one's talents is considered an asset in a business so rife with rejection. Should success come, one's narcissism is stroked to an even higher gloss by others trying to get to the top of the heap, or struggling to stay there. The transient nature of success is also said to inflame, rather than humble, the egoism of those with tenuous status in the industry.

Beyond pure financial gain, the power and privilege granted by the system to successful players has risen substantially, especially to those associated with a blockbuster. Tremendous "clout" is concentrated in a charmed circle of executives, producers, agents, and a few producer-directors. Stars wield an even greater influence. Studio chiefs stand in awe—if not downright fear—of them, and shrink from advising them, let alone controlling their excesses.

Star participation in a production may herald fortunes, just as withdrawal may precipitate financial catastrophe. Stars are courted like royalty; their word often constitutes a law unto itself. They may overrule direction, rewrite scripts without consulting a writer, and thus generate a McMovie—e.g., Stallone's tampering with *Rhinestone*'s reportedly excellent first script into mediocrity.[18]

By no means are all stars prima donnas, but the mechanisms for them to indulge in narcissistic excess are well entrenched. A powerful actor with serious narcissistic tendencies is easily lured into emblazoning his ego—and his emptiness—across his screen persona. Few are willing to risk his displeasure by interposing common sense. In cutting a character to fit his own grandiose measure, projecting what he imagines to be his strengths into a role, the actor may unwittingly project his narcissism as well. Hence, the gagging insensitivity toward others, the yawning emptiness masked by the surface virtue and wholeness of the action McMovie male superhero.[19]

Directorial excesses arguably stemming from heightened narcissism may also impact upon the McMovie narrative. After Michael Cimino garnered an academy award with *The Deer Hunter* (1978), he undertook *Heaven's Gate,* a western based on the Johnson County land war. Despite plentiful early warnings about massive budget override, executives were unwilling to reign in the director's profligacy. *Heaven's Gate* finally cost some forty-four million dollars, was an aesthetic and critical disaster—an early McMovie—and brought down United Artists. Despite widespread censure, Cimino remains unrepentant to this day, representing himself as the embattled protector of his artistic vision against studio philistines.

In Cimino's next film, *Year of the Dragon,* detective Stan White's grandiose, entitled behavior is justified by his obsession with justice. White ignores general disapproval in his headlong pursuit of the tong leader. An implicit parallel is there to be drawn between the hero and the director's ultimate vindication, after vanquishing the corporate criminal "dragon." So is the unintended parallel between the catastrophes wrought by White's narcissism and Cimino's uncritical self-regard upon their respective associates.

Film and the collective psyche are widely held to be imbricated in a complex feedback process. Cinema constantly recycles conscious and unconscious preoccupations through its scenarios. Beyond the direct impact of powerful narcissistically inclined individuals on the McMovies, these films may reflect the introjection and reprojection of inchoate trends toward self-aggrandisement widely prevalent in our culture.

Lasch, Schickel, and others have discussed the narcissistic thrust of contemporary American society, manifested by slavish worship of fame and celebrity, wholesale absorption in personal prestige and power, the raging sense of entitlement at the expense of others, so forth.[20] Reliable statistics on the actual prevalence of pathological narcissism among normal or clinical populations are virtually impossible to come by. I can only cite subjective impressions within my profession.

Over the past ten to fifteen years, I have encountered more severely troubled narcissistic personalities, and noted a substantive rise in narcissistic tendencies in patients with other disorders. My cases include adolescents and young adults from fortunate backgrounds treated in an urban private practice, as well as teenagers from impoverished circumstances whose treatment I supervised in various public settings.

Thirty or so colleagues across the country report similar findings. Several wondered if narcissistic personality disorder could be considered the disease of the day, much as hysteria was conceived to be the signal illness of Freud's time. The burgeoning clinical literature on the subject over the past decade and a half is another possible index of escalating narcissistic pathology.

Some may argue that a cohort of psychiatric patients comprises too idiosyncratic a sample on which to base conclusions about the status of character traits abroad in general society. My sense is that our narcissistic clientele only exhibit blatantly the greedy self-absorption that flourishes outside our offices and hospitals in more "functional" adaptations.

I have wondered if the McMovie's narcissistic emptiness is as natively congenial to its audience as its hero. Whatever their artistic failings or biases, most classic Hollywood films called forth warm feelings of empathy at some point from the public—witness the legions of women who wept through Crawford and Davis's travails, the public's sympathy for Bogart's tough but tender bank robber in *High Sierra* (1941) or John Wayne's Indian hunter in *The Searchers* (1956). But I look in vain for complex empathic affinities between public and protagonist at the McMovies. A simplistic—indeed, witless—identification seems to join the audience to Rambo and Dirty Harry as these baleful straw men go about savaging the opposition.

Television

Television's trivializing potential has concerned social critics from its inception. Postman has asserted that meaningful intellectual discourse in America is threatened by television's questionable tutelage, its "dangerous and absurdist" epistemology.[21] His well-reasoned polemic has little to say about the degrading influence of video upon cinema. Kael, Shales, and Denby comment on the issue briefly.[22]

Once hostile to each other's fortunes, the television and film industries are now indissolubly wedded, often coexisting under the same conglomerate umbrella. Film studios regularly produce television programs. Television personnel regularly migrate to cinema. Their negative impact on the movies has been (rather impressionistically) attributed to inadequate training, or to the dulling of skill and creativity by chronic association with mediocre products.

Responsibility for the McMovie's fatuousness may to some degree rest with executives from the higher reaches of television management, who carry to film studios and production companies their philosophy of profitably pleasuring the most with the least. Wherever it originates, the spoor of television praxis is certainly evident in the McMovie's negligible content and fragmented visual strategies. The McMovie notably abounds with the idiosyncratic signature of high-production-value commercials and MTV videos[23]—accelerated pacing; jittery editing; short takes and quick cuts; loud, fast music; swooping camera; imparting of minimal diegetic information in compressed blips; the general privileging of style (or what is taken for style) over substance.

Cocaine

The central nervous system stimulant cocaine can produce an impressive subjective sense of heightened competence, while warping judgment and jeopardizing work performance. Grandiosity, disinhibition of aggressive impulses, impulsiveness, and irresponsibility often are encountered in heavy abusers. The drug may temporarily enhance energy and concentration in some individuals, but long-term effects on creativity are frequently devastating. Chronic abuse leads to other florid symptoms—deranged attention, driven restlessness, paranoid thinking veering into delusions, gut-wrenching depression during the post-cocaine "crash," so forth.[24]

While experimentation is common, the extent of hard-core drug addiction in Hollywood is uncertain. Movie people generalize ominously or optimistically, but names and films made "under the influence" are rarely forthcoming, except postmortem. The impression prevails that overall drug abuse in the industry has substantially increased over the past five to ten years. Cocaine is said to be the drug most ruinously abused next to alcohol; its deleterious influence supposedly can impact upon every step of filmmaking and marketing, from first deal to final cut.[25]

While Hollywood is facilely associated in the public imagination with scandalous behavior, its drug problems may actually be no greater than those of any other high-pressure workplace. The role of cocaine in the genesis of the McMovie must be rated *absolutely* speculative. Certainly, other causes adduced throughout this paper are sufficient to explain the McMovie's coked-up aura. But the drug may dovetail with them, to function as a potent "X" factor enabling the irritable grandiosity of McMovie characters; the McMovie's frantic pace; its jury-rigged construction; its resolution of complication through violence or mere agitated motion.

A movie is a collaborative effort involving an army of administrative, creative, and on-line technical personnel. However, the harm caused by an addicted gaffer cannot match the havoc wrought by a working star or director coked to the retinas. Clearly, the more powerful the influence of the serious abuser(s) on the basic conception or execution of a film, the greater the likelihood that cocaine's influence may be sutured into the McMovie's mise-en-scène.

Declining Literacy and the Death of Imagination

Critics have objected to Hollywood's low estimate of its public's intelligence, arguing that because audiences may be getting younger does not necessarily signify they are getting dumber. It has been suggested that many people would choose quality films if studios would only abandon their obsession with profit (and, one presumes, McMovies) to back riskier, more substantial pictures.

I suspect the McMovie's prevalence *is* largely dictated by an unrepentant lust after gain, and that the manipulation of viewers toward accepting bad films often proceeds from a Barnumesque view of their intellect. However, it's naive to think that filmgoers who keep attending McMovie after McMovie are merely passive victims of Hollywood's greed, with plentiful taste in reserve for better fare.

The McMovie maker's degraded perception of an audience composed of retarded early adolescents with attention deficit disorder may hyperbolically reflect an ominous truth. America is sinking into illiteracy, and no correction is in sight. High school dropout rates, particularly among the impoverished, have risen alarmingly over the past generation. Several major studies indicate a serious decline in learning—and teaching—competence at every educational level. It has been stated that the United States faces a serious depletion of young adults "who read and write well enough to perform the complex technological, scientific, and managerial tasks on which the nation's future depends."[26]

Despite the inroads of the VCR, despite critical lament about the sorry state of cinema, movie grosses are still enormous. One or more billions of tickets are sold yearly. By no means do adolescents buy all of them. McMovies and semi-McMovies now constitute the bulk of Hollywood's output. Viewers do not visit such films out of sheer force of habit, nor do the majority sit through them bitterly unhappy, as Denby suggests (one wonders if the disaffected moviegoers he cites might be urban cineasts).

Consider that McMovie producers, writers, and directors are often barely out of their twenties, children of the day's ignorance and narcissism. Schooled in little art or culture beyond cinema, they imagine a visual quote of Frank Capra profound. Perhaps they are not always as cynical as they seem. Perhaps they esteem their creations past profit and power, not intimating fully how they, too, are bound up in what they have created.

Vacuous as the McMovie may be, it seems to serve many of its viewers well, else they would not return for more and provoke McMovie makers to newer inanities. It is alarming to contemplate that the intellectual horizons of the audience may have become as constricted as the McMovie itself, more alarming to conceive that the McMovie may bear some signature of a general heightened narcissism and ego impoverishment—*in sum, that product, producer, and consumer may be participating in a cybernetic of emptiness, makers and viewers resonating with each other's profound intellectual deficits and possibly characterological deficits as well.*

Today the power of discourses other than cinema to move, educate, or inform the literate and less literate in America is steadily being eroded. The trivializing thrust Postman decries is ubiquitous. A stifling of imaginative effort, a general shrinking of creativity can be perceived throughout media, highbrow, and popular art.

The signet of the McMovie's barrenness is recognizable in *USA Today,* the blather of the local "Eyewitness News" anchorstar; in the unsubtlety of the average Saturday morning cartoon; in the starvation-bloat of James Clavell novels; in Andreas Vollenweider's inane arpeggios; in Neil Simon's attenuated one-liners, and in Andrew Lloyd Webber's hypertrophied productions. Over a few short years, our culture has been inundated by McNews, McArt, McBooks, McMusic, McPlays.

It is unlikely that television or cocaine per se can be blamed for this unprecedented cascando of *kvatch*. If a monistic cause is to be invoked, it resides within the same intrusion of late twentieth-century capitalist practices into the arts and media that already has infected other markets. The hallmarks of relentless mercantilism include the unslakable obsession with profit over value, the escalation of commodification, and the suppression of variety—all attendant upon the march toward conglomerate oligarchy.

We are far from powerless before these massive ills—certainly not at the box office. As this is written, there is growing evidence that older viewers may be returning to the Bijou to watch somewhat better fare. But until we deny Hollywood our dollars, Hollywood will assuredly continue seducing us to affirm our identities in the tarnished mirror of the McMovie's debased entertainments. We will, in sum, have the McMovies—as well as the other meager artifacts of a throwaway culture—we deserve.

After the "McMovie"

My principal psychoanalytic brief in the preceding pages was to explore the articulating narcissism of product, actor, and creator in a species of big, bad film that threatened to become endemic during Reagan's reign. By 1988, the entity I had termed a "McMovie" was being read by other critics as yet another signifier of the era's greedy corporate practices. Many pictures mentioned in my essay would clearly fall into the domain of the "high-concept" production analyzed by Wyatt and Rutsky. [27] In retrospect, my inquiry scanted the extent to which Hollywood's output was already sutured into the consumerist strategies of megalithic entertainment conglomerates like Coca-Cola (Coke acquired a shade less than half of Columbia Studio's stock in 1982, then sold its control to Sony in 1989).

Rather than being merchandised sui generis, the McMovie (and somewhat better filmfare) increasingly served as the springboard for vastly profitable spin-offs of toys, food, clothing, theme park rides, so forth. The *cascando* of hectic hawking proceeded under the umbrella of a single huge company, or with the help of its agreeable brethren, beggaring analogous previous campaigns—such as the spin-off of apparel lines from forties women's films.

My study only touched briefly on the orgies of the McMovie's merchandising and other aspects its derivation, i.e., the role of television. These have been analyzed at length in *Seeing through Movies,* a book of studies by prominent film/media theorists edited by Mark Crispin Miller. [28] The collection is indispensable for a proper understanding of the blockbuster phenomenon and its detritus. I will skim off a few apposite insights.

In his chapter on TV's impact on contemporary filmmaking, Todd Gitlin argues that Hollywood has passed from anxious derision to companionable, even reverential accommodation of the small screen (doubtless facilitated by the increasing migration of creative and business personnel back and forth between the two media).[29] He specifically holds commercials and music videos responsible for the high-concept film's often violent content and pervasive homogeneity of directorial style—i.e., for the quick cuts and verbal restrictions I alluded to—noting that "the exchange of speeches more than two crude sentences long comes to be considered a *longeur,* a distraction from action."[30]

Douglas Gomery discovers sobering corollaries between the decline of cinema and the site of its reception.[31] Today's film theaters are often owned or franchised by a subsidiary of the same corporation which owns the studio that sponsors the McMovie's genesis. The average "multiplex" now offers a degraded viewing environment oddly reminiscent of the early nickelodeon in all save the latter's minimal price. More often than not, films are viewed in a noisy, dirty box, on a screen whose dimensions and state of repair are often inadequate for appropriate projection.

Ever fewer theaters are available for revivals and foreign films, a lack that television and the VCR cannot currently redress. In his mordant piece on the colorizing controversy, Stuart Klawans observes that even when a film is broadcast in a reasonable state of preservation and unsullied by interruptions its pleasures are still diminished by compromised clarity, resolution, and reframing practices (panning, scanning), which substantively deface the original images.[32]

I described the crafting of the McMovie for a hypothecated younger viewer's lowest common *jouissance.* Peter Biskind argues that the cinema of Steven Spielberg and George Lucas actually aims at reconstituting the audience at large into awestruck children.[33] Gone is the ironic, distanciation of seventies antigenre directors like Altman and Kubrick. Polysemia is exchanged for Pollyanna, in stupendous restorations of the action/adventure genres treasured by the younger filmmakers during their youth and film school days.

Spielberg/Lucas enlist formidable Industrial Light and Magic wizardry in the service of stripped down narratives that privilege an American imaginary's simplistic virtues and Manichean worldview. Heroes like Indiana Jones or Luke Skywalker renounce dangerous grown-up sexuality, "progressing" through regression. Oedipal conflict is resolved by deeding independence over to a potent father figure or supernally benevolent paternalistic "Force." A dim approbation of the sixties counterculture ethos, drained of deeper intellectual content, insinuatingly lays the groundwork for uncritical acceptance of the Great Communicator's paternalistic blather.

Miller's elegant concluding essay analyzes the most blatant corporate incursion into filmmaking yet. Plugsters now profit richly from bringing advertisers and producers together to broker "product placement" within the body of a movie. The impact of this practice reaches far beyond merely displaying beer or borax, to encompass cinema's total look and content. More and more films appear designed rather than directed, pervaded by the unsubtle stylistics of the TV commercial. The formal norm consists of

close-ups, two shots, and other sets whereby the action is (just as in advertising) repetitiously foregrounded. . . . there are few scenes shot in deep focus. . . . Likewise, we rarely see the kind of panoramic composition that allows a generous impression of quasi-global simultaneity . . . *pictures* comprising pleasurable "touches," moving tableaux that often (as Bazin argued) give their viewers some choice, and require (often minimal) interpretive attention. . . .

Today's Hollywood movie works without, or against, the potential depth and latitude of cinema, in favor of that systematic overemphasis deployed in advertising. . . . Each shot presents a content closed and unified, like a fist, and makes the point right in your face: big gun, big car, nice ass.[34]

Minimalized medium informs meager message. Miller believes that film "problems" now tend to be much slighter, their solutions more perfunctory and blatantly ridden with wish fulfillment than previously (see the peculiar congratulatory mode of the adolescent "go-for-it" subgenre discussed above).

Rather than extol lucky/plucky characters, the high-concept Mc-Movie incessantly constructs the *star* who becomes the sole focus of attention, a shining cynosure for our identification. Miller acutely notes additional signets of McMovie narcissism: e.g., the egregious piling on of surplus triumphs for the star, "not as a quick way to end the film, but as its very purpose."[35] The star is also set against a panoply of ridiculed inferiors—"jerks, creeps, dweebs, dworks, dips, freaks, shmucks, bastards, phoneys, fags, and sleazeballs"[36]—further inflating an unmerited "greatness."

When these feel-good films allude nostalgically to past pictures, the latter's most discordant, uncanny, or tragic moments are usually erased. Earlier stringent indictments of the status quo are smoothed over, replaced by hyperbolic approbation of Our Way Of Life. The sense of real history evaporates into thin air. Beset by what Miller perceives as an agonizing fear of loss (wholesale loss of the post–World War II prosperous dream?), Hollywood frantically has turned to generating relentless uppers, redolent with "constant solace, flattery, and affirmation."[37]

If Hollywood history has taught us anything, it is wariness about pronouncements on the decline and fall of cinema. Bad movies have always been with us, although not so many have been laden with the McMovie's peculiar melding of expense and emptiness until the last decade. While Miller and several of his colleagues remain fairly pessimistic, I am not as doubtful about the state of this still new art now, compared with four years ago.

In 1991 McMovies and semi-McMovies are still being filmed. Sometimes they are well attended, but just as often their reception is lackluster. More to the point, since *Batman* (1989)—that ultimate monument to vacuity—the cost of producing star vehicle McMovies has escalated staggeringly (e.g., *Dick Tracy* [1990]), without *Batman*'s fabulous returns.

Many McMovie clones of previous successes (e.g., *Robocop II* [1990]) have also done poorly. At this writing, critics are even wondering if *The Godfather, Part III*'s (1990) disappointing box office might presage an end to the sequel trend. Meanwhile, modestly budgeted and promoted films like *Ghost* (1990) have proven incredibly lucrative. The unexpected blockbuster is no new phenomenon, testifying once more to the eternal, fatal vagaries of viewer preference.

Setting aside the enormous youthful audiences for *Teenage Mutant Ninja Turtles* (1990) and *Home Alone* (1991), more mature viewers now seem to be starting to drive the market again. Statistics are problematic on this score, but in Hollywood the mere perception a thing is so is often enough to make it so. Current industry perception seems to be that audiences expect better fare than a decade ago. They are often receiving it—and occasionally are being shown very good pictures indeed.

The final essays in this collection address several current tiers of filmmaking. The subject of adaptation is taken up again in a study of Steven Spielberg's *Always* (1990), the director's McMovie rehash of *A Guy Named Joe* (1943). My focus is an Oedipal dynamic that may be implicit in the remaking process. *Working Girl* (1989) is discussed as an example of the "co-opt" movie with a seemingly liberal agenda, which mocks or subverts the very social advances of the sixties and seventies it would seem to affirm. I conclude by analyzing the neurotic and creative strategies of post-traumatic Holocaust survival set forth in *Enemies: A Love Story* (1989). Mazursky's best film to date represents the tentative but hopeful recuperation of quality in post-Reagan Hollywood, despite the incursions of the McMovie and its equally suspect fellow travelers.

9

Raiders of the Lost Text: Remaking As Contested Homage in *Always*

You cannot speak "on" such a text, you can only speak
"in" it, in its fashion, enter into a desperate plagiarism.
—Roland Barthes, *The Pleasure of the Text*

TOP: Oedipal triangulation in *A Guy Named Joe*. Courtesy of Museum of Modern Art/Film Stills Archive. BOTTOM: Oedipal triangulation in *Always*. Is there an Oedipal dynamic embedded in the remaking process itself, waiting to be evoked by the eternal triangle between remaker, maker, and the original film?

*I*n poker, when cards are poorly shuffled and redealt the result is often a "ghost hand." If the last hand was good, its ghost is likely to be a poor, watered-down thing better left unplayed. In their long Hollywood history, most remakes of earlier films have been ghost hands, shallow attempts to trade in on an original's smash success via new stars, new technology, sometimes a new setting—rarely as profitable as the first movie and artistically best left unmade.[1]

By no means is remaking necessarily dictated by pursuit of gain alone. The new version may be sincerely or ironically intended as homage or satire; may seek to open up psychological/political possibilities latent in the original movie which its makers weren't aware of, or which they couldn't pursue because of censorship (e.g., Blake Edwards's *Victor, Victoria* [1982]—a remake of a now forgotten German film of the thirties with a much more suppressed homoerotic subtext).[2]

Steven Spielberg's purposes in rehashing the World War II chestnut *A Guy Named Joe* (1943) into *Always* (1990) would appear to be highly personal, located well beyond the profit principle. The war has been the director's preferred locale in many of his pictures—e.g., in *1941* (1979), two of the *Indiana Jones* cycle (*Raiders Of The Lost Ark* [1981], *Indiana Jones and the Last Crusade* [1989]), and the underrated *Empire of the Sun* (1987). His father served as a radio operator with a B-25 bomber squadron in Burma as a young man.[3] Spielberg is proud of this, but has not spoken of any influence his parent's military career played specifically on his filmmaking choices. He clearly admires the hometown and frontline virtues commended by the media of the time—all that boyish spunk and good-humored doing without. He has been particularly enchanted by *A Guy Named Joe* since adolescence, has seen the film numerous times, greatly admires its director, Victor Fleming; has said he always wanted to make an old-fashioned love story like the one in *Joe,* instead of the action spectaculars that have been his hallmark.[4]

A Guy Named Joe was actually a slight, sentimental piece of business scripted rather lumpishly by Dalton Trumbo, redeemed by Victor Fleming's crisp direction. Daredevil pilot Spencer Tracy, madly in love with free-spirited airperson Irene Dunne, loses his life diving on a Nazi ship, then joins a spectral squadron of dead heroes with a mission to instruct a new generation of live ones. Tracy's prize student, Van Johnson, falls for Dunne. By the conclusion, Tracy has renounced his jealousy, recapitulating the renunciation theme privileged in *Casablanca* and other World War II movies. He proudly lets Dunne go "out of my heart" into a star-spangled future with Johnson.

Tracy's sidekick in *A Guy Named Joe* is the sturdy Ward Bond. At the beginning of *Always,* John Goodman, the oafish replicant of Bond's Al Yackey, states:

> AL: What this place reminds me of is the war in
> Europe . . . which I personally was never at, but think
> about it. . . . The beer is warm, the dance hall's a
> quonset, there's B26's outside, hotshot pilots inside, an
> airstrip in the woods. . . . It's *England,* man, every-
> thing but Glenn Miller! Except you go to burning
> places and bomb 'em until they stop burning. You see,
> Pete, there is no war here. This is why they don't make
> movies called *Night Raid in Boise, Idaho,* or *Firemen
> Strike at Dawn.* And this is why you're not exactly a
> hero for taking the chances you take. You're more of
> what I would call—a dickhead.

Having asserted that no good war can be found to fight in contemporary America, it's Spielberg's enterprise to have it fought anyway—by the pilots who extinguish raging forest fires with chemicals dropped from ancient planes, like the ones his father flew in. There are such pilots, working in outfits roughly like the one Yackey describes, and they do run enormous risks. But the director reduces his relocated narrative into negligible sound and fury, roaring piffle unable to carry the weight of the original's perilous combat context.[5]

As the leads, Richard Dreyfuss and Holly Hunter own the sexual spark of *Peanuts* kids. Both are literally dwarfed by their earlier counterparts—particularly Hunter, compared with Dunne's luminous persona. Spielberg makes a nod at feminism by using Hunter in a role meant to reprise her feisty producer in *Broadcast News* (1987), much as he deployed Karen Allen in *Raiders of the Lost Ark* as a tough-minded foil for Harrison Ford. By the end of *Raiders,* Allen had been reduced to an impotent screaming Mimi. In *Always,* whether due to direction or scripting, Hunter is rendered into a querulous tomboy. Dunne's image is vastly more adult, competent, and sensuous on or off the ground. Her (and Tracy's) eroticism gains a keener edge from their passion's implicit lack of consummation. Hunter beds Dreyfuss tastefully, without a jot of sensuality.

The couple's dialogue in *Always,* reaching for the lucid sassiness of those thirties and forties movies that conspicuously foregrounded equal footing between the sexes, rings like *The Goonies* (1985) instead of *Adam's Rib* (1949). Lacking the poignant edge of universal wartime insecurity, Dreyfuss and Hunter indulge in inane New Age chatter about commitment, your thing, my thing, so forth.[6] The oddly juvenile—and asexual—quality of their relationship infects Spielberg's work more definitively than ever, thoroughly subverting the intended romanticism of his project in and away from the bedroom.

For example, in *A Guy Named Joe,* Tracy slow dances with Dunne at the officer's club, while a single flyer eyes her speculatively. In *Always,* at the firefighter's canteen dance, Hunter is besieged by a horde of grimy smokejumpers who ogle and paw at her like moonstruck boy scouts. The sequence could have been filmed at sleepaway camp.

In the main, *Always* rates as an unfortunate ghost hand (about ghosts). The screenplay unwittingly telegraphs its own obituary in Yackey's initial admonition to Pete. *Always is* instructive about Spielberg's increasing blindspots: his childlike predilection for wretched excess, visually and aurally; his simpleminded admiration for the male-bonded professionalism celebrated in the movies of Howard Hawks and John Ford; and, above all, his unreflective hankering—similar to Pete's—after what the director evidently valorizes as an ideologically simpler era he never lived through (he was born in 1947), but chiefly experienced via its pop culture artifacts.

Essentially, *Always* interprets as a postmodern fantasy based on an agitprop version of the war—one cracked mirror held up to another, Baudrillardian simulacra both. Whatever its shortcomings, *A Guy Named Joe* did possess a substantive ideological agenda. The film sought to console audiences that their loved ones weren't *really* dead—only translated to a newer realm of struggle.[7] It was pitched at alleviating the guilt of women who had found new men after their husbands or boyfriends had been killed. It virtually elided any notion of fear or panic in combat, purveying the message that no matter how rough the fighting got, an American soldier would still acquit himself with grace and good humor, even as he died.[8] Finally, *A Guy Named Joe* intensively promoted the necessity for teamwork rather than classic American rugged individualism. In a sense, Pete had to die to learn from his ghostly fellowship that the war could not be survived and won by seat-of-the-pants soloists.[9]

Compared to its source, *Always* is radically drained of ideological freight. Yackey's "dickhead" speech usefully reads as Barthesian "inoculation" against the attainder that practically *nothing* except tepid New Age romance is at stake in this juvenile text, with its infantilized protagonists.[10] Spielberg centrally privileges nostalgia and pastiche, that mimesis of dead styles from the "imaginary museum" analyzed by Jameson and other cultural critics.[11] The film is resolutely ignorant or uncaring about actual history;[12] for all its feminist pretensions, its sexual politics are deeply—if unpolemically—conservative. It is profoundly informed by the "aesthetic *frisson* in emptiness" so often encountered in recent remakes and sequels.[13]

My specific psychoanalytic interest resides in the intensely rivalrous spirit inhabiting Spielberg's "homage." In his seminal *Anxiety of Influence,* Harold Bloom theorizes that many of the strongest poets were compelled by their anxiety about a predecessor's power to deviate sharply from his praxis.[14] Instead of Bloom's "swerve," Spielberg plunges unabashedly into *A Guy Named Joe.* The metaphor is literally fleshed out in *Always*'s establishing sequence, a peaceful scene of two men fishing on a lake. Behind them, a huge PBX seaplane descends, its foreshortened image slowly filling the screen; wavering ominously in the lambent air, until the men, alerted by the sudden, terrifying roar of its engines, dive out of their canoe, barely escaping destruction as the plane hurtles upon them.

This arresting sequence is extremely difficult to place within *Always*'s narrative schema. It can only be linked with an anecdote Dorinda/ Hunter tells much later in the film to her new lover, about a flying vacation she took with Pete/Dreyfuss in a PBX seaplane rigged as a "scoop" craft. From the air, Pete saw a fire in a small-town courthouse. He onloaded water from a nearby lake, dove on the conflagration, but completely missed the courthouse and disastrously flooded the town. Dorinda bubbles with laughter as she relates the episode. Her humor appears curiously callous for a character presented as so empathic, particularly when one considers the misery that must have attended Pete's blunder.

Always's introduction may have been intended as a "raid" on audience sensibility—reminiscent of the thunderclap establishing sequence of *Close Encounters of the Third Kind* (1977). It perhaps also anticipates Dorinda's tale of Pete's scooping up water from the town lake. The connection in the "conscious" narrative between the two cinematic events is, at best, obscure. I would suggest that this very tenuousness, along with Dorinda's oddly unsympathetic humor, may be understood analytically as symptoms of an intriguing textual uneasiness, exemplifying strategies of isolation and crude denial, defenses directed against the occulted recognition within *Always's* text of its own bristling competitiveness with *A Guy Named Joe.* Under this rubric, *the men in the boat, the town and its people can be taken as one entire symbol of the source film, which Spielberg has raided and swamped in transgressive adulation.*

Throughout *Always,* Spielberg and his writers tamper egregiously with quite unproblematic scenes from *A Guy Named Joe,* adding a punched-up soundtrack and overwrought visuals. To cite but one example: in the original film's climax, Dunne steals the plane Van Johnson was supposed to pilot in a solo suicide mission, and bombs a Japanese ammunition dump, aided by the ghostly Tracy. The explosions and gunfire of the bombing sequence are modest for a war film of the time. As they return to home base, Tracy speaks eloquently of the wonderful life waiting for Dunne. She lands, and Tracy bids her goodbye.

Spielberg has Hunter steal the plane to extinguish a blaze trapping a platoon of smokejumpers in a hard-to-reach mountain site. The pyrotechnics and acoustics of Hunter's overflight rival Luke Skywalker's run at the Deathstar. Afterward, Dreyfuss gives the Tracy farewell speech, virtually unchanged. The plane then stalls, crashes into the water, and sinks like a stone. Hunter, in extremis and goggle-eyed, then momentarily *sees* Dreyfuss. He pulls her to the surface, a few feet from the runway where her new lover is waiting. She walks toward him, Dreyfuss bids her goodbye, end of story.

Spielberg obviously must have believed these hyperbolic, clumsy changes (of which making Dreyfuss *visible* is the most risible, the latent rendered absurdly blatant) were artistically justifiable, satisfying elaborations. But inflicting them upon the yeoman work of the original appears as questionable as the enterprise of the Yiddish theater entrepreneur who earlier in the century advertised his company's production of *Hamlet* as a *"shoyshpil fun Vilyam Shekspir—farendert un farbesert"*—drama by Shakespeare, changed and improved.[15] One cannot know if the impresario was only repeating a hoary theatrical precedent, by convincing himself that he was after all only doing for Shakespeare what he believed Shakespeare had accomplished for Hollingshead.

The central issue for the purposes of this discussion is not *Always*'s merits relative to *A Guy Named Joe*. Rather, the issue is the extraordinary merit the latter has "always" held for Steven Spielberg, and the attendant possibility that an unconscious, Oedipally driven competitiveness constitutes the dark side of Spielberg's intense admiration for the original and its director. Some evidence can be adduced on this score from several anecdotes in Spielberg's biography.

The senior Spielberg has a background in electrical engineering, and helped design early computer technology. He comes across as a pragmatic, hard-driving individual, intensely passionate about scientific progress, equally passionate about conveying the wonders of the universe to an impressionable, admiring little boy:

With Dad everything was precision, accuracy, "head-on." He had the fastest slide rule in Arizona and spoke two languages: English and Computer.[16]

When I was a five-year-old kid in New Jersey . . . my dad woke me up in the middle of the night and rushed me into our car in my night clothes. . . . He had a thermos of coffee and had brought blankets, and we drove for about half an hour. We finally pulled over to the side of the road, and there were a couple hundred people, lying on their backs in the middle of the night, looking up at the sky. My dad found a place, spread the blanket out, and we both lay down. . . . He pointed to the sky, and there was a magnificent meteor shower.[17]

This memory would later form the organizing stimulus for *Close Encounters of the Third Kind*.

Spielberg's first filmmaking experience involved emulation of, and competition with, his father, however lighthearted:

A long, long time ago, I became interested in moviemaking simply because my father had an eight-millimeter movie camera, which he used to log the family history. I would sit and watch the home movies and criticize the shaky camera movements and bad exposures until my father finally got fed up and told me to take over. I became the family photographer and logged all our trips.[18]

It would not be unfair to say that Spielberg's father thus inadvertently launched his career.

Another episode speaks to more pointed youthful rivalrous feelings. When Spielberg was eleven, his father came home and gathered the family in the kitchen:

He held up a tiny little transistor he had brought home and said: "This is the future." I took the transistor from his hand . . . and I swallowed it. Dad laughed, then he didn't laugh; it got very tense. It was like the confrontation scene between Raymond Massey and James Dean in *East Of Eden*. One of those moments when two worlds from diametrically opposite positions in the universe collide. It was as if I was saying, "That's your future, but it doesn't have to be mine."[19]

Spielberg's quotation from *East Of Eden* is illuminating. In the movie, James Dean gives a classic performance as a rebellious late adolescent, Cal Trask, desperately struggling to overcome his father's perennial displeasure, while wrestling with his own strong ambivalence. The father is a stern, religious farmer who, like Spielberg's parent, greatly valorizes scientific progress. He sustains massive losses in an ill-advised effort to send iced-down vegetables by rail cross-country. The scene Spielberg alludes to occurs after the father refuses to accept the gift of "dirty" money Cal made in crop future speculation during World War I. One notes that Cal's "tainted" agricultural enterprise was a spectacular success, whereas the father's project failed abysmally (albeit "honorably" from the latter's censorious viewpoint).

Steinbeck's novel, and the film derived from it, are elsewhere rich in Oedipal resonances. Cal competes keenly with his brother Aaron for the father's love, as well as for Aaron's fiancée. Aaron's "good" persona obviously prefigures the preternaturally upright, idealized/envied paternal imago for Cal.

One may inquire if Spielberg has discovered an analogous idealized father/rival in Victor Fleming. The leitmotif of *A Guy Named Joe* is the struggle in its hero's heart with another aviator over the same love object. Did a similar competition exist in Spielberg's psyche with Fleming, "ownership" of the original film its aim, anxiety at the prospect of fulfilling that aim inevitable?

From this perspective, Pete's "accidental" flooding of the town in

Dorinda's tale takes on the ambiguous valence of a Freudian slip, where conflicted motive lies concealed beneath a gratuitous facade. Pete's rather surprising incompetence may be construed as a mask for Spielberg's ambivalent designs upon *A Guy Named Joe* and its creator. It may be speculated that the director aimed consciously to "hit the target," i.e., to render appropriate obeisance toward Fleming and his work, but could not resist indulging in a species of cinematic overkill, and went considerably wide of the mark.

No proof should be drawn from the above that Spielberg is particularly "neurotic." One speaks here only to the presence—and possible influence—of unconscious conflictual residues in the director's films. On the evidence of biographical material as well as his own brief autobiography, he seems an engaging, assertive individual, who has labored exceptionally well under the stresses of his idiosyncratic craft, is devoted to family and friends off the job. [20]

Setting aside the incidents previously described, there seems to have been little overt, serious conflict between Spielberg and his father. He speaks of him consistently with affection, and evidently remained close to him following his parents' divorce in his mid-teens. Spielberg has spoken of his mother with equal approval, and not a little awe:

She had more energy than a hundred mothers her age. The image I have of her is of this tiny woman climbing to the top of a mountain, standing there with her arms out and spinning around. My mom was always like a little girl, who never grew out of her pinafore. . . . She left a large wake. [21]

While somewhat estranged from peers during late childhood and adolescence—the nature, degree, and hurtfulness of his alienation varies considerably from one report to the next—Spielberg indicates that life at home was generally happy. The temperamental differences between his parents did cause him distress, related by the director with characteristic boyish diffidence:

My mom and dad were so different. That's probably why they were attracted to each other. They both love classical music . . . aside from that, they had nothing in common. . . . My mother was a classical pianist. She would have chamber concerts with her musician friends, in the living room, while in another room my father would be conferring with nine or ten other men in the business about how to build a computerized mousetrap. These opposite lifestyles would give me circuit overload. My tweeters would burn out and my only insulation would be my bedroom door which remained closed for most of my life. I had to put towels under the jamb so I couldn't hear the classical music and the computer logic.[22]

Spielberg's account could have been drawn from the pages of a Thomas Mann novel. He depicts himself as a suburban Tonio Kröger, his identifications riven between an artistically inclined, emotive mother and a burgherlike father, firmly anchored in scientific and business reality.

It can be reasonably argued on the basis of available sources that the director emerged from the Oedipal vicissitudes of early childhood with balanced, loving perceptions of his father, indeed both parents. Against this favorable background, with further unstinting parental affection he was able to weather the internal turmoil and external stresses of his adolescence. Drawing upon his native creative endowment, he eventually forged a primary identification with his mother's artistic inclinations, but also internalized his father's scientific interests and business acumen. The result is the adult of today—an auteur-producer-entrepreneur extraordinaire, exceptionally skillful at Hollywood's intricate business; passionate in advancing the technical parameters of filmmaking; eyes fixed literally and figuratively upon the stars.

However, even an immensely successful, stable son who enjoys a harmonious relationship with his parents may still harbor considerable unconscious fantasy referable to childhood traumata, including the Oedipal struggle. When that son is an artist, such fantasies may fuel his art, successfully or quite otherwise. For instance, Spielberg has little to say about the impact of his parents' separation, but its signature is written poignantly across the character of Elliot in *E.T.* and Cary Guffey's wonderful toddler in *Close Encounters*.

Both are children of divorce, each the apple of his mother's eye (like Spielberg), uncontested victor on the Oedipal field—a contest no little boy really wants to win. Each bears the stigmata of paternal loss—loneliness and longing openly articulated by Elliot, wordlessly by the younger child in his delighted tropism toward the blinding presence on the other side of the door. Recuperation of the father's absence is accomplished for both in a relationship with alien voyagers, themselves condensations of omnipotent father and achingly vulnerable child.

Human paternal surrogates in these and other Spielberg films are frequently portrayed as impersonal authoritarian oppressors or benevolent facilitators. Alternately, positive and negative paternal imagos are condensed in a single character. In *Close Encounters*, the polarization is manifested on the one hand by the officers who attempt to thwart Roy Neary and his fellow visionaries from realizing their quest; on the other by Lacombe, the luminously intelligent director of the secret mountain project whose intervention sends Neary across the galaxy.

In *E.T.*, Keys, the leader of the team dispatched by the government to apprehend Elliot's "visitor," is initially presented as a cold, impersonal bureaucrat (Spielberg deliberately keeps him and his minions faceless in their early appearances). As the tale unfolds, Keys evolves into an increasingly sympathetic character. He can empathize with Elliot's neediness because of his own childhood yearning for an "E.T."

These divided representations may be taken as embodiments of the child Spielberg's ambivalent perceptions of paternity—Oedipally shaded, as yet unintegrated imagos of the powerful, beloved father who unveils the heavens to his adoring son, or the no less powerful, harsh authority figure who seeks to impose his iron will upon his resentful offspring. The negative side of the equation is further darkened by the specter of paternal abandonment, which conceivably still haunts the director's imagination—abandonment through divorce in *E.T.* and *Close Encounters* (Spielberg's adolescent experience, projected backward upon those films' youngsters?); or through rank indifference, in the case of Indiana Jones's work-obsessed father. [23]

I have noted in an earlier essay on Fellini that "the connection between the artist's triumphs or disasters in his creative life and his mundane affairs is incompletely understood at this stage of psychoanalytic theory." [24] Pathobiography is an especially risky venture, often vitiated by dubious reportage, bias (including the myths artists spin around themselves), and scant clinical information. Freud himself acknowledged the limitations of interrogating Leonardo's oeuvre on the basis of a few historical details and a single, if trenchant dream.

Acknowledging the fragmentary and inferential nature of supporting evidence, I submit that an Oedipal gloss does offer modestly plausible grounds (internally plausible, that is, in terms of depth psychology) upon which to explicate *Always*'s overreaching and excessive contrivance. The only Spielberg film to treat heterosexual romance at length imbricates sexuality in a triangulation between two heroes and the woman they both love. The theme is common and ancient—and one which would seem to have proven particularly thorny for the director.

However, other causes within and external to Spielberg's psychic life that may have contributed to the film's aesthetic deficiencies must also be properly recognized: these include other directorial psychodynamics[25] and the dynamics of collaborators; financial and other "realistic" exigencies; the creative limitations of other major or minor players in the production.

Setting aside Spielberg's specific difficulties in remaking *A Guy Named Joe,* it does not seem untoward to suggest that an intrinsic Oedipal configuration lies deeply embedded in the remaking process, waiting to be evoked in the triangle between remaker, maker, and the original movie—all the more troublesome to the degree that the source is perceived by its remaker as a mysterious, ultimately unavailable plenitude.[26] Barthes's remarks on the text as maternal object, and the Oedipal thrust of narrativity seem apposite here: "The writer is someone who plays with his mother's body . . . in order to glorify [and] embellish it";[27] "Doesn't every narrative lead back to Oedipus? Isn't storytelling always a way of searching for one's origin, speaking one's conflict with the Law, entering into the dialectic of tenderness and hatred?"[28]

Pace other contributing factors, one speculates on the extent to which the shape (perhaps the quality, as well) of remaking depends upon the project's Oedipal significance for the remaker—notably, on how competitive strivings evoked by the maker and source are processed intrapsychically and artistically.[29] (An Oedipal dynamic would clearly have greatest impact when a director, or another personality under its sway, exerts central influence over the remaking project.)[30]

In-depth exploration of this issue lies beyond the scope of this inquiry but several possible outcomes can be tentatively advanced for those cinematic "cases" where significant Oedipal inflection of the original constitutes a problematic for the remaker:

1. The text exists under the sign of unwavering idealization; the remaker forswears competitive designs and remains unreflectively—even stultifyingly—"faithful" to it.

2. The remaker, analogous to a creative resolution of childhood and adolescent Oedipal conflict, eschews destructive competition with the maker, taking the original as a point of useful, relatively unconflicted departure.

3. The original, as signet of paternal potency and maternal unavailability/refusal, incites the remaker's unalloyed negativity. This precipitates a savage, contemptuous attack on the original, in which its significant elements are erased, disfigured, and/or parodied.

4. The remaker, simultaneously worshipful and envious of the maker, enters into an ambiguous, anxiety-ridden struggle with a film he both wishes to honor and eclipse. Caught up in contested homage, he eclipses his own native gifts—I venture this was the case with Spielberg in *Always*—dwindling down into a hopelessly compromised raider of the lost text.

10

Working Girl: Leveraged Sellout

Working Girl: Tess McGill, co-opt cinema's canny reinvention of the dumb blonde, makes her daily pilgrimage from the cultural barrens of Staten Island to Manhattan's tainted New Jerusalem.

*H*ollywood's ideology trends toward the comfortable Right. In the first half of the century, socially conscious films like *I Am a Fugitive from a Chain Gang* (1932) and *The Grapes of Wrath* (1940) were aberrations. The average studio picture was likely to endorse middle-class heartland values, patriarchy, and the profit motive. Sexism, racism, or the evils bred out of greedy big business practice were rarely confronted at the Bijou.

An upswing of serious social critiques and "problem films" followed World War II, issuing from Hollywood's liberal wing. But notwithstanding the McCarthyites' haunted fantasy of an industry festering with fellow travelers, films like *Home of the Brave* (1949) and *The Defiant Ones* (1959) still remained an exception rather than the rule. The movies sustained a brief flirtation with the Left during the upheavals of the sixties, reaching its zenith when Jane Fonda bearded the blacklisters in her Academy Award acceptance speech for *Coming Home* (1978). But as the Reagan era gathered momentum, Hollywood was quick to resurrect its native conservatism with Ramboesque enthusiasm, a state of affairs tempered but little since the Great Communicator passed the torch.

Whether one approves or condemns the decerebrate jingoism of the Stallones, the ideology of the New Right McMovie is at least blatantly up front. Much more problematic is a peculiar subgenre of pseudo-engaged cinema that has been intermittently surfacing since the counterculture went belly-up. Huey Long once asserted we would surely have fascism in America—"but we'll call it anti-fascism." In this vein, the pseudo-engaged movie with liberal premises covertly mocks, subverts, and/or co-opts the very social transformations of the sixties and seventies it would seem to be affirming.

A few examples.

The radicalism of the "healthy" sixties survivors in *The Big Chill* (1983) has been safely mainstreamed (one of its heroes has graduated from making revolution to hawking running shoes with few qualms of conscience and little regret). Their former political struggles are now perceived through a nostalgic haze, as a function of understandable but unrealistic adolescent idealism.

Personal Best (1982) allows a lesbian relationship between a pair of athletes, but implies that the affair is a provisional holding action for the younger, less troubled of the two until Mr. Right comes along (he does).

In *The Big Fix* (1978), an Abbie Hoffman clone who disappeared into the underground in the seventies reemerges as a high-salaried ad agency hack.

Mississippi Burning (1988) rewrites the history of the civil rights movement to propose that crusading agents of J. Edgar Hoover's FBI were largely responsible for bringing racial justice to the South.

The latest example of co-opt cinema, *Working Girl* (1988), enlists a facile feminism to rationalize the corporate smash-and-grab tactics scathingly criticized in *Wall Street* (1987), as well as earlier antibusiness pictures like *The China Syndrome* (1979) and *Silkwood* (1984). Its heroine, Tess McGill (Melanie Griffith), is a feisty Staten Island beauty who lacks the Ivy League credentials and social gloss to gain admission into a Manhattan stockbroker training program. She's marooned in the secretarial pool; her job as much a dead end as her relationship with a lowbrow neighborhood hunk who reads *Motor Trends* in bed before making love.

Fed up with an equally chauvinist boss—he picks her brains while fobbing off her body on lecherous buddies—Tess quits. She goes to work for Catherine Parker (Sigourney Weaver), a mergers-and-acquisitions hotshot with a blueblood background and the professional ethics of a jackal. Catherine takes Tess under her wing, exploits her shamelessly, teaching her just enough to turn her into an unthreatening disciple.

When Catherine is laid up out of town by a skiing accident, Tess discovers her erstwhile mentor has stolen her plan to broker the sale of a radio network to Oren Trask, a formidable elder statesman of the leveraged buyout. She also catches her boyfriend in flagrante delicto with a pneumatic bimbette from down the block.

Disgusted at playing patsy on and off the job, Tess moves into Catherine's posh Park Avenue apartment, borrowing her clothes, accent, and office. She contacts Jack Trainer (Harrison Ford), a handsome venture capitalist Catherine had planned to use for the Trask project and (unbeknownst to Tess) also hoped to marry. Tess passes herself off to Jack as an experienced player. In Jack's world, you're only as good as your last deal; his have been falling through. He gets fired up for the Trask action, and for Tess, too.

In a series of madcap exploits, gutsy Tess and intrepid Jack wangle an introduction to Trask, sell him on the network buyout, and enter into a torrid affair. Then Catherine returns, unmasks Tess, and represents to Trask that the project was her baby. Jack temporarily suspects Tess's passion was feigned. Once he realizes the depth of her love, he refuses to do the deal without her. Tess now convinces Trask that *she* put the network project together. She's read in *People* magazine that Slim Slicker, the network's star, may be about to bolt for richer pickings elsewhere. Catherine knows nothing about the rumor of his defection and, as it turns out, nothing about the original nuts and bolts of the deal. Trask has her fired on the spot, and hires Tess to start training with his firm's financial division. Tess moves in with Jack. The film ends as Tess exuberantly phones her working-class friends from her new office.

Various film theorists have pointed out that the classic Hollywood movie is so skillfully crafted as to efface viewer awareness of the mechanics of its production. Instead, one has the odd sense the picture is somehow being created and projected from within one's own brain. In the process, one is easily seduced away from examining questionable notions being pitched. Filmmakers are often quite as unconscious of the ideological bias in their work: their efforts can be more persuasive than heavy-handed propaganda when bad politics, sexism, or economic injustice are uncritically accepted as "givens" of the system.

Working Girl is exemplary in this regard. It's impeccably directed by Mike Nichols in the high style of those thirties and forties "screwball" comedies with a feminist thrust (*The Awful Truth* [1937], *Adam's Rib* [1949]), handsomely photographed (by Michael Ballhaus), and persuasively acted (Griffith and Ford are particularly good). It's hilarious, engrossing, and appallingly subversive of a generation's progress in women's rights.

Between scenes in the executive boardroom, Nichols has his knowing camera linger on knots of office women swapping gossip, taking up collections, so forth. He cleverly insinuates that the entire corporate apparatus, with its high profits for the privileged "classy" few, is fueled by low-cost labor, much of it woman's work. The cutthroat, demeaning competitiveness of the business jungle is also witheringly satirized.

But nowhere is it suggested that the rapacious system needs changes more fundamental than an infusion of the vital democratic spirit Tess embodies a là Frank Capra—Ms. Deeds Comes to Town. Nor can one glean from *Working Girl* that any working stiff or middle-management employee in the heartland could be harmed by buyout fallout—no assets sold off, no factories mercilessly shut down. The film ratifies Gordon Gekko's *Wall Street* dictum that greed is good. The only one who is going to get hurt in the film's world is a dealmaker who can't pull off a deal.

Despite his acknowledged ruthlessness in pursuit of an unholy buck, *Working Girl* admires Oren Trask—"the man who applied Japanese management principles, instead of kowtowing to the unions"—at least as much as Tess. "Mr. Trask knows *everything,*" breathes one of his awestruck execs. Trask is patriarchy personified, his power godlike. Cutting a deal for him is Tess's way out of the working class. In the end, his intervention (spurred by Jack) saves her skin and gives her the chance "to prove her mettle," by satisfying him that the network deal isn't a onetime flash in the pan.

But what chance does Trask really give her? Absent its aura of tinseltown fantasy, the entry-level job he majestically confers is really a crumb from the corporate table. Would a man who had just pulled off a megamillion score for his boss be so meanly rewarded? Tess's gratitude for Trask's meager bounty reflects the film's assumption that it's "natural" for those of humble origins—and female to boot—to come up the hard way if they want to fulfill the American dream. Horatio Alger's poor boys set the standard a century ago: the truth now, no less than then is that an uncomfortably large number of working-class Americans, particularly women and members of minority groups, wind up stuck in entry-level jobs. And today their typical level of entry is likely to be selling Big Macs at minimum wage.

For all her supposed braininess, Tess emerges as a reconstructed dumb blonde—not quite the Monroe airhead, rather an update of Billy Dawn in *Born Yesterday* (1950). Tess's chief asset—an uncanny knack for tuning into pop culture and intuiting what the Slim Slickers of medialand are up to—is subtly attributed to the working-class crudeness the film smugly implies is a hallmark of Staten Island life (it's simultaneously intimated that the parched spirit of the WASP executive could benefit from an injection of her barbarian blood).

Beyond her smarts, Tess succeeds because she's able to paper over her slob background with the signatures of class lifted from Catherine Parker to revenge Catherine's exploitation. (In *Working Girl* women have learned to trample over each other like men as they claw their way up the corporate ladder. If this is liberation, what constitutes bondage?) The film's depiction of Catherine's prissy villainy compares instructively to *Fatal Attraction*'s (1987) twisted construction of a vibrantly sexual, ambitious career woman into a frustrated psychotic caricature of women's lib.

Clinical experience with various Wall Street men indicates the real, as well as intrapsychic threat women like Catherine Parker often pose, especially when their education and skill articulate with an absolute imperviousness to flirtation. If the package also includes beauty and chic, the menace to male egos unaccustomed to dealing with a feminine business counterpart on equal footing can loom even more substantial.

Working Girl contrives to eliminate macho angst by deriding Catherine into a repellent Yuppie cliché, then humiliating her out of existence. Trask, echoing Tess, orders her to "get your bony ass out of here!" Bereft of employment and mate, Catherine exits with a curious dignity, a sacrifice on the altar of patriarchy. In the film's bitch-eat-bitch fantasy, Tess appears quite the Oedipal victor. But she has actually lost any meaningful potential for liberation, consigned to work her presumably softer ass off for the likes of Oren Trask.

Mindful of Catherine's former shabby use of her services, Tess gently advises her new secretary, "Don't get coffee unless you're getting it for yourself. We'll make up the rest as we go along." Shortly thereafter, the closing credits roll over Carly Simon's heart-swelling ballad, "Let the River Run." Simon's lyrics speak poignantly about actualizing the dream of "a new Jerusalem," as the camera pulls back from Tess's office window to pan across the blank facade of the Trask building, glittering in the bright morning sun.

The song, written by an acknowledged counterculture heroine, is set against a chilling image of the corporate monolith. The film's co-optation of the principles women like Simon—and Tess—and Catherine— went to the barricades for in the sixties is complete. How far Nichols has traveled from his own facile anticorporate bias of *The Graduate* (1967) and *Silkwood!* In a different movie and a different world, Tess might have crossed her river to become a physician, architect, educator, politician. In *Working Girl*'s corrupted New Jerusalem, where the risk arbitrageurs neither reap nor sow, Tess is well embarked on fulfilling her tarnished dream—becoming a kinder, gentler corporate raider.

11

Enemies: A Love Story—Awful Plausibility

Enemies: A Love Story: Already torn
between a wife in Brooklyn and a lover
in the Bronx, Broder finds the wife he
had thought slain by the Nazis
resurrected in Manhattan. "You're a lost
man, Herman," says Tamara. "You need
a manager."

*H*arry Stack Sullivan once said that the human tribe was characterized by its awful plausibility. He was probably referring to our infinite capacity for rationalizing questionable motivation. But his enigmatic remark seems peculiarly relevant to the curious admixture of courage, almost perverse stubbornness, and denial deployed by victims of catastrophic trauma like concentration camp survivors to struggle on.

It's not uncommon for camp victims to be perceived as intrinsically noble simply because they were *there* and managed to endure. While there was no shortage of heroic deeds, survival itself seems to have been mainly a matter of luck, slimly aided by the ability to think quickly on one's feet. To grasp the true enormity of Nazi evil, one more properly contemplates the stark variety of the butchered multitudes.

Everyone went into the camps, young and old; rich and poor; noble, ignoble, and (the majority, as always) those in between. Even though they may have behaved with exceptional fortitude while imprisoned, the few who came out weren't heroes anymore, just ordinary people who somehow had to suppress the extraordinary horrors they had beheld, or wrestle whatever meaning they could from their experiences, in aid of taking up life again. To this task they brought the same character mechanisms, psychological virtues, and neurotic liabilities which had helped or hindered them prior to the camps—supplemented by desolating post-traumatic pathology.

Unsophisticated investigations have ignored the articulation between Holocaust experience and the preexisting givens of personality. Poignant awareness of this connection hallmarks the sensibility of *Enemies: A Love Story* (1990), the deeply satisfying film Paul Mazursky has directed from Isaac Bashevis Singer's novel. Set in 1949, its definitively unheroic protagonist, Herman Broder, is a Polish intellectual who was away on business when a Nazi death squad invaded his town, executing his wife and two children. Broder was hidden in a barn for the duration of the occupation by Yadwiga, a Catholic servant. After the war, he wed his pliant savior and emigrated to America, where he now works itinerantly as a ghostwriter for an entrepreneurial rabbi.

According to Broder's awfully plausible reasoning, he married the none-too-brilliant Yadwiga out of gratitude. One infers he was also compelled by an ambivalent dependency on women that informed his pre-Holocaust adaptation, as well as his wrenching loneliness after the war. His sort of vulnerable neediness can be insidiously attractive, particularly in someone of Broder's slippery charm. The other side of the coin is often a formidable fear of engulfment by the feminine, energizing exuberant promiscuity.

In Poland, Broder was chronically unfaithful to his wife. In Brooklyn, he gulls the adoring Yadwiga into accepting outrageous yarns about bookselling trips, while he travels to the Bronx for steamy trysts with Masha, a camp survivor whose withering nihilism on all save sex matches her alarming beauty. "A backward country, this America . . . Where are the Nazis?" she asks. Before the war, Masha was locked in chronic struggle with her hysterical mother. After the camps, Masha found her mother near death, nursed her back to health, and took their perennial combat to the new world. Broder comments acidly that if these two were the last on earth they'd still be at each other's throats.

Broder's metastable arrangement is threatened when Masha starts pushing for more commitment, even though her estranged husband won't divorce her, just as Yadwiga is pressing him for a baby and approval of her conversion to Judaism. Then, the ultimate complication: his wife appears, resurrected! Two bullets in her hip, Tamara managed to clamber out of an SS mass grave, escape to Russia, and finally emigrate.

A newspaper advertisement brings Broder to Tamara's Lower East Side Manhattan apartment. Moments after their reunion, the two are quarreling as if the Holocaust never parted them. He objects to her unflattering appraisal of him, she mocks his remarriage, which she views as only the latest proof of his roving eye. She accuses him of having an affair with Yadwiga before the war, but suddenly (with a largeness of heart we learn is as characteristic as her sarcasm) backs off. She has no claim on him, for he had thought her dead, and in truth she views herself a living corpse.

Broder retreats in cowardly confusion. But as the demands of his other women escalate, he returns to Tamara and, briefly, to her bed; not out of any great physical desire, rather for the consolation of memory, particularly of their dead babies, and—after he tells her about Masha—for the clearheaded, not unfriendly read she gives him of a life grown so duplicitous Broder himself can't keep track of it.

Yadwiga and Masha both announce their pregnancies. Masha, ignorant of Tamara's return, now wants to marry Broder; it's utterly plausible to her that his marriage to a gentile is invalid. Her odious husband, Tortshiner, grants her a divorce, but secretly tells Broder she slept with him to obtain it. Like many of his ilk, Broder is insanely jealous. A compulsive seducer, he trembles with almost delusional anxiety that the women he has made love to might be seduced by another. Masha maintains Tortshiner lied, and Broder is persuaded to take yet a *third* wife! His dilemma is embodied hilariously in a scene where he stands, bewildered, on a subway platform, pondering which train to take to which borough or woman.

His tangled web begins to unravel when Yadwiga finds out about Masha, and Tamara visits Yadwiga. Once Yadwiga realizes Tamara isn't a ghost (a wonderfully comic turn), she offers to leave, or to stay on as the couple's servant. Instead, Tamara takes the betrayed Yadwiga under her wing like a benevolent godmother. Masha's pregnancy turns out to be a pseudocyesis. She is further demoralized—and infuriated—at discovering Tamara's presence in Broder's world. "You're a lost man, Herman," says Tamara, "You need a manager."

Tamara "manages" Herman's return to Yadwiga and to life as a rational being. But—"we're both devils"—he soon rejoins Masha. On the verge of their flight to California, Masha's mother dies and her apartment is robbed. The despondent Masha makes her terminal demand upon Broder—double suicide, to which he nearly assents, until he wheedles her into admitting she had indeed let Tortshiner bed her to get the divorce. In his most awful piece of plausibility, he lets her lie free him from the *Liebestod* she proposes, by signifying she's a whore (and, unlike his other, idealized women, a liar like himself), hence not worth his death. He leaves her to her fate. After her funeral and Yadwiga's delivery, we see Tamara and Yadwiga feeding Broder's new daughter, a baby girl named for Masha. The only trace of Broder, an envelope from points unknown, with a twenty dollar bill . . .

My summary scants the novel and film's tangled plotline, which is highly reminiscent of the bedroom farces of Goldoni and Feydeau. The manic energy propelling their plays seems almost a force of nature, bred out of the adulterous characters' ornery lustfulness and terror of exposure. *Enemies'* hectic propulsion likewise proceeds from Broder's relentless adulteries. However, beyond pure concupiscence, Broder—and Masha—are poignantly driven by post-traumatic denial. A therapist who herself survived the camps said she regularly discovered such rampant promiscuity in not a few survivors. She believed they sought to erase their despair, to suppress catastrophic memories through the balm of endlessly repeated orgasms.

The film opens on Broder's recurring dream of hiding in the hayloft while German soldiers beat Yadwiga below. The sequence ends on a close-up of her screaming, bloody mouth. It is, as critic Georgia Brown has aptly observed, a ruling symbol for Broder: of Yadwiga's sacrifice, but also of the damage that woman herself might inflict upon him. One theorizes that his dependence on Yadwiga during his long "imprisonment" has sharpened his considerable prewar ambivalence on both ends; death lay waiting for him should her care fail; death lay waiting for him precisely *because* he had put himself in her hands instead of attempting escape.

Broder's oscillation between dependency and flight from feminine entrapment comprises *Enemies'* narrative mainspring. Months or years of passive, frightened watchfulness in the barn have generated a frantic modus vivendi, in which no woman (really no *one*) will ever pin him down, and memory is held at bay by literally reinventing his life from one day to the next. Yet always on the other side of his restless running is the craving for protection in a woman's arms. His flashbacks to the Nazis are often dictated by the threat of rupture in his relationship with Masha, his most exciting object—for in her quarrelsome eroticism resides his most potent denial of terrible remembrance.

He, in turn, is Masha's exciting object. But she has been through the camps (the only one of the major characters to be actually imprisoned), does not share Broder's feckless desire to survive. Her overheated eroticism is thinly layered over an increasingly unambivalent wish for death, the ultimate remedy against memory.

Broder's ambivalence about his mother may only be intimated; Masha's hostile symbiosis with hers is glaring. The original struggle to be quit of her mother possibly caused wrongheaded affairs with rejecting or unavailable men (a frequent clinical finding in such women). However, as with many young adult survivors, the camp experience radically foreclosed her opportunity for psychological growth, and profoundly fixated her previous neurotic inclinations.

Masha has grown more entangled than ever with her mother after the awful sundering of their European world. She has been primed for a hateful marriage, then a no-win affair with Broder. A succession of narcissistic blows erode her brittle defenses; her mother's death overwhelms them. Reunion with mother in the blissful forgetfulness of the grave is such a blessing that she's positively radiant with gratitude when Broder refuses to join her. It is a quite ineffable moment of a soul in mortal torment, laid bare to the amazed truth of its wish to simply cease being.

Yadwiga and Tamara embody more integrative possibilities of survival. Broder views Yadwiga impatiently as a lovestruck simpleton, but she's a model of constancy and quiet piety (in successive faiths). She also proves to be nobody's fool, revealing an unexpected depth of character as awareness of Broder's hypocrisy ripens.

Tamara, despite her assertions of deadness, contrives to split off the part of her spirit deadened by loss and carry on. Her first act of affirmation is remedying her crippling from Nazi bullets. Her ironic morality and a genuine sense of indebtedness to Yadwiga preclude resuming her marriage. Instead, she jury-rigs an ambiguous but healing relationship with the couple, first as Broder's "manager," then as surrogate mother of his new child. Significantly, it's on the night before her operation that she visits Yadwiga. In time these two betrayed, honorable women draw on their mutual vitality and courage to find the anchor in each other that the craven, elusive Broder could never provide.

After Paul Mazursky's not particularly profound accounts of American midlife angst (*Bob and Ted and Carol and Alice*, [1969] *An Unmarried Woman*, [1978] *Down and Out in Beverly Hills* [1986]), *Enemies* comes as a revelation. Mazursky directs powerfully, each sequence a jewel in composition and shot rhythm, from the script he wrote with Roger L. Simon. Singer's characters are considerably deepened, and the New York milieu of my own youth is captured with mellow accuracy down to the most uncanny details of dress, architecture, and design.

The casting of the film's major and minor parts is impeccable. Angelica Huston plays an elegant, mordantly witty Tamara. Yadwiga's luminous sweetness is delightfully portrayed by Polish actress Margaret Sophie Stein, in a strong American film debut. Lena Olin, from Ingmar Bergman's group in Stockholm, acutely depicts Masha's impatient lust, her astringency, her quicksilver shifts around the certainty of her doom.

Ron Silver, one of our best stage actors, renders Broder artfully plausible, as sympathetic as the character's essential weakness and shadiness allows. Mazursky himself is properly brutal in a cameo role as the vile Tortshiner. Judith Malina is utterly convincing as Masha's chronically overwrought mother. Maurice Jarre has written an idiomatic score that colorfully cites Yiddish *klezmer* music (note the great swooping performance of clarinet virtuoso Giora Feidman).

Like the Grand Inquisitor's meditation in *The Brothers Karamazov*, *Enemies: A Love Story* is centrally preoccupied with the meaning latent in the death of children. The cruelty of the Holocaust is epitomized by the murder of Tamara's youngsters. They speak to her in her sleep; visions of their faces haunt her abortive attempts at lovemaking after the war. Broder opposes Yadwiga's pregnancy because he cannot tolerate losing another child. On Yom Kippur eve he refuses defiantly to join her in synagogue, then weeps over the photographs of his slaughtered babes. For a moment one glimpses the shattering grief underpinning his frenzied philandering, and can pity him. The termination of Masha's false pregnancy mocks her search for meaning beyond the orgasmic. Her mother, who had wished for a baby to name after "all the dead Jews," is equally devastated.

Masha resolves her existential crisis by suicide. For Broder, a God who could sanction the extermination of His children is either an omnipotent monster or a fiction. Yet he still fears Him, or the judgments of his murdered father upon his faithless, disordered life. Broder's solution, as always, is to run. He flees the struggle to divine God's purposes, the responsibility of generativity, the responsivity parenthood would urge, and becomes a rootless wanderer.

But Yadwiga, who never lost her faith in life or God, is joined by the truly resurrected Tamara in caring for the baby Masha; hope reborn in the name of one who had lost all hope. *Enemies* concludes on a prolonged lovely shot of Coney Island's famous "Wonder Wheel"; seen marginally throughout the film, it now becomes a marvelous, condensed symbol both of the ceaseless, empty turning of Broder's wretched spirit, and of life triumphantly renewed in the very teeth of death.

Notes

Introduction

Unless otherwise indicated, works by the authors mentioned in this introduction are fully referenced in the next chapter, "Reel Significations."

1. Norman Holland, "I-Ing Lacan," in Patrick Colm Hogan and Lalita Pandit, eds., *Criticism and Lacan: Essays and Dialogues on Language, Structure, and the Unconscious* (Athens: University of Georgia Press, 1990), pp. 87–108; "Review of *The Works of Jacques Lacan: An Introduction*," *Psychoanalytic Psychology* 7(1) (1990):139–49; Marshall Edelson, *The Trouble(s) with Lacan*, in press. Edelson also raises serious doubts about the usefulness of Lacanian theory on language for psychoanalysis. See Edelson, *Language and Interpretation in Psychoanalysis* (New Haven: Yale University Press, 1975), pp. 6–13.

2. With the exception of Julia Kristeva's recent admirable study of depression, citing her analysis of severely depressed patients (*Black Sun: Depression and Melancholia*, Leon S. Roudiez, trans. [New York: Columbia University Press, 1989]). Kristeva was trained and analyzed by Lacan; her project is influenced as much by Barthesian semiology as Lacanian psycholinguistics. It is not clear to me whether she can be unambiguously located within the Lacanian camp on the basis of her current practice: thus, *Black Sun*'s views on ego functioning in melancholia seem surprisingly "orthodox." (Since Lacan's death and the violent dispersion of his inheritors, qualifications for *echt* Lacanian status often appear moot in any case.) Kristeva is one of the few analysts of her persuasion to cite biochemical factors in psychiatric illness and to approve of drug therapy.

Other relevant writings on actual Lacanian clinical practice include M. H. Spiro, "Psychoanalytic Reflections on a Particular Form of Language Distortion," *Psychoanalytic Quarterly* 59(1) (1990):54–74; D. Moss, "From the Treatment of a Nearly Psychotic Man: A Lacanian Perspective," *International Journal of Psychoanalysis* 70 (1989):275–86; R. D. Chessick, "Lacan's Practice of Psychoanalytic Psychotherapy," *American Journal of Psychotherapy* 41(4) (1987):571–79; J. E. Gorney, "The Clinical Application of Lacan in the Psychoanalytic Situation," *Psychoanalytic Review* 69(2) (1982):241–48; Catherine Clement, *The Lives and Legends of Jacques Lacan*, Arthur Goldhammer, trans. (New York: Columbia University Press, 1983); and Stuart Schneiderman, ed. and trans., *Returning to Freud: Clinical Psychoanalysis in the School of Lacan* (New Haven: Yale University Press, 1980).

3. The widespread usefulness of psychotherapy whose theory and practices derive from Freudian/neo-Freudian psychoanalysis is documented in several well-designed clinical studies: M. L. Smith, G. V. Glass, and T. I. Miller, *The Benefits of Psychotherapy* (Baltimore: Johns Hopkins University Press, 1980); D. A. Shapiro and D. Shapiro, "Meta-Analysis of Comparative Outcome Studies: A Replication and Refinement," *Psychological Bulletin* 92 (1982):581–604; L. Luborsky et al. *Who Will Benefit from Psychotherapy?: Predicting Therapeutic Outcomes* (New York: Basic Books, 1988). To the best of my knowledge no similar thorough investigations have been undertaken regarding the outcome of therapy based on Lacanian theory and technique.

4. Notably, the Freudian ego psychologists (Hartman et al.), with their vision of an autonomous, "unsplit" ego/subject. Among the many areas virtually neglected by Lacan's project is the depth psychology of adolescence, including pubertal, cognitive, and linguistic development.

5. In France the popularizing of Lacanian theory has proceeded for some time. Insofar as I can determine, this mainly involves other venues than the mental health establishment and does not much parallel the helpful incorporation of orthodox Freudian and neo-Freudian concepts into various widespread extra-analytic psychotherapies that has occurred elsewhere.

Sherry Turkle argues that the incorporation of Lacanian psychoanalysis into Gallic popular discourse can be related to the May 1968 uprisings. She analogizes to the general fascination with existentialism in France after World War II and Occupation/Resistance:

Both theories offered historically appropriable "things to think with," theoretical materials for a cultural process analogous to . . . *brico-lage.* . . . After the events [of May], people were left hungry for a way to continue to think about sexuality and self-expression as part of a revolutionary movement. . . . French social and political theory tended to accept the fundamentals of Lacan's theoretical scaffolding: in particular, the notions that people are constituted by language, that our discourse embodies the society beyond, and that there is no autonomous ego. . . . Lacanianism became a bridge between French Marxism, French feminism, French anti-psychiatry, and French psychoanalysis.

(Sherry Turkle, " 'Dynasty': Review of *Jacques Lacan and Co.: A History of Psychoanalysis in France, 1925–1985*," *London Review of Books* [December 6, 1990]:8.) For further information on the reception of Lacan by the French, see Elisabeth Roudinesco, *Jacques Lacan and Co.: A History of Psychoanalysis in France, 1925–1985*, Jeffrey Mehlman, trans. (London: Free Association Books, 1990).

6. "*Psycho:* The Apes at the Windows," essay 5 of this volume.

7. In *The Movies on Your Mind* (New York: E. P. Dutton, 1975), I theorized about the conscious and unconscious fulfillment of omnipotent/omniscient fantasy by cinema. The subject merits further study, e.g., regarding the possibility that watching a film energizes regressive fantasies of blissful satiation at the maternal breast, replete with omnipotent claims upon the mother. See the work by Bruce Kawin, Marsha Kinder, and Robert Eberwein, discussed in the next essay, on the relationship between the cinematic and dream "screens."

8. The present collection contains little pathobiographic study; for example, see my essay on narcissistic pathology in Fellini's oeuvre, "*8½:* The Declensions of Silence," in *The Movies on Your Mind*, pp. 138–68.

9. Greenberg, *The Movies on Your Mind*, p. 11.

10. "The determining, identifying feature of a film genre is its cultural context, its community of interrelated character types whose attitudes, values, and actions flesh out dramatic conflicts inherent within that community. The generic community is less a specific place (although it may be [so] . . .), than a network of characters, actions, values, and attitudes" (Thomas Schatz, *Hollywood Genres: Formulas, Filmmaking, and the Studio System* [New York: Random House, 1981], pp. 21–22).

"All film genres treat some form of threat—violent or otherwise—to the social order. However, it is the attitudes of the principal characters and the resolutions precipitated by their actions which finally distinguish the various genres from one another" (ibid., p. 26).

11. Christian Metz, *The Imaginary Signifier*, Celia Britton et al., trans. (Bloomington: Indiana University Press, 1982), p. 14.

12. Ibid., p. 15.

1. Reel Significations: An Anatomy of Psychoanalytic Film Criticism

The epigraph is from Denis Diderot, *Rameau's Nephew: D'Alembert's Dream* (London: Penguin, 1966), p. 47.

1. Sigmund Freud, "Delusions and Dream in Jensen's *Gradiva*," in J. Strachey, ed., *Standard Edition of the Complete Psychological Works of Sigmund Freud*, vol. 9 (London: Hogarth Press, 1959), p. 3.

2. The lack of analytic criticism in the nonverbal arts foregrounds inherent problems with applied psychoanalysis. Written or spoken literature is generally a more comfortable habitat for the psychoanalyst; study of other art forms demands an appreciation of media and symbolic languages not familiar to most

clinicians. The shortcomings of pathobiography in these fields are especially evident. Fine arts and music "convey their messages wordlessly—they rely on the nature of their themes as content to a much lesser degree than does literature, so that psychoanalytic attempts to explain their aesthetic form based . . . on a search for typical conflicts [are] bound to be unproductive" (J. E. Gedo, "Thoughts on Art in the Age of Freud: A Review," *Journal of the American Psychoanalytic Association* 18 [1970]:219).

Music presents particular difficulties for psychoanalysis due to its lack of obvious connotations and denotations, as well as the formidable obstacles of conceptualizing a fluid, nonideational medium. Several investigators have linked the infant's oceanic perception of the mother's voice and heartbeat to the adult listener's unreflective immersion in the medium's sensuous sounds. See D. Anzieu, "L'envelope sonore du soi," *Nouvelle revue de psychoanalyse* 13 (1976):161–79; and G. Rosolato, "La voix: Entre corps et langage," *Revue française de psychoanalyse* 38(1) (1974):74–94.

Doubtless because of the problems cited above, the psychoanalytic study of cinematic music and sound is even more sparse than other limited investigations into these subjects. See the admirable anthology, E. Weis and J. Belton, eds., *Film Sound: Theory and Practice* (New York: Columbia University Press, 1985); C. Gorbman, *Unheard Melodies: Narrative Film Music* (Bloomington: Indiana University Press, 1987); and C. Flinn, " 'The Most Romantic Art of All': Music in the Classic Hollywood Cinema," *Cinema Journal* 29(4) (199):35–50.

3. Many of mainstream cinema's narrative strategies evolved from analogous textual practices in nineteenth-century novels and melodramas (flashbacks, intercutting between parallel action, dramatic rescues, etc.). Movies today still continue to process the same themes, plots, and characters which made their literary/dramatic antecedents such fertile ground for analytic criticism. *Gradiva,* for instance, readily "visualizes" as a Hitchcock or De Palma thriller like *Vertigo* (1961) or *Obsession* (1976).

4. E. Jones, *The Biography of Sigmund Freud,* vol. 3 (London: Hogarth Press, 1957), p. 121.

5. H. C. Abraham and E. L. Freud, eds., *A Psychoanalytic Dialogue: The Letters of Sigmund Freud and Karl Abraham, 1907–1926* (New York: Basic Books, 1965). See also B. Chodorkoff and S. Baxter, *"Secrets of a Soul:* An Early Psychoanalytic Film Venture," *American Imago* 31(4) (1974):319–34, for an extensive discussion of the project.

6. H. Sachs, *"Secrets of a Soul": A Psychoanalytic Film* (Berlin: Lichtbild-Buhne, 1926).

7. *Closeup*'s editors, McPherson and Bryher, had intriguing ties with the psychoanalytic community. Irving Schneider discusses the magazine's history and content at length (*Closeup* and its contributors, in preparation).

8. See H. Sachs, *The Creative Unconscious* (Boston: Sci-Art Publishers, 1942), for his work on cinema and the arts.

9. H. Münsterberg, *The Photoplay* (New York: Dover, 1970).

10. Ibid., p. 95.

11. R. Durgnat, *Films and Feelings* (Cambridge, Mass.: MIT Press, 1971), p. 67.

12. M. Wolfenstein and N. Leites, *The Movies* (New York: Atheneum, 1970).

13. See my analysis in essay 2 of this collection.

14. P. Tyler, *The Hollywood Hallucination* (New York: Simon and Schuster, 1944).

15. Tyler was nevertheless quite acute on occasion. See his study of the homoerotically tinged relationship between *Double Indemnity*'s (1944) sleazy insurance salesman and his older principled mentor. Long before the semiotic/Marxist critics, Tyler observed that "Hollywood is but the industrialization of the mechanical worker's daylight dream . . . extended ritualistically into those hours reserved by custom for relaxation and amusement" (ibid., p. vii).

16. Greenberg, *The Movies on Your Mind,* p. 11.

17. K. Gabbard and G. O. Gabbard, *Psychiatry and the Cinema* (Chicago: University of Chicago Press, 1987), p. 187.

18. The dedicated auteurist would counter that a unique signature of directorial style and preoccupation—neurotic or otherwise—is present in *any* film, however obscured by constraints of studio, star, or other agency.

19. S. Weissman, "Chaplin's *The Kid,*" in J. W. Smith and W. Kerrigan, eds., *Images in Our Souls: Cavell, Psychoanalysis, and Cinema* (Baltimore: Johns Hopkins University Press, 1987), pp. 183–86.

20. J. Beebe, "At the Movies: Alfred Hitchcock, 1899–1980," *San Francisco Jung Institute Library Journal* 1(3) (1980):36–37; Beebe, "Film as Active Imagination," audiotape of seminar, San Francisco C. G. Jung Institute, October 10–11, 1981; Beebe, "Film and the Unconscious," audiotape of seminar, San Francisco C. G. Jung Institute, February 1982; and Beebe, "Creativity in the Movie Image: *Vertigo* and *North by Northwest,*" audiotape of seminar, San Francisco C. G. Jung Institute, October 10–11, 1986.

21. Holland is one of the few academic literary/film theorists to undergo formal psychoanalytic training. He was instrumental in founding the Center for the Psychological Study of the Arts at the State University of New York at Buffalo, and subsequently the Institute for Psychological Study of the Arts at the University of Florida, Gainesville. Over the past several decades these institutions and the programs they inspired have generated a wealth of psychoanalytic research into the humanities and cinema. Holland's work on film includes "The

Puzzling Movies: Their Appeal," in R. A. Smith, ed., *Aesthetics and Criticism in Art Education: Problems in Defining, Explaining, and Evaluating Art* (New York: Rand McNally, 1966), pp. 453–61; "I-Ing Film," *Critical Inquiry* 12 (1986): 654–71; and "Film Response from Eye to I: The Kuleshov Experiment," *South Atlantic Quarterly* 88 (1989):415–42.

22. N. Frye, *Anatomy of Criticism* (Princeton: Princeton University Press, 1957); Frye, *Fables of Identity* (New York: Harcourt, Brace, and World, 1963).

23. D. Frederickson, "Jung/Sign/Symbol/Film, part 1," *Quarterly Review of Film Studies* 4(2) (1979):167–92; Frederickson, "Jung/Sign/Symbol/Film, part 2," *Quarterly Review of Film Studies* 5(4) (1980):460–78.

24. C. Branson, *Howard Hawks: A Jungian Study* (Santa Barbara, Calif.: Capra Press, 1987).

25. For an excellent sampling of such criticism, see J. Hillier, ed., *Cahiers du Cinema: The 1950s—Neo-Realism, Hollywood, New Wave* (Cambridge, Mass.: Harvard University Press, 1985).

26. C. Metz, *Language and Cinema,* D. J. Umiker-Sebeok, trans. (The Hague: Mouton, 1971); Metz, *Film and Language: A Semiotics of the Cinema,* M. Taylor, trans. (New York: Oxford University Press, 1974); and Metz, *The Imaginary Signifier.*

27. K. Silverman, *The Subject of Semiotics* (New York: Oxford University Press, 1983).

28. J. P. Oudart, "Cinema and Suture," *Screen* 18(4) (1978):35–47.

29. D. Dayan, "The Tutor Code of Classical Cinema," in B. Nichols, ed., *Movies and Methods* (Berkeley: University of California Press, 1976), p. 438.

30. See E. A. Kaplan, *Women's Pictures: Feminism and the Cinema* (London: Routledge and Kegan Paul, 1982); M. A. Doane, "Film and the Masquerade: Theorizing the Female Spectator," *Screen* 23(3–4) (1982):74–87; Doane, *The Desire to Desire: The Woman's Film of the 1940s* (Bloomington: Indiana University Press, 1987); A. Kuhn, *Women's Pictures: Feminism and the Cinema* (London: Routledge and Kegan Paul, 1982); and T. De Lauretis, *Alice Doesn't: Feminism, Semiotics, Cinema* (Bloomington: Indiana University Press, 1984).

31. This account is drawn from Gabbard and Gabbard, *Psychiatry and the Cinema,* p. 182.

32. L. Mulvey, "Visual Pleasure and the Narrative Cinema," in G. Mast and M. Cohen, eds., *Film Theory and Criticism,* 3d ed. (New York: Oxford University Press, 1985), pp. 803–16.

33. See Gabbard and Gabbard, *Psychiatry and the Cinema,* p. 183.

34. Silverman, *The Subject of Semiotics,* p. 212.

35. See also my essay on *Psycho,* essay 5 in this book, for further analysis of the psychiatrist's role.

36. R. Wood, *Hollywood from Vietnam to Reagan* (New York: Columbia University Press, 1986), p. 247.

37. R. Durgnat, "Review of *The Imaginary Signifier*," *Film Quarterly* 36(2) (1982):61.

38. S. Heath, *Questions of Cinema* (Bloomington: Indiana University Press, 1981).

39. C. McCabe, *Tracking the Signifier: Theoretical Essays—Film, Linguistics, Literature* (Minneapolis: University of Minnesota Press, 1985).

40. L. Althusser, "Ideology and Ideological State Apparatuses (Notes Towards an Investigation)," in *Lenin and Philosophy, and Other Essays*, B. Brewster, trans. (London: New Left Books, 1971), pp. 127–86.

41. S. Cavell, *The World Viewed* (Cambridge, Mass.: Harvard University Press, 1979); Cavell, *Pursuits of Happiness: The Hollywood Comedy of Remarriage* (Cambridge, Mass.: Harvard University Press, 1981); and Cavell, "Psychoanalysis and Cinema: The Melodrama of the Unknown Woman," in Smith and Kerrigan, eds., *Images in Our Souls*, pp. 11–43.

42. R. Wood, *Hitchcock's Films* (New York: A. S. Barnes, 1965; revised ed., New York: Columbia University Press, 1989).

43. B. Kawin, *Mindscreen: Bergman, Godard, and First-Person Film* (Princeton: Princeton University Press, 1978); M. Kinder, "The Adaptation of Cinematic Dreams," *Dreamworks* 1 (1980):54–68; R. T. Eberwein, *Film and the Dream Screen* (Princeton: Princeton University Press, 1984).

44. N. Chodorow, *The Reproduction of Mothering* (Berkeley: University of California Press, 1978); G. Studlar, "Masochism and the Perverse Pleasures of the Cinema," In Nichols, ed., *Movies and Methods*.

45. G. Studlar, *In the Realm of Pleasure: Von Sternberg, Dietrich, and the Masochistic Aesthetic* (New York: Columbia University Press, 1992).

46. R. B. Ray, *A Certain Tendency of the Hollywood Cinema, 1930–1980* (Princeton: Princeton University Press, 1985); D. Polan, *Power and Paranoia: History, Narrative, and the American Cinema, 1940–50* (New York: Columbia University Press, 1985).

47. B. Singer, "Film, Photography, and Fetish: The Analyses of Christian Metz," *Cinema Journal* 27(4) (1988):4–22.

48. D. Bordwell, *Making Meaning: Inference and Rhetoric in the Interpretation of Cinema* (Cambridge, Mass.: Harvard University Press, 1989).

49. N. Carroll, *Mystifying Movies: Fads and Fallacies in Contemporary Film Theory* (New York: Columbia University Press, 1988).

50. Ibid., p. 70.

51. K. Silverman, *The Acoustic Mirror: The Female Voice in Psychoanalysis and Cinema* (Bloomington: Indiana University Press, 1988); C. Penley, *The Future of an Illusion: Film, Feminism, and Psychoanalysis* (Minneapolis: University of Minnesota Press, 1989); M. A. Doane, "Remembering Women: Psychical and Historical Constructions in Film Theory," in E. A. Kaplan, ed., *Psychoanalysis and Cinema* (New York: Routledge, 1990); S. Flitterman-Lewis, *To Desire Differ-*

ently: Feminism and the French Cinema (Urbana: University of Illinois Press, 1990); E. A. Kaplan, *Motherhood and Representation: The American Maternal Melodrama, 1830 to the Present* (forthcoming).

52. J. Bergstrom and M. A. Doane, eds., "Special Issue: 'The Spectatrix,' " *Camera Obscura* 20–21 (1990).

53. M. Hansen, "Pleasure, Ambivalence, Identification: Valentino and Female Spectatorship," *Cinema Journal* 25(4):7. Mulvey has modified this, taking into account later work in the field, in two subsequent considerations of her original essay. See L. Mulvey, *Visual and Other Pleasures* (Bloomington: Indiana University Press, 1989).

54. T. Modleski, *The Women Who Knew Too Much: Hitchcock and Feminist Theory* (New York: Methuen, 1988); L. Williams, *Hard Core: Power, Pleasure, and the "Frenzy of the Visible"* (Berkeley: University of California Press, 1989).

55. Williams, *Hard Core*, p. 206.

56. M. Turim, *Flashbacks in Film: Memory and History* (New York: Routledge, 1989).

57. Ibid., p. 20.

58. S. White, "Male Bonding, Hollywood Orientalism, and the Repression of the Feminine in Kubrick's *Full Metal Jacket*," *Arizona Quarterly* 44(3) (1988):120–44.

59. I. Bick, "Outatime: Re-creationism and the Adolescent Experience in *Back to the Future*," *Psychoanalytic Review*, forthcoming.

60. T. Elsaesser, "Film History and Visual Pleasure: Weimar Cinema," in P. Mellencamp and P. Rosen, eds., *Cinema Histories, Cinema Practices* (Frederick, Md.: University Presses of America, 1984); P. Petro, *Joyless Streets: Women and Melodramatic Representation in Weimar Germany* (Princeton: Princeton University Press, 1989).

61. I. Schneider, "The Theory and Practice of Movie Psychiatry," *American Journal of Psychiatry* 144(8) (1987):996–1002.

62. R. Huss, *The Mindscapes of Art: Dimensions of the Psyche in Drama and Film* (Rutherford, N.J.: Fairleigh Dickinson University Press, 1986).

2. *Cult Cinema:* Casablanca—*If It's So Schmaltzy, Why Am I Weeping?*

The epigraph is from Norman Rosten, "Nobody Dies Like Humphrey Bogart," in Paul Michael, ed., *Humphrey Bogart: The Man and His Films* (New York: Bobbs-Merrill, 1965), p. 5.

1. Pauline Kael, *Kiss, Kiss, Bang, Bang* (New York: Bantam, 1969), p. 303.

2. Andrew Sarris, *The American Cinema* (New York: E. P. Dutton, 1968), p. 176.

3. Howard Koch, *"Casablanca"—Script and Legend* (New York: Overlook Press, 1973).

4. All quotes from the film are taken from ibid.

5. Ibid., p. 24.

6. See Richard Corliss, essay on *Casablanca*, ibid., p. 198.

7. Harvey Greenberg, *"The Treasure of the Sierra Madre:* There's Success Phobia in Them Thar Hills," in *The Movies on Your Mind,* pp. 33–52.

8. See essay 3 in this book.

9. See R. Harris Smith, *OSS* (Berkeley: University of California Press, 1972).

10. Smith addresses this issue at some length (ibid.).

11. A conclusion based on Smith's account (ibid.), as well as the observations of one of my teachers, who escaped the *Anschlüss* to spend several months in Casablanca before emigrating to Canada, thence to the United States.

12. Ibid., p. 39.

13. General Maxime Weygand, 74-year-old Vichy governor of North Africa, supposedly the bastard son of Maximilian of Mexico. Although the person of Weygand was real, no "letters of transit" with such absolute irrevocability could ever have been issued by him.

Some *Casablanca* buffs insist Lorre flubbed the reference to Weygand, and said "General de Gaulle." Supposedly the flub was not picked up due to production pressure. Repeated hearings reveal that Lorre's accent obscures Weygand's name, making it sound—by a stretch—like "de Gaulle."

14. Barbara Deming, *Running Away from Myself* (New York: Grossman Publishers, 1969), see chapter 2; Corliss, essay on *Casablanca* in Koch, *"Casablanca."*

15. Krin Gabbard and Glen O. Gabbard. "Play It Again, Sigmund: Psychoanalysis and the Classical Hollywood Text," *Journal of Popular Film and Television* 18(1) (1990):6–17.

16. Silverman, *The Acoustic Mirror.*

17. Ray, *A Certain Tendency.*

18. Gabbard and Gabbard, "Play It Again, Sigmund," p. 15.

19. Including the frisson of renunciation, commented upon variously throughout this book.

20. Gabbard and Gabbard, "Play It Again, Sigmund," p. 16.

See also the following: Bruce A. Austin, "Portrait of a Cult Film Audience: *The Rocky Horror Picture Show," Journal of Communications* 31 (1981):450–65; Umberto Eco, *"Casablanca:* Cult Movies and Intertextual Collage," in *Travels in Hyperreality,* William Weaver, trans. (New York: Harcourt Brace Jovanovich, 1986) (Eco veers between Barthesian profundity and pixillation. *Casablanca* as postmodern icon; the ultimate incoherent, "unhinged" text; clotted with genre and mythic referents; a melange of "intertextual archetypes"; frames, moments, speeches, so forth, "cited or in some way recycled by innumerable other texts" [p. 200]. The film "is not *one* movie. It is 'movies.' . . . When all the archetypes burst out shamelessly, we plumb Homeric profundity. . . . The extreme of banality allows us to catch a glimpse of the Sublime [pp. 208, 209]); Gary Green, "The Happiest of Happy Accidents: A Reevaluation of *Casablanca*," *Smithsonian Studies in American Art* 1(2) (1987):3–14 (Green asserts that *Casablanca* was no happy accident, due to the underrated talents of Michael Curtiz [my essay was as dismissive of Curtiz as other criticism at that time]. Green marshals impressive evidence for Curtiz's intervention at every level of production [inter alia, he was responsible for the insertion of the Paris flashback into the script]. This exquisite sense of composition was influenced by the German Expressionist style he encountered during his early days at Berlin's UFA studio. Green believes the director was deeply drawn to *Casablanca*'s underlying dark themes, and imparted a strong noirish sensibility to the film which has been insufficiently appreciated); J. Hoberman and Jonathan Rosenbaum, *Midnight Movies* (New York: Harper and Row, 1983) (the authors discuss cult films, notably the more weird and horrific. For the emergence of the *Casablanca* cult, see p. 30); Canham Kingsley, *Hollywood Professionals* (New York: A. S. Barnes, 1973) offers biographic material on Michael Curtiz; and Jack Nachbar, "*Casablanca* and the Home Front," presentation at the Popular Culture Association meeting, Chicago, 1987 (Nachbar offers fascinating data on determinants of the film's horizon of reception at its release; e.g., the World War II period's record consumption of alcohol and tobacco, immense popularity of radio "hit parades" in the context of gasoline rationing. Nachbar wonders if "stranded" viewers were particularly primed to identify with the entrapped emigrés of the Cafe Americain as they transacted escape, brooded about the lack thereof over cocktails, and danced the nights away in a haze of cigarette smoke).

3. The Detective Film: The Maltese Falcon—Even Paranoids Have Enemies

The first epigraph is from Raymond Chandler, "Casual Notes on the Mystery Novel," in S. Burack, ed., *Writing Detective and Mystery Fiction* (Boston: The Writer, Inc., 1945), pp. 81–89. The second is from Raymond Chandler, *The Little Sister* (New York: Ballantine, 1971), p. 280.

    1. G. Pederson-Krag, "Detective Stories and the Primal Scene," *Psychoanalytic Quarterly* 18 (1949):203–14.

    2. Leo Bellak, "On the Psychology of Detective Stories and Related Problems," *Psychoanalytic Review* 32 (1945):403–7.

    3. Raymond Chandler, *The Simple Art of Murder* (New York: Ballantine, 1972), p. 16.

    4. Dashiell Hammett, *The Maltese Falcon* (New York: Random House, 1972).

    5. Ernest Jones, *Hamlet and Oedipus* (New York: Norton, 1949).

    6. Deming, *Running Away from Myself*, pp. 140–71.

7. William Luhr, "Tracking *The Maltese Falcon:* Classical Hollywood Narration and Sam Spade," in Peter Lehman, ed., *Close Viewings: An Anthology of New Film Criticism* (Tallahassee: Florida State University Press, 1990).

8. Ibid., p. 12.

9. Ibid., pp. 10–11.

10. Jon Tuska, *Dark Cinema: American Film Noir in Cultural Perspective* (Westport, Conn.: Greenwood Press, 1984), pp. 149–98; J. P. Telotte, *Voices in the Dark: The Narrative Patterns of Film Noir* (Urbana: University of Illinois Press, 1989).

11. Telotte, *Voices in the Dark,* p. 218.

12. By the same token, viewing Rick Blaine's paranoid tendencies in *Casablanca* today, I'm equally impressed by Rick's schizoid defenses (in the sense of English object relations theory)—the self, perceived both as agent and recipient of harm, precipitates chronic withdrawal and isolation. Under this rubric, Rick's paranoid maneuvers may be interpreted as another function of his schizoid adaptation.

4. War Movies: Dangerous Recuperations—Red Dawn, Rambo, *and* the New Decaturism

1. See General Bruce J. Palmer, Jr., *The 25-Year War: America's Military Role in Vietnam* (New York: Simon and Schuster, 1984). Palmer, General Westmoreland's deputy commander in Vietnam, analyzes the failure of American civilian and military leaders to grasp the complex historical roots of the conflict or the strength of the enemy's resolve. Palmer's study is remarkably measured and free of polemic. He still believes our cause was neither expansionist nor unjust.

2. Sigmund Freud, *Civilization and Its Discontents,* 6th ed. (London: Hogarth, 1953).

3. *Rambo*'s combat and torture scenes repeatedly feature "beefcake" displays. Its yeasty blend of macho narcissism and masochistically tinged homoeroticism locates the film squarely within the tradition of 1950s "sword and sandal" epics. In the "Hercules," "Maciste," and "Jason" movies, a mythic strongman and his band of male followers tested their mettle in journeys far from home (and feminine intrusion). The hero's pectorals were much in evidence; his interest in a white-bread heroine appeared theoretical.

I have elsewhere indicated how diverse Hollywood genres from westerns to war films privilege the woman-hating companionship of the preadolescent/ adolescent gang (inter alia, "In Search of Spock: A Psychoanalytic Inquiry," *Journal of Popular Film and Television* 12 [1983]:52–65). *Red Dawn* and *Rambo* both keep feminine sexuality safely checked. Rambo hardly pledges his heart before his Vietnamese girlfriend is killed. The partisans of *Red Dawn* are too busy for romance (one of the girls moons briefly over the downed air force officer, shortly before *he* dies). Women are presented as frailties to be protected or avenged. Or they gain entrance into the charmed male circle by showing they can "cut it" as competent warrior buddies. Nowhere do they exert a softening influence upon masculine aggression.

4. See Elaine Scarry's fascinating study of literary devices employed in military and diplomatic writing to deny the reality of battlefield injury: "Injury and the Structure of War," *Representations* 10 (1985):1–51.

5. Cf. Michael Rogin's essay on the grip of Ronald Reagan's film roles upon his political decisions: "Ronald Reagan, the Movie," in *Ronald Reagan, the Movie: and Other Episodes in Political Demonology* (Berkeley: University of California Press, 1987), pp. 1–43.

6. Sigmund Freud, "Why War?" in James Strachey, ed., *Collected Papers,* vol. 5 (New York: Basic Books, 1959), pp. 273–87.

7. Sam Keen, as stated in *The Face of the Enemy,* KQED-TV, San Francisco, 1987.

5. Psycho: *The Apes at the Windows*

The first epigraph is from Freud, *Civilization and Its Discontents,* p. 123. The second is found in François Truffaut, *Hitchcock* (New York: Simon and Schuster, 1967), p. 240.

1. Erik Erikson, *Childhood and Society* (New York: W. W. Norton, 1950), pp. 81–82.

2. Ibid., p. 252.

3. Freud, *Civilization and Its Discontents,* p. 55.

4. Truffaut, *Hitchcock,* p. 244.

5. For some examples, see ibid., and the following essays in Albert J. La-Valley, ed., *Focus on Hitchcock* (Englewood Cliffs, N.J.: Prentice-Hall, 1972): Budge Crawley, Fletcher Markle, and Gerald Pratley, " 'I Wish I Didn't Have to Shoot the Picture': An Interview with Alfred Hitchcock," pp. 22–27; Peter Bogdanovich, "Interviews with Alfred Hitchcock," pp. 28–31; Alfred Hitchcock, "Direction (1937)," pp. 32–39; and Hitchcock, "Rear Window," pp. 40–46.

6. Bernard Herrman's impressive score was written for unaccompanied strings. The composer's skill is the more evident for the absence of instruments traditionally—and all too often artificially—used to heighten suspense.

7. James Naremore, *Filmguide to "Psycho"* (Bloomington: Indiana University Press, 1973), p. 56.

8. Ibid., p. 64.

9. A feminine maternal surrogate or a father pathologically entwined with his child may inflict a similar regime of paralyzing dependency (the father in the famous Schreber case is a notable case in point). I have seen more than a few

patients where the father's intrusions in the earliest stages of life overrode the mother's healthier rearing.

10. Some children demonstrate an early exceptional neediness, due to poorly understood constitutional factors, physical illness of one sort or another, so forth. In these situations, heightened maternal ministrations may be more a function of the child's needs/problems rather than the mother's.

11. The birds of *Psycho,* as Naremore observes, are overdetermined images, admitting of multiple interpretations. They are the silent "watchers," symbolic of passive victimization or predatory attack. Marion, perennial victim, "eats like a bird" according to Norman. Mother's depredations are accompanied by birdlike keening. Hitchcock's next film, *The Birds* (1963), depicts an avian onslaught on a California seaside town like Fairvale, mysteriously related to the anger of a jealous mother when her bachelor son brings home an attractive young woman.

12. Given separation anxiety of psychotic proportions, and his own malevolence, Norman certainly would have been capable of killing his mother and lover, particularly if they were planning to incarcerate him.

13. André Bazin, "Hitchcock versus Hitchcock," in LaValley, ed., *Focus on Hitchcock,* pp. 60–69; Eric Rohmer and Claude Chabrol, "The Wrong Man," in LaValley, ed., *Focus on Hitchcock,* pp. 111–15. See also the introduction by Albert LaValley to the same collection, p. 2.

14. Raymond Durgnat, "The Strange Case of Alfred Hitchcock, Part Three," in LaValley, ed., *Focus on Hitchcock,* pp. 91–97.

15. William Shakespeare, *King Lear,* in *The Complete Works of William Shakespeare,* W. J. Craig, ed. (New York: Oxford University Press, 1949), p. 930.

16. Leo Braudy, "Hitchcock, Truffaut, and the Irresponsible Audience," in LaValley, ed., *Focus on Hitchcock,* pp. 116–26.

17. Naremore, *Filmguide,* p. 71.

18. Wood, *Hitchcock's Films,* p. 123.

19. William Rothman, *Hitchcock: The Murderous Gaze* (Cambridge, Mass.: Harvard University Press, 1982), p. 255.

20. Ibid., p. 341.

21. Modleski, *The Women Who Knew Too Much,* p. 8.

22. Ibid., p. 107.

23. Ibid., pp. 120–21.

24. R. Barton Palmer, "The Metafictional Hitchcock: The Experience of Viewing and the Viewing of Experience in *Rear Window* and *Psycho,*" *Cinema Journal* 25(2) (1986):4–19.

25. Ibid., p. 18.

26. Stephen Robello, *Alfred Hitchcock and the Making of "Psycho"* (New York: Harper Perennial, 1990).

6. *Reimagining the Gargoyle: Psychoanalytic Notes on* Alien *and the Contemporary "Cruel" Horror Film*

1. Harvey Greenberg, "Horror and Science Fiction: The Sleep of Reason," in *The Movies on Your Mind,* pp. 195–206.
2. See essay 5 in this book.
3. Robin Wood, "The Return of the Repressed," *Film Comment* (August 1978):25–32.
4. Ibid., p. 32.
5. "Special *Alien* Issue," *Cinefantastique* 9(1) (1979).
6. Victor Tausk, "On the Origin of the 'Influencing Machine' in Schizophrenia," *Psychiatric Quarterly* 2 (1933).
7. Daniel Dervin, "The Primal Scene in Film Comedy and Science Fiction," *Film/Psychology Review* 4(1) (1980):115–47.
8. Ibid., p. 131.
9. Walter H. Abell, *The Collective Dream in Art: A Psycho-Historical Theory of Culture Based on Relations between the Arts, Psychology and the Social Sciences* (Cambridge, Mass.: Harvard University Press, 1957).
10. Wood, "The Return of the Repressed," p. 32.
11. Abell, *The Collective Dream in Art.*
12. Lyn Davis and Tom Genelli, "*Alien*: A Myth of Survival," *Film/Psychology Review* 4(2) (1980):240.
13. Ibid.
14. Wood, "The Return of the Repressed," p. 32.
15. Thomas Merton, *Zen and the Birds of Appetite* (New York: New Directions, 1968), pp. 82–85.
16. For a more extensive Marxist critique, the reader is referred to the Science Fiction Studies Symposium on *Alien,* Jackie Byars, moderator, in *Science Fiction Studies* 7 (1980):278–305. See also Douglas Kellner, "*Blade Runner:* A Diagnostic Critique," *Jump Cut* 29 (1984):6–8.

7. *Fiction into Film—Problems of Adaptation: Improper* Bostonians

1. Henry James, *The Bostonians* (New York: Signet Books, 1979), p. 370.
2. Ibid., p. 273.
3. See this book, essay 5.
4. Gerald Peary and Roger Shatzkin, eds., *The Classic American Novel and the Movies: Exploring the Link between Literature and Film* (New York: Ungar Film Library, 1977), p. 4.
5. Joyce Gould Boyum, *Double Exposure: Fiction into Film* (New York: Universe Books, 1985), offers a definitive dethronement of the myth that inferior fiction makes better material for adaptation. See also George Bluestone, *Novels into Film* (Berkeley: University of California Press, 1966); John L. Fell, *Film and*

the Narrative Tradition (Norman: University of Oklahoma Press, 1974); Gerald Mast, "Literature and Film," in Jean-Pierre Baricilli and Joseph Gibaldi, eds., *Interrelations of Literature* (New York: Modern Language Association, 1982), pp. 276–306; Bruce Morrissette, *Novel and Film: Essays in Two Genres* (Chicago: University of Chicago Press, 1985); Robert Richardson, *Literature and Film* (Bloomington: Indiana University Press, 1969); Susan Sontag, "A Note on Novels and Films," in *Against Interpretation* (New York: Dell, 1972), pp. 245–50; and Geoffrey Wagner, *The Novel and the Cinema* (Cranbury, N.J.: Fairleigh Dickinson University Press, 1975).

8. On the McMovie: Less is Less at the Simplex

The second epigraph is from Neil Postman, *Amusing Ourselves to Death* (New York: Penguin, 1985), p. 155.

1. Pauline Kael, "Why Are Movies So Bad, or, the Numbers," in *Taking It All In* (New York: Holt, Rinehart, and Winston, 1980), pp. 8–20; David Denby, "Can the Movies Be Saved? David Denby on the Hollywood Blues," *New York* (July 21, 1986):24–35; Tom Shales, "Seen Any Good Movies Lately?" *Esquire* (July 1986):93–96.

2. Denby, "Can the Movies Be Saved?," p. 25.

3. The list of films cited in each category is not intended to be exhaustive. Readers will inevitably disagree about specific nominations—your trash is somebody else's treasures, goes the old antique dealer's mot.

4. See essay 4 in this book.

5. See Noel Carroll, "The Future of Allusion: Hollywood in the Seventies (and Beyond)," *October* 21 (Spring 1982): 51–81. Carroll attributes the rise of allusions in recent Hollywood cinema to the flourishing of academic film study programs since the seventies, the increasing number of directors (and, one assumes, other key movie personnel) schooled in such programs, and the emergence of a film-sophisticated audience prepared to recognize and enjoy allusions. The literacy of the various participants in this feedback loop beyond their knowledge of cinema is, as we shall see, a different, sadder matter.

6. Robert Spitzer et al., eds., *The American Psychiatric Association Diagnostic and Statistical Manual of Mental Disorders,* 3d ed. (*DSM-III*) (Washington, D.C.: American Psychiatric Association Press, 1980), p. 317.

7. See, among others, Otto Kernberg, *Borderline Conditions and Pathological Narcissism* (New York: Jason Aronson, 1975); Heinz Kohut, *The Analysis of the Self* (New York: International Universities Press, 1971); Kohut, *The Restoration of the Self* (New York: International Universities Press, 1977); and Arnold Goldberg, ed., *The Psychology of the Self: A Casebook* (New York: International Universities Press, 1978).

8. Kernberg, *Borderline Conditions,* pp. 231–32.

9. Ibid., p. 232.

10. Laura Mulvey, "Visual Pleasure and Narrative Cinema," *Screen* 16(3) (1975):6–18, and other well-known related work on this subject.

11. With the exception of Prince's egregious self-stroking in *Purple Rain* (1984) and the quintessential McMusical, *Under the Cherry Moon* (1986).

12. Kael, "Why Are Movies So Bad?"; James Monaco, *American Film Now* (New York: Plume, 1979); David McClintock, *Indecent Exposure* (New York: William Morrow, 1982); Mark Litwak, *Reel Life: The Struggle for Influence and Success in the New Hollywood* (New York: William Morrow, 1986); and Steven Bach, *Final Cut: Dreams and Disaster in the Making of "Heaven's Gate"* (New York: Plume, 1985).

13. Litwak, *Reel Life*, p. 113.

14. "Incidence of Motion Picture Attendance, August 1984," Motion Picture Association of America, study conducted by Opinion Research Corporation, Princeton, New Jersey, as cited in ibid.

15. Ibid., p. 115.

16. See Michael B. Druxman, *Make It Again, Sam: A Survey of Movie Remakes* (New York: A. S. Barnes, 1975), for a comprehensive exploration of previous industry remaking practice. Today's remakes and sequels would not seem to stem from the cost-cutting or shortage of product that dictated earlier remakes, but are rather created as a function of the relentless quest for blockbuster-associated megaprofit. Establishing a film's credibility through allusion is frequently essential toward this end (Carroll, "The Future of Allusion"). The filmmaker's desire to affirm knowledgeability and sophistication vis-à-vis the medium can be rated an added factor in contemporary remaking.

17. Compare Charles Bronson's ironic military policeman in *Rider on the Rain* (1970) with his robotized Paul Kersey in *Death Wish III*. The actor no longer plays the role, but vice versa. Recall the case of Eugene O'Neill's father, accounted one of the most promising young actors of his day, until success as *The Count of Monte Cristo* brought him matinee-idol status and financial reward. For the rest of his life he could never risk being quit of the part. It bankrolled him, and bankrupted his talents.

18. Litwak, *Reel Life*, pp. 21–29.

19. There are still more Stallones than Streisands in Hollywood. With rare exceptions, male superstars own greater, more enduring power than their female counterparts.

20. Christopher Lasch, *The Culture of Narcissism* (New York: Warner Books, 1979); Lasch, *The Minimal Self: Psychic Survival in Troubled Times* (New York: Norton, 1984); Richard Schickel, *Intimate Strangers: The Culture of Celebrity* (New York: Doubleday, 1986).

21. Postman, *Amusing Ourselves to Death*, p. 27.

22. Kael, "Why Are Movies So Bad?"; Shales, "Seen Any Good Movies Lately?"; and Denby, "Can the Movies Be Saved?"

23. Like the McMovie, these are produced with at least competent, and often very considerable, technical skill.

24. Herb D. Kleber and Frank H. Gaber, "Cocaine," in "Drug Abuse and Drug Dependence," in Allen J. Rances and Robert E. Hales, eds., *American Psychiatric Association Annual Review*, vol. 5 (Washington, D.C.: American Psychiatric Association Press, pp. 160–85.

25. Litwak, *Reel Life*, pp. 279–81.

26. Fred M. Hechinger, "Stubborn Pockets of Illiteracy," *New York Times* (December 12, 1986):C-13.

27. Justin Wyatt and R. L. Rutsky, "High Concept: Abstracting the Post-Modern," *Wide Angle* 10(4) (1988):42–49.

28. Mark Crispin Miller, ed., *Seeing through Movies* (New York: Pantheon, 1990).

29. Todd Gitlin, "The Medium," in Miller, ed., *Seeing through Movies*, pp. 14–48.

30. Ibid., p. 46.

31. Douglas Gomery, "The Theater: If You've Seen One, You've Seen the Mall," in Miller, ed., *Seeing through Movies*, pp. 49–80.

32. Stuart Klawans, "Colorization: Rose Tinted Spectacles," in Miller, ed., *Seeing through Movies*, pp. 150–85.

33. Peter Biskind, "Blockbuster: The Last Crusade," in Miller, ed., *Seeing through Movies*, pp. 112–49.

34. Mark Crispin Miller, "Advertising: End of Story," in Miller, ed., *Seeing through Movies*, p. 205.

35. Ibid., p. 214.

36. Ibid., p. 217.

37. Ibid., p. 233.

9. *Raiders of the Lost Text: Remaking as Contested Homage in* Always

The epigraph is from Roland Barthes, *The Pleasure of the Text* (New York: Hill and Wang, 1975), p. 22.

1. Druxman's *Make It Again, Sam* remains the most comprehensive investigation of Hollywood remaking practice. Druxman views remaking as a function of industry pragmatism, variously undertaken due to a shortage of "product," the cost-effectiveness of recycling previous scripts, the profit potential of deploying new stars and techniques in proven vehicles, so forth. He documents the transformation of some 30 films at length, and cites many other remakes briefly in an approach avowedly more anecdotal than hermeneutic.

The following common remake categories derive from Druxman's work and my overview of the subject:

The acknowledged, close remake. The original film is replicated with little or no change. Advertising and pressbook material may inform viewers of the remaker's intention to hew to the previous movie's narrative and characters. Verisimilitude can constitute a strong selling point. Notable examples are found in the biblical epic subgenre (e.g., *Ben Hur*, 1907, 1925, 1959).

The acknowledged, transformed remake. Transformations of character, plot, time, and setting are more substantive than in the previous category. The original movie is openly but variably mentioned as a source, ranging from a small screen credit to significant foregrounding in promotion. Remakes in this category during the past two decades include *A Star is Born* (1976), *Heaven Can Wait* (1978), *Stella* (1990), and *Always* (1990).

The unacknowledged, disguised remake. Major alterations are undertaken in time, setting, gender, or—most particularly—in genre. The audience is deliberately uninformed about the switches. Disguised remaking peaked roughly from the thirties through the early fifties—the heyday of the studio system, when the relentless demand for new films, wedded to a perennial lack of fresh material, compelled frequent reuse of earlier screenplays. Any list of disguised remakes would be formidable. See Bruxman, *Make It Again, Sam,* particularly pp. 13–24, for examples.

2. The second volume of William Luhr and Peter Lehman's study of Blake Edwards's oeuvre (*Returning to the Scene: Blake Edwards,* vol. 2 [Athens: Ohio University Press, 1989]) contains an elegant inquiry into the more complex esthetic and ideological premises behind remaking. Edwards is highlighted as a model of the consummate improviser who refuses to valorize the original as a historically fixed, complete project. He assays "not so much . . . to remake the film as . . . to replicate the conditions that allowed the film to be made . . . [returning] to the creative moment when the original film could have developed in any number of directions" (pp. 209–10). Again, his "remakes often question the premises of what they reprise, and often attempt to reformulate the mainstream cinema of which they are a part" (p. 224).

Corollary to Luhr and Lehman's study, Robert Eberwein suggests that a remake always exists under the sign of erasure, effecting "a kind of reconstruction of the original. . . . Erasing it [presents] an opportunity to recuperate the voyeuristic lack we experience in our view of the original" ("Remakes: Writing under Erasure," presentation at the Florida State University Conference on Literature and Film, 1988). Eberwein theorizes that the remaker's efforts invade implicitly forbidden territory, redolent with primal scene associations.

Allusions to material from previous films have been escalating in American cinema since the seventies. In effect, these are remakes in miniature, embedded *pars pro toto* in the new movie's associative matrix. Noel Carroll's investigation provides valuable insights into remaking a whole film, as well as its parts ("The Future of Allusion").

3. Jerry Tallmer, "Jawing with Steven Spielberg," *New York Post* (June 28, 1975):1, Entertainment.

4. "The Most Powerful Man in Hollywood: Spielberg—From *E.T.* to TV," *Rolling Stone* (October 1985):77; "Behind the Camera: A Candid Conversation about the Past and Future Films of Steven Spielberg," *Prevue* (November 1981):46.

5. Consultation with government and private agencies concerned with combating forest fires occurred during the production of *Always*. The numerous departures from firefighting realities thus do not proceed from ignorance, but would seem to be dictated by a melding of melodramatic license (had Pete in reality dropped chemicals from his craft on Al Yackey's burning plane, it would most certainly have crashed), the director's penchant for hyperbole, and sexism. Thus, Hunter and one or two other women are the only female personnel at the firefighting station and related locales; in fact, the percentage of feminine smokejumpers ranges anywhere from 25 to 30 percent. The pilots, however, are exclusively male as of this writing. (Information supplied by Arnold Hartigan, Public Affairs Officer, Boise Interagency Fire Center.)

6. In *A Guy Named Joe* Pete is still subject to military discipline after his death. His squadron of ghostly "advisors" is commanded by a general modeled after Billy Mitchell, who rebukes Pete for letting his jealousy toward Van Johnson affect his guidance with a stirring homily on making the world safe for democracy. Corollary to its transformation of *Joe*'s protagonists into New Age post-Reaganites, *Always* metamorphoses the squadron and its commander into Hap, a feminine angel-cum-EST facilitator (played with tooth-grinding sweetness by Audrey Hepburn) who gently chides Pete with no-brainer epigrams that could have been culled from the back of Celestial Seasonings teabag packages.

7. A point made by Pauline Kael in her review (*New Yorker,* January 8, 1990, pp. 92–93).

8. I am indebted to Krin Gabbard for these observations.

9. The tutoring of the American "loner" on the communitarian values required by the war in films like *Casablanca* and *Air Force* (1943) is discussed at length by Ray in *A Certain Tendency*.

10. Ariel Dorfman comments tellingly on the trend toward infantilization in the mass culture of late twentieth-century capitalism. See "The Infantilizing of Culture," in Donald Lazere, ed., *American Media and Mass Culture: Left Perspectives* (Berkeley: University of California Press, 1988), pp. 145–53. Dorfman's arguments are exceptionally pertinent to much of Spielberg's oeuvre as director and producer in recent years.

11. "Pastiche is . . . the imitation of a peculiar or unique style, the wearing of a stylistic mask, speech in a dead language. . . . In a world in which

stylistic innovation is no longer possible, all that is left is to imitate dead styles, to speak through the masks and with the voices of the styles in the imaginary museum" (Fredric Jameson, "Postmodernism and Consumer Society," in E. Ann Kaplan, ed., *Postmodernism and Its Discontents: Theories, Practices* (New York: Verso, 1988), p. 16, 18.

12. "The very style of nostalgia films [is] invading and colonizing even those movies today which have contemporary settings: as though . . . we were unable today to focus our own present, as though we have become incapable of achieving aesthetic representations of our own current experience. . . . [This is] an alarming and pathological symptom of a society that has become incapable of dealing with time and history. . . . We seem condemned to seek the historical past through our own pop images and stereotypes about that past, which itself remains forever out of reach" (Ibid., p. 20).

13. "American political life has never been a consistently reliable source of sustenance; and most people who grew up in the '50s and '60s have come to count, for their sense of value and style and even identity, on the ambient culture that has given postwar American life its special richness. . . . This culture seems to have reached a very high level of technical accomplishment, and then to have run out of anything fresh to say. . . . [It] seems thrillingly vacant. The wonderful package has nothing inside. . . . There is a genuine aesthetic frisson in emptiness" (Louis Menand, "Don't Think Twice: Why We Won't Miss the 1980s," *New Republic* [October 9, 1989]:22).

14. Harold Bloom, *The Anxiety of Influence: A Theory of Poetry* (New York: Oxford University Press, 1973).

15. I am indebted for this transliteration to Zachary Bayer, chief librarian of the YIVO Institute for Jewish Research.

16. Steven Spielberg, "The Autobiography of Peter Pan," *Time* (July 15, 1985):62.

17. Herbert Margolis and Craig Modderno, "Interview with Steven Spielberg," *Penthouse* (February 1978):102.

18. Ibid., pp. 142, 144.

19. Spielberg, "Autobiography," p. 62.

20. See above interviews. Also see Donald R. Mott and Cheryl McAllister Saunders, *Steven Spielberg,* Twayne's Filmmakers Series (Boston: Twayne Publishers, 1986); and Dian G. Smith, "Steven Spielberg," in *American Film Makers Today* (Poole/Dorset: Blandford Press, 1983), pp. 135–45.

21. Spielberg, "Autobiography," p. 62.

22. Ibid.

23. According to the history supplied by *Indiana Jones and the Last Crusade* (1989), Professor Henry Jones is a noted medievalist caught up with proving the historical reality of the Holy Grail. The death of his wife left him to raise his son. His scholarly obsession and unremitting criticism made his son revolt

against his authority. During his teens, Indy left home to pursue his own peculiar archaeological ambitions. The stormy relationship of Jones Senior and Junior echoes the fractiousness of Adam and Cal Trask in *East of Eden*, previously cited by Spielberg in describing the signatory moment of rebellion against his own father.

The *Last Crusade* openly portrays angry division between father and son as in no other Spielberg film. The Joneses' search for the grail is a rather heavy-handed symbol of their quest to heal their rift. Their mutual competitiveness is enormous; vis-à-vis *Always's* Oedipal motif, the film has Indy unknowingly sleep with the same woman his father had bedded in aid of finding the grail.

24. Harvey Greenberg, "*8½:* The Declensions of Silence," in *The Movies on Your Mind*, p. 167.

25. Such as, for instance, a pre-Oedipal/oral relationship between the remaker and the original film, hallmarked by the primitive drive toward fusion with and incorporation by the "maternalized" source. In this regard, see Norman Holland's analysis of the reader's oral relationship with the literary text: "The 'Willing Suspension of Disbelief,' " in *The Dynamics of Literary Response* (New York: Oxford University Press, 1968), pp. 63–103.

26. My remarks are obviously pitched at the Oedipal relationship between a male remaker and his subject, predicated upon the industry-driven reality that virtually all remaking has been done by men of films made by other men. I have so far been unable to discover remaking of a "male" original undertaken by a female director or other key female cinema figure (and welcome information on this subject). In the highly unlikely circumstance of a woman remaking another woman's film, the elaboration of an Electra "complex" corresponding to the male Oedipal dynamic around the source is plausible.

27. Barthes, *The Pleasure of the Text*, p. 37.

28. Ibid., p. 47.

29. The articulation between neurotic conflict and artistic effectiveness must be viewed as exceptionally problematic. It is analytically naive to suppose that in all instances a "serious" Oedipal conflict related to the original film would necessarily compromise the aesthetic effectiveness of the remake. For instance, Oedipally motivated, hostile "defacement" of the source film could still be accomplished through great art, if in a spirit of great contempt.

30. Since emerging as a major force in Hollywood, Spielberg usually wields this sort of influence over the pictures he directs. While in most cases he has not written the screenplay of his films (*Close Encounters* was one notable exception), crucial conceptual, narrative, and visual elements are often his. He is intimately bound up with script selection, then rewriting and/or interpretation during film production. Thus, it may reliably be assumed that, much like Hitchcock, the salient psychodynamics of the screenplays he chooses to "process" closely reflect his own preoccupations.

Additional Suggested Reading

The literature in psychoanalytic film scholarship is substantial. The following references comprise a representative sampling of papers and books in the field. Several useful overviews of general film theory, as well as relevant journals are also listed.

Altman, C. F. "Psychoanalysis and the Cinema: The Imaginary Discourse." In Bill Nicholas, ed., *Movies and Methods*, vol. 2. Berkeley: University of California Press, 1985.

Bellour, Raymond. "Psychosis, Neurosis, Perversion." *Camera Obscura* 3(4) (1980):105–32.

Bick, Ilse J. "Outatime: Recreationism and the Adolescent Experience in *Back to the Future I and II*." *Psychoanalytic Review* 79(4) (1990):587–608.

Brody, M. "The Wonderful World of Disney—Its Psychological Appeal." *American Imago* 33 (1976):350–80.

Brown, Royal S. "*Dressed to Kill:* Myth and Male Fantasy in the Horror Suspense Genre." *Film/Psychology Review* 4(2) (1980):169–82.

Calef, Victor, and Edward M. Weinshel. "Some Clinical Consequences of Introjection: Gaslighting." *Psychoanalytic Quarterly* 50(1) (1981):44–80.

Cavell, Stanley. "Knowledge as Transgression: Mostly a Reading of *It Happened One Night*." *Daedalus* 109(2) (1980):147–75.

Charney, M., and J. Rippen, eds. *Psychoanalytic Approaches to Literature and Film.* Rutherford, N.J.: Fairleigh Dickinson University Press, 1987.

Copjec, J. "The Orthopsychic Subject: Film Theory and the Reception of Lacan." *October* 49 (1989):53–71.

Deleuze, Gilles. *Cinema I: The Movement-Image.* Minneapolis: University of Minnesota Press, 1986.

————. *Cinema II: The Sound-Image*. Minneapolis: University of Minnesota Press, 1986.

DeNitto, D. "Jean Cocteau's *Beauty and the Beast*." *American Imago* 33 (1976): 123–54.

Dervin, Daniel. *Through a Freudian Lens Deeply: A Psychoanalysis of Cinema*. Hillsdale, N.J.: Analytic Press, 1985.

Drezner, J. L. "*E.T.:* An Odyssey of Loss." *Psychoanalytic Review* 70(2) (1983): 269–75.

Erikson, Erik H. "Reflections on Dr. Borg's Life Cycle." *Daedalus* 105(2) (1976):1–28.

Fleming, M., and R. Manvell. *Images of Madness: The Portrayal of Insanity in the Feature Film*. Rutherford, N.J.: Fairleigh Dickinson University Press, 1985.

Flitterman-Lewis, Sandy. "*Imitation*(s) *of Life:* The Black Woman's Double Determination as Troubling 'Other.'" *Literature and Psychology* 34(4) (1988): 44–57.

Gabbard, Glen O., and Krin Gabbard. "The Female Psychoanalyst in the Movies." *Journal of the American Psychoanalytic Association* 37(4) (1989):1031–49.

Gordon, N., and A. Gordon. "DePalma's *Dressed to Kill:* Erotic Imagery and Primitive Aggression." *American Imago* 39 (1982):273–84.

Kaplan, E. Anne, ed. *Psychoanalysis and Cinema*. London: Routledge, 1990.

Kinder, Marsha. "The Art of Dreaming in *Three Women* and *Providence:* Structures of the Self." *Film Quarterly* 31 (Fall 1977):10–18.

Kline, T. Jefferson. *The Dream Loom: A Psychoanalytic Study of the Films of Bernardo Bertolucci*. Amherst: University of Massachusetts Press, 1987.

Krutnik, Frank. *In a Lonely Street: Film Noir, Genre, and Masculinity*. New York: Routledge, 1991.

Leaming, Barbara. "Towards a Psychoanalytic Reading of a Contemporary American Film." *Cine-Tracts* 1(3) (1978):15–29.

Lu, F. G., and G. Heming. "The Effect of the Film *Ikiru* on Death Anxiety and Attitudes toward Death." *Journal of Transpersonal Psychology* 19(2) (1987): 151–60.

Miller, M., and R. Sprich. "The Appeal of *Star Wars:* An Archetypal Psychoanalytic View." *American Imago* 38 (1981):203–20.

Moellenhoff, Fritz. "Remarks on the Popularity of Mickey Mouse." *American Imago* 42(2–3):105–19.

Neustadter, Roger. "PHONE HOME: From Childhood Amnesia to the Catcher in Sci-Fi—The Transformation of Childhood in Contemporary Science Fiction Films." *Youth and Society* 20(3) (1989):227–40.

Penley, Constance. *The Future of an Illusion: Film, Feminism, and Psychoanalysis*. Minneapolis: University of Minnesota Press, 1989.

Petric, V., ed. *Film and Dreams: An Approach to Bergman*. South Salem, N.Y.: Redgrave Press, 1981.

Rodowick, D. N. *The Difficulty of Difference: Psychoanalysis, Sexual Difference, and Film Theory.* New York: Routledge, 1991.

Roffman, P., and J. Purdy. *The Hollywood Social Problem Film: Madness, Despair, and Politics from the Depression to the Fifties.* Bloomington: Indiana University Press, 1981.

Rutsky, R. L., and Justin Wyatt. "Serious Pleasures: Cinematic Pleasure and the Notion of Fun." *Cinema Journal* 30(1) (1990):3–19.

Ryan, M. "The Politics of Film: Discourse, Psychoanalysis, Ideology." In C. Nelson and L. Grossberg, eds., *Marxism and the Interpretation of Culture.* Chicago: University of Illinois Press, 1988.

Smith, Joseph H., and William Kerrigan, eds. *Images in Our Souls: Cavell, Psychoanalysis, and Cinema.* Baltimore: Johns Hopkins University Press, 1987.

Stam, Robert. "Hitchcock and Buñuel: Desire and the Law." In R. Barton Palmer, ed., *The Cinematic Text: Methods and Approaches,* pp. 23–46. New York: AMS Press, 1989.

Studlar, Gaylyn. "Midnight S/excess: Cult Configurations of 'Femininity' and the Perverse." *Journal of Popular Film and Television* 17(1) (1989):2–14.

Telotte, J. P. "The Call of Desire and the Film Noir." *Literature/Film Quarterly* 17(1) (1989):50–58.

Twitchell, James B. *Preposterous Violence: Fables of Aggression in Modern Culture.* New York: Oxford University Press, 1989.

White, M. " 'They All Sing': Voice, Body, and Representation in *Diva.*" *Literature and Psychology* 34(4) (1988):33–43.

Williams, Linda. *"Personal Best:* Women in Love." In C. Brundson, ed., *Films for Women,* pp. 146–54. London: British Film Institute, 1986.

Williams, T. *The Family in American Horror Films: Society under Siege.* Ann Arbor: UMI Research Press, 1988.

Zisek, S. "Rossellini: Woman as Symptom of Man." *October* 54 (1990):18–44.

Overviews of Film Theory

Andrew, Dudley. *Concepts in Film Theory.* New York: Oxford University Press, 1984.

Eberwein, Robert T. *A Viewers' Guide to Film Theory and Criticism.* Metuchen, N.J.: Scarecrow Press, 1979.

Holland, Norman N. *Holland's Guide to Psychoanalytic Psychology and Literature-and-Psychology.* New York: Oxford University Press, 1990.

Mast, G., and M. Cohen, eds. *Film Theory and Criticism: Introductory Readings.* 3d ed. New York: Oxford University Press, 1985.

Nichols, Bill, ed. *Movies and Methods.* Berkeley: University of California Press, 1976.

———. *Movies and Methods.* Vol. 2. Berkeley: University of California Press, 1985.

Rosen, P., ed. *Narrative, Apparatus, Ideology: A Film Theory Reader*. New York: Columbia University Press, 1986.

Wollen, Peter. *Signs and Meanings in the Cinema*. Bloomington: Indiana University Press, 1969.

Film Theory Journals and Other Journals Publishing Psychoanalytically Oriented Film Criticism

Camera Obscura: A Journal of Feminism and Film Theory

Cine-Action!: A Magazine of Radical Film Criticism and Theory

Cineaste

Cinema Journal

Critical Studies

Differance

Discourse

Enclitic

Film and Psychology Review (no longer published)

Film Quarterly

Journal of Popular Film and Television

Jump Cut

Literature and Psychology

Literature/Film Quarterly

October

Persistence of Vision: The Journal of the Film Faculty of the City University of New York

PostScript

Quarterly Review of Film and Video

Representations

Science Fiction Studies

Screen

The Velvet Light Trap

Wide Angle: A Film Quarterly of Theory, Criticism and Practice

Other Publications by Harvey Greenberg on Cinema, Media, and Popular Culture

"Clouseau Observed, Bond Revisited." *Film and Psychology Review* 4 (1980): 149–51.

"Dracula, Erect (and Otherwise): *Dracula, Nosferatu the Vampire, Love at First Bite*." *Psychoanalytic Review* 67:409–14.

"Germinal Dread: Review of '*Caligari's Children': The Film as Tale of Terror*." *Quarterly Review of Film Studies* 7 (1982):191–96.

"Anti-Brideshead." *Academy Forum* 26 (1982):21–23.

"In Search of Spock: A Psychoanalytic Inquiry." *Journal of Popular Film and Television* 12 (1983):52–65.
"*The Dresser:* Played to Death." *Psychoanalytic Review* 72 (1985):347–52.
"Titanic Warnings: The Challenger Disaster." *Academy Forum* 30 (1986):8–10.
"On Boesky Diagnostics." *Academy Forum* 31 (1987):1, 20, 22.
"Fembo: *Aliens'* Intentions." *Journal of Popular Film and Television* 15 (1988): 164–79.
"Bring the Lady a Bug: *Fatal Attraction.*" *Psychiatric Times* 5 (April 1988):22–23.
"Forsyth's Drift: *Housekeeping.*" *Psychiatric Times* 5 (May 1988):17.
"Garbagemen: *Full Metal Jacket.*" *Psychiatric Times* 5 (June 1988):18–19.
"Congealed History: *The Last Emperor.*" *Psychiatric Times* 5 (July 1988):12, 34.
"Re-enforcer: *The Manchurian Candidate.*" *Psychiatric Times* 5 (September 1988):25, 27.
"Cavils: or, How I Learned to Recuperate Reality When I Thought That's Where I Was All Along. Review of *Images in Our Souls: Cavell, Psychoanalysis, and Cinema.*" *Psychiatry* 51(4) (1988):432–47.
"Corpus Christi: *The Last Temptation of Christ.*" *Psychiatric Times* 6 (January 1989):28–30.
"Cruel Algebra: *The Thin Blue Line.*" *Psychiatric Times* 6 (March 1989):34–36.
"Future Imperfect: *Star Trek: The Next Generation.*" *Psychiatric Times* 6 (July 1989):20–21.
"*Indiana Jones and the Last Crusade:* Serial Mythmash." *Tikkun* 4(5) (September/October 1989):78–80.
"Batflop: *Batman.*" *Psychiatric Times* 6 (October 1989):20–21.
"Cinna the Poet: *The Morton Downey Junior Show.*" *Journal of Popular Film and Television* 17(3) (Fall 1989):123–25.
"Hopper Country: *sex, lies, and videotape.*" *Psychiatric Times* 6 (December 1989):34–36.
"Review Essay: *Psychoanalytic Approaches to Literature and Film.*" *Psychoanalytic Review* 76(4) (Winter 1989):607–11.
"Lacunae: *Crimes and Misdemeanors.*" *Psychiatric Times* 7 (March 1990):54–55.
"Just How Powerful Are Those Turtles: The 'Teen-Age Mutant Ninja' Film May Shell-Shock Its Young Audience." *New York Times* (April 15, 1990): Arts and Leisure, 1, 21–22.
"Celluloid Shrinkage: Review Essay on *Psychiatry and Cinema.*" *Quarterly Review of Film and Video* 12(1–2):141–56.
"Unread Books: *Born on the Fourth of July.*" *Psychiatric Times* 7 (May 1990):69–71.
"All of Hell We Need: *Through the Wire.*" *Psychiatric Times* 7 (June 1990):28.
"Introduction: Celluloid and Psyche," Special Issue on Psychoanalysis and Cinema, *Journal of Popular Film and Television,* 18(1) (1990):3–5.

"Review of *In the Realm of the Senses.*" *Movieline* 11(3) (November 1990):68.

"Rescrewed: *Pretty Woman*'s Co-opted Feminism." *Journal of Popular Film and Television* 19(1) (1991):9–13.

"Devilish Appeal: *Reversal of Fortune.*" *Psychiatric Times* 8 (January 1991):43–44.

"Privileged Moments, Guilty Pleasures." *Psychiatric Times* 8 (February 1991): 58–59.

"Corleone at Colonus: *The Godfather, Part III.*" *Psychiatric Times* 8 (March 1991):21–23.

"Motiveless Malignity: *The Silence of the Lambs.*" *Psychiatric Times* 8 (April 1991):56–57.

"Rooted Sorrows: *Sweetie.*" *Psychiatric Times* 8 (May 1991):62–64.

"Inwardly, Downwardly: *Where the Heart Roams.*" *Psychiatric Times* 8 (June 1991):53–54.

"Wellespring: *Citizen Kane.*" *Psychiatric Times* 8 (July 1991):48–49.

"Nothing Left to Lose: *Thelma and Louise.*" *Psychiatric Times* 8 (August 1991):40–41.

"Short Takes: Reel Personalities; Frankenstein—New and Improved (*Terminator 2: Judgment Day*); Badfellas (*State of Grace*); Glasnote (*The Russia House*)." *Psychiatric Times* 8 (October 1991):51–53.

"Short Takes II: Iron Men, Wooden Ships (Patrick O'Brien's Aubrey/Maturin Novels); Questionable Occupation (*The Story of Women*); Unholy Collaboration (*Uranus*)." *Psychiatric Times* 8 (December 1991):33–35.

"Spielberg on the Couch." *Movieline* (December 1991):44–48, 80, 83.

Index

Albuquerque Academy Library
6400 Wyoming Blvd. NE
Albuquerque, NM 87109